Joe Holmes –
Here I Am Amongst You

Songs, Music and Traditions of an Ulsterman

Len Graham

FOUR COURTS PRESS

Set in 10.5 pt on 13.5 pt Garamond by
Carrigboy Typesetting Services, for
FOUR COURTS PRESS LTD
7 Malpas Street, Dublin 8, Ireland
www.fourcourtspress.ie
and in North America for
FOUR COURTS PRESS
c/o ISBS, 920 NE 58th Avenue, Suite 300, Portland, OR 97213.

ISBN 978–1–84682–251–3 hbk
978–1–84682–252–0 pbk

Printed in Spain
by Graficas Castuera, Pamplona.

And when the first surprise of flight
Sweet songs excite, from the far dawn
Shall there come blackbirds loud with love,
Sweet echoes of the singers gone.

From *Lament for the Poets: 1916,*
Francis Ledwidge (1891–1917)

For Eoghan and Macdara
and to John Campbell (1933–2006)

Contents

Acknowledgments

I AM GRATEFUL TO the following for contributing to the funding of the many aspects of the research that led to this overall work: the Slieve Gullion Festival of Traditional Singing who initiated funding from the National Lottery Fund through the Arts Council of Northern Ireland; Prof. David Cooper, University of Leeds and the Sonic Arts Research Centre at Queen's University, Belfast for the digital enhancement of field recordings.

To those whose kind assistance and expertise was vital to the completion of this work: Andy Dickson and Anne Bailie for the music transcriptions of all the songs and dance tunes; Nicholas Carolan and the staff of the Irish Traditional Music Archive, Dublin; the staff of the Linen Hall and Central Libraries, Belfast; the staff of the National Library; the Library of the Royal Society of Antiquaries of Ireland, Dublin; the Library of Congress, Washington, DC; Harvard College Library; the British Library; the Bodleian Library, Oxford University; Cambridge University Library; the National Library of Scotland, Edinburgh; the School of Scottish Studies at the University of Edinburgh; the Mitchell Library, Glasgow; the Ulster Museum; Robbie Hannon and the staff of the Ulster Folk & Transport Museum; Terry Moylan and the staff of Na Píobairí Uilleann; Peta Webb and the staff of the English Folk Dance and Song Society; to those who gave me recordings including Cathal and Maura McConnell, Aodán Mac Póilín, Tom Davis, Geoff and Evelyn Harden; to Dr John Moulden, Dr Hugh and Lisa Shields, Dr Hamish Henderson and Dr Tom Munnelly for their encouragement over the years and for their generosity in sharing material and research and to Dr Patrick McKay of the Northern Ireland Place-Name Project.

My special thanks are also due to the following for their support and practical assistance: the family of Joe Holmes: Nancy Currie (sister), Jean Currie (niece), Robin Harper (grand-nephew); Billy McKee of the Antrim and Derry Fiddlers' Association, Labhrás Ó Murchú and staff of Comhaltas Ceoltóirí Éireann, Gerry O'Hanlon, Micil 'Ned' Quinn, Dr Ríonach uí Ógáin, Patricia Flynn, Prof. Ciaran Carson, Ken McLeod, Dr John Kirk, Dr Martin Dowling, Jeannie McGrath, Prof. Micheál Ó Suilleabháin, Jackie Devenney, Dr Andrew Noble, Dr Sheila Douglas, Frank Harte, Robin Morton, Colin Harper, Liz Weir, Paul Flynn, Prof. Paul Muldoon, Dr Julie Henigan, Peter Cassidy, Jimmy McBride, Paul Brady, Breda McKinney, Jim Carroll and Pat Mackenzie, Dr Michael O'Leary, John Kennedy, Jackie Boyce, Antóin MacGabhann, Joe Hickerson, Eamon Stinson, Ian Kirk-

Smith, Jack Lynch, Brendan O'Hare, Alison McMorland and Geordie McIntyre, Róisín White, Dr Ian Russell, John Fyfe, Robbie Haldane, James Foley, and to Dr Pádraigín Ní Uallacháin for her constant help and inspiration throughout the entire project.

Introduction

ONE WINTER'S NIGHT IN 1963, I was at a gathering of the Antrim and Derry Fiddlers[1] in Dunminning near Ballymena in Co. Antrim where songs were a welcome inclusion during the night's fiddling. I was nineteen years of age at the time and I sang *The Murlough Shore*[2] which I learned in my own family. I was approached by an older man – one of the fiddlers – who asked me for the words of this song which he had heard sung by his grandmother in his youth. This man was Joe Holmes and we arranged that I would deliver the song to him in his home at Killyramer near Ballymoney, Co. Antrim. I called over the following week to where he lived with his brother Davy and I gave him the song words. We got talking about songs. Although he was one of the best traditional singers that I ever met, I discovered then that he was a singer who didn't sing outside the confines of his own home. He told me that as a boy at primary school one of his teachers remarked that he couldn't sing and that he was tone-deaf. With his confidence undermined, he applied himself to fiddle playing and stopped singing in public. His musical ear and good memory however, had absorbed a great store of songs from his mother and other visitors to their home, but with her death in the 1950s the singing of songs in the Holmes' household had ceased. My then youthful

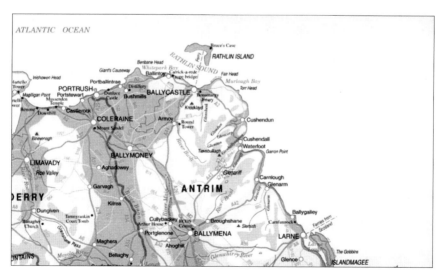

Map of the area mentioned in book, in counties Antrim and Derry.

Market Day in Ballymoney, Co. Antrim, *c.*1910 (photograph courtesy of Jean Currie).

The Aul' Lammas Fair in Ballycastle, Co. Antrim, *c.*1960
(photograph courtesy of Ballycastle Urban District Council).

enthusiasm for singing and my curiosity about songs had stirred memories in him that winter's night by his stove and he slowly began to release his great store:

> It happened for to be on a cold winter's evening,
> A fair maid sat waiting all alone.
> She was thinking of her father, likewise her aged mother,
> Aye, and also her true lover John.[3]

This was the opening verse of a classic ballad *True Lover John* and was to be my introduction to his rich repertoire of Ulster song and music, and the beginning of a musical friendship and partnership that would span a further fifteen years until Joe's sudden death in January 1978.

This friendship and musical collaboration of solo and unison singing, which is a common feature in the north of Ireland song tradition, led to our recording of two albums: *Chaste Muses, Bards and Sages* in 1975 and *After Dawning* in 1978 shortly before his death.[4] A selection of field recordings of Joe have been published in *Early Ballads in Ireland* and also in an early publication of my own field recordings: *'It's of my Rambles …'*[5] As a result his songs are now widely sung and recorded by many other singers and groups including The Chieftains, Boys of the Lough, Planxty, Battlefield Band, Voice Squad and by solo singers like Tríona Ní Dhomhnaill, Dolores Keane, Andy Irvine, Róisín White, Frank Harte, Dick Gaughan, John Doyle and many others throughout the singing world.

Joe Holmes was from Killyramer and was born in 1906. He finished his formal education in 1920 at the age of fourteen 'before the schoolroom tamed his lively tongue'.[6] Joe's ability to recall numerous poems, songs and tunes and stories from memory never failed to amaze me. His extensive repertory covered a whole gamut of themes and human experience in wide ranging song types including early classic ballads, broadside ballads, local songs, come-all-ye's, lyric folksongs, music hall pieces, songs on politics, murder, love, emigration and so on. He was a fine fiddle player too who came from a long line of musicians and singers and from a home that was steeped in music. His grandfather and his elder brother Harry played the fiddle and at the age of twelve Joe was presented with his first fiddle by Harry in 1918 on his return from France at the end of the First World War. His mother Jane Getty was a celebrated traditional singer from whom Joe inherited many songs. Their home was a popular céilí-house frequented by musicians such as fiddlers and singers John McAfee and Jimmy Kealey, and the singing coachman, Jimmy Currie, who worked for the Leslie's of Leslie Hill, Ballymoney. These were all contributors to the great collection of Ulster song in Sam Henry's *Songs of the People* newspaper column.[7] Other visitors to Joe's family

Jane Holmes (*née* Getty) *c.*1920, Joe Holmes' mother
(photograph courtesy of Jean Currie).

home were Paddy 'Stump' McCloskey, who also contributed to Henry's column and to Sean O'Boyle and Peter Kennedy's BBC survey in the early 1950s,[8] and also to Kennedy's *Folksongs of Britain and Ireland.*[9] As his home was a well-known music house others from farther afield would call there including the travelling Wexford uilleann pipers Johnny and Felix Doran while on their way to the popular Aul' Lammas Fair in Ballycastle in August. He once told me that dancing was a regular feature in his home and on bigger occasions the dance or ball would be held in a barn. One of the local farmers had a large barn with a wooden floored loft above, which was popular as the wooden floor acted as percussion for the dancers. When the grain, potato and flax (lint-pulling) harvests were saved, these

Left to right: Joe's mother, Joe Holmes, Nancy (sister) and Johnny (brother)
(photograph courtesy of Jean Currie).

were some of the occasions for which the bigger venue of a barn was required.[10] In Joe's time this sort of céilíng with song, story and dance was common to many houses in Co. Antrim and other parts of Ulster, irrespective of religious affiliation and background. The sub-culture of the céilí-house which was the scene of fireside philosophers, rustic bards, storytellers, songsters, balladeers, traditional musicians and dancers was that of ordinary people with extraordinary skills and imaginations. The Holmes' hearth and homestead was a welcome oasis bringing together neighbours, tailors, tinkers, itinerant musicians and singers which was the 'university' of Joe's learning and experience.

Joe's first job at the age of fourteen was carrying the red danger flag in front of a steamroller for a north Antrim road contractor. This brought him around many of the Co. Antrim villages and towns and into contact with local musicians and singers. He would always carry his fiddle with him in the hope of meeting other musicians on the road. At that time the steamroller would also tow a wooden caravan in which the workers had their meals and slept. By the late 1920s Joe had taken up employment as a scutcher with the local Killyramer Scutch

Broken-down steamroller and caravan in the Glens of Antrim, 1933.
This was the same type of steamroller and caravan that Joe Holmes worked
with in his first job in the 1920s (photograph courtesy of MAGNI).

Mill.[11] In the mid-1930s he purchased a motorcycle and travelled to the Milltown
Flax Mill in Ballymoney and he worked here as a scutcher until the mid-1950s.
This motorcycle also provided Joe with the means to travel to other céilí-houses,
dances and other gatherings (with the fiddle tied to his back!), especially after his
mother's death. With the decline in the linen industry during the 1950s Joe took
up employment as a green-keeper with the Ballymoney Bowling Club and worked
at this job up unto his death in 1978.

When I came to live in the Ballymoney area in the early 1960s, I found there
an atmosphere of tolerance and kindness generally among its people and formed
many life-long friendships there, in particular the friendship and singing
partnership with Joe Holmes. He was very typical of the character of the people
of Ballymoney described in the Co. Antrim Ordnance Survey Memoirs of the
1830s by the surveyor James Boyle:

Scutchers' berths in a scutch mill near Toome Bridge, Co. Antrim, c.1960.
This is similar to the Killyramer Scutch Mill where Joe Holmes worked
in the 1920s and 30s (photograph courtesy of MAGNI).

The general character of the people of this parish is orderly and peaceable, their dispositions generous and humane. They are remarkably kind and attentive to strangers. Amongst themselves too, they are in a great measure free from those party dissensions and bickerings which unhappily prevail in most of the neighbouring parishes … The result of this mutual good-feeling towards each other is that the people are contented and happy.[12]

Joe was a joyful singer, always smiling and rearing-to-go for a session wherever it would take him, whether to visit Eddie Butcher over in Magilligan, the local Antrim and Derry Fiddlers gathering, south to the Keanes of Cahirlistrane in Co. Galway, or to the fiddle players of Slieve Luachra in Co. Kerry or Donegal. When I reflect on my time spent with him, with the great Magilligan singer from Co. Derry, Eddie Butcher (1900–80), and the numerous other singers, musicians and characters I

17

Len Graham and Joe Holmes performing at Féile na Bóinne, Drogheda, Co. Louth, 1976
(photograph by Joe Dowdall courtesy of ITMA).

encountered along the road, I liken it to attending a twentieth-century bardic school where ideas, songs, stories, poems and tunes were exchanged, revised and enjoyed. Séamus Heaney has eloquently expressed this exchange and continuity:

> to an imaginative person, an inherited object becomes a point of entry into a common emotional ground of memory and belonging. It can transmit the climate of a lost world and keep alive in us a domestic intimacy with realities that might otherwise have vanished.[13]

During his lifetime Joe Holmes led many of us into this common emotional territory with his inherited repertoire of songs and tunes. It is my hope that some of these riches, which I had the privilege to share with Joe and which are compiled in this publication, may also lead other future generations to a place of intimacy and belonging through the continuity of folk memory.

RECORDING EQUIPMENT

My interest in collecting songs began in earnest in the early 1960s, mainly with pen, paper and memory. Outside of my family circle of singers, many of these early encounters with older singers happened during my travels as a member of the *Youth Hostelling Association of Northern Ireland* and its south of Ireland counterpart, *An Óige*.

When I acquired my first recorder in 1967, it was a Sharp 5" reel-to-reel. It was expensive at the time, *c*.£30, which was twice my weekly earnings of £15. As the tape was also expensive I used the very economical speed of 1 ⅞ rpm for the earliest recordings but, on advice, I notched this up to 3 ¾ rpm. The Sharp recorder began giving trouble sometime in the mid-1970s and I changed to a Sony cassette recorder. Neither of these recorders was of a professional standard, consequently the sound quality of my field recordings could be better. John Doherty the great Donegal fiddler once said to me: 'I have always been blessed with a bad fiddle!' and so was I with my tape recorders. However, I make no apologies for the quality of the material that I was so privileged to share with Joe Holmes and all the other wonderful people who gave so generously of their songs, good company and hospitality. I recorded in all sorts of situations and conditions; in competition halls of Fleadh Cheoils, in smokey public houses, in my car and even in a gents' toilet! However, the majority of the recordings I made of Joe Holmes were made in the comfort of his home at Killyramer with the only background sound being the metronomic tick-tock of his old wag-on-the-wall clock. Many of the recordings of Joe Holmes have been digitally enhanced by the staff in the Sonic Arts Research Centre, Queen's University, Belfast, and also Prof. David Cooper, University of Leeds.

During the compilation of this work, I have been given some extra recordings of songs which were recorded on better equipment and include tunes and solo singing by Joe and sometimes in duet with me. They are acknowledged above. In all cases they are additional copies of songs and tunes which I myself recorded from Joe Holmes over the years. These recordings were generally made at more public events and they capture the atmosphere of sessions and concerts and live audience. It is my intention to make all of the songs and tunes in this book available on future audio recordings. Recording details will be included for all tracks and will be available from www.storyandsong.com, www.lengraham.com.

Len Graham
An Mullach Bán,
Co. Armagh, 2010

Part One

THE SONGS

THE SONGS

1 Annie Moore

As I roved out one evening fair, in the month of sweet July,
Through groves and shady valleys and streams I did pass by,
The small birds they sat murmuring, on each green shady grove,
They changed their notes all for that youth lamenting for his love.

He tore his hair distracted, oft-times his hands he wrung,
The tears ran down his rosy cheeks like an uneasy stream,
Oft-times he cried, 'My darling's lost, the girl I did adore,
By a sudden call to her long home, will I ever see her more?'

Being on the twelfth day of July, Orange arches we did form,
When Scully and his cavalry thought to cut them down by storm,
But all his efforts were in vain for they would not comply,
And as we advanced, – 'No Surrender', was our cry.

In riding forth to cut them down we received a mortal blow,
You know a stone from David's sling, did lay Goliath low,
When the Light Infantry got an order to fire a round of ball,
'Twas at that fatal moment, my true-love she did fall.

A ball did enter in her breast and pierced her body through,
She fell and gently waved her arm, but could not bid adieu,
As I held her milk-white hand in mine, it grieved my heart full sore,
For to see those lips I had oft-times kissed, now whiter than the snow.

Oh, Annie Moore was my love's name of credit and renown,
She was the flower of this country and the rose of Belfast town,
The Protestant cause she dearly loved, William's sons she did adore,
And round her neck to the very last, an orange ribbon wore.

Now the Protestants of Belfast town turned out like heroes brave,
To carry her remains to a cold and silent grave,
And many hearts are merry, but my poor heart is dry,
For it makes me sigh, when I think on the twelfth day of July.

During the nineteenth century, sectarian violence in Belfast flared up repeatedly in the years 1813, 1832, 1835, 1843, 1852, 1864, 1872 and 1886. The events in this song took place in Belfast during one of those outbreaks on the 12 July 1835. The Party Procession Act of 1832 failed to stop Orange Lodges from Sandy Row and Ballymacarrett areas from marching in Belfast on the 'Twelfth' of 1835. Police and troops came under attack from Orangemen with sticks and stones in the vicinity of the Barrack Street area when they tried to stop the march. Police magistrate Captain Arthur Skinner (and not Scully, as sung by Joe in this song) was attacked and knocked from his horse. The Riot Act was read, and troops counter-attacked with sabres and musket fire. Two people died, William Trainor and the unfortunate girl, Annie Moore, named in this song. The *Belfast News Letter* of 14 July 1835 had this to say:

> It is truly lamentable to witness the ferocious spirit by which citizens of the same country and natives of the same town are actuated in regard to each other, merely, because their respective creeds are called by different names.

It is worth noting that another Annie Moore, a fifteen-year-old Irish girl, who sailed from Queenstown (Cobh), County Cork, was the first immigrant to pass through the newly opened Immigration Station at Ellis Island, New York in 1892. Her statue now adorns the harbour at Cobh, as well as Ellis Island.

2 The Banks of Boyne

I am a fair young damsel that loved my laddie well,
My heart was always dear to him, more than tongue can tell,
'Twas in my father's garden that he stole this heart of mine,
And caused me to wander from the lovely banks of Boyne.

His hair it hangs in ringlets, his cheeks are like the rose,
His teeth are as white as the ivory and his eyes as black as sloes,
His promise is the same sincere and his aspects bold and fine,
But his heart was false to Flora on the lovely banks of Boyne.

He courted me a while and then he promised me to wed,
Until he gained my favours, then away from me he fled,
His love is flew like morning dew, when the sun begins to shine,
And he quite forsook young Flora, on the lovely banks of Boyne.

Now I understand that this young man to London went straightway,
I packed up my jewels all on that very day,
I bid adieu to my parents who now in sorrow mourn,
And forsook my father's castle on the banks of Boyne.

Then quickly I posted for famous London town,
Where there I found my love was wed to a lady of renown,
Young girls can guess my feelings I will now resign,
It proved my ruination on the lovely banks of Boyne.

No more by yon purling streams that are so far away,
Where me and my bonny boy so carelessly did stray;
It's in the walls of Bedlam I am forced to remain,
Amidst tyrant bars and galling chains far from the banks of Boyne.

Now fond memories come back to me of joys that now are flown,
Of broken-hearted Flora lamenting far from home,
So come all young girls be careful how you spend your youthful time,
And think of poor young Flora on the lovely banks of Boyne.

The river Boyne is in Co. Meath and was the scene of the Battle of the Boyne in 1690. This song however has no political significance. It is a song of unrequited love which is a common theme in the Irish song tradition and it came from Joe's mother. The young girl in this song is jilted in love and she leaves her father's castle on the banks of the river Boyne and follows her unfaithful lover to London. There she finds her young man married to another and the young girl loses her reason and is admitted to Bedlam.[1] In other versions she becomes a nun and enters a convent.[2]

3 The Banks of Claudy

As I roved out one evening, being in the month of May,
Down by the banks of Claudy, I carelessly did stray,
I overheard a fair young maid, in sorrow did complain,
All for her absent lover and Johnny was his name.

I step-ped up unto her and I took her by surprise,
I own she did not know me, I being in disguise,
Said I, 'My fairest creature, my joy and heart's delight,
Pray pardon me what takes you here, this dark and dismal night?'

'Kind sir, the road to Claudy would you be pleased to show?
Take pity on a stranger that knows not where to go,
I am in search of a young man and Johnny is his name,
And it's on the banks of Claudy I'm told he does remain.'

'This is the banks of Claudy, the place whereon you stand,
But do not trust young Johnny, for he's a false young man,
Take no delight in Johnny, for he'll not meet you here,
But tarry with me in these green woods, no danger need you fear.'

'Oh, if my Johnny was here tonight, he'd keep me from all harm,
But he's in the field of battle all in his uniform,
He's in the field of battle, his foes he does defy,
Like a royal king of honour, who fought in the wars of Troy.'

'It's six long weeks and better, since Johnny left these shores,
And on the briny ocean, where the foaming billows roar,
'Twas on the briny ocean for honour and for fame,
His ship was wrecked, I have been told upon the coast of Spain.'

Oh, when she heard this dreadful news, she was in deep despair,
With the wringing of her hands and the tearing of her hair,
'Oh, if my Johnny he is drowned, no other man will I take,
Through these lonesome hills and valleys, I will wander for his sake.'

When Johnny saw her loyalty, he could no longer stand,
He fell into her arms, saying, 'My dear, I am your man,
Oh, Betsy I am your young man, the cause of all your pain,
And since we've met on Claudy's banks, we ne'er shall part again.'

This song enjoys enormous popularity throughout Ireland, Britain and North America. The 'in disguise' motif is common and in some versions of this song the 'broken-token' motif also occurs. The 'broken-token' means that when two lovers were about to part, usually because the man had joined the army or navy, they would divide a coin or token in half. Each took one piece as a token of love separated but not ended. The young soldier in Joe's version has no token but returns in disguise and puts his love to the test; she successfully passes.

The English folksong collector Cecil Sharp collected a version from Joanne Slade of Minehead, Somerset in 1904 very similar in text to Joe's, entitled *The Banks of Cloddy*. The famous Sussex singing family, The Coppers, made popular another similar version, but shorter and to a different air which they called *Claudy Banks*. They sing it with wonderful harmonies. The Irish group The Voice Squad based their musical inspiration and harmonies on The Coppers. This brings to mind an occasion in the early 1990s in the Glens Traditional Singing Club in Cushendall, Co. Antrim. The Voice Squad were the special guests in the club. The resident singer and elder of the club was Archie McKeegan. On the night in question several floor singers, including Archie, sang and, when it came round for the three-piece Voice Squad to perform, they were only about half-way through their first song when Archie shouted out from the corner – 'That's enough of that – one singer, one song!'

4 The Banks of the River Ness

I am a brisk young sailor lad, just lately come ashore,
To have some recreation and spend my gold in store,
Where there I spied a maiden fair all in a silken dress,
I heard her sigh as she passed by on the banks of the river Ness.

I step-ped up to this fair maid and unto her did say,
'Are you engaged to any young man? Come tell to me, I pray,
Are you engaged to any young man?' and she modestly answered, 'Yes,
To a sailor lad, but he's on the sea, far from the banks of the river Ness.'

I said, 'My charming fair maid, pray tell me your love's name,
'Tis William, he has a ring and I should know the same,
It's on his little finger, may God my sailor bless,
A ploughboy was my William fair, from the banks of the river Ness.'

I then replied, 'Young William you ne'er will see no more,
For he is bound in irons upon the Turkish shore.'
Said Mary, 'I will wonder and mourn my love's distress,
I will wander broken-hearted on the banks of the river Ness.'

I gazed in raptures on her and could no longer stand,
I showed her my little finger with the ring on my left hand,
She said, 'I've land and houses – throw off your tarry dress,
And put on your moleskin britches on the banks of the river Ness.'

Then to the church we hastened and wed we did with speed,
No more to sea he'll ramble, this couple they agreed,
For they have gold in plenty to relieve them from distress,
They live happy and contented on the banks of the river Ness.

This song came from one of Joe Holmes' workmates from Co. Derry when they were
working on road surfacing in North Antrim in the 1920s. Here we have the 'in disguise'
and 'token' motifs with a sailor involved this time. He puts the poor girl to the test and
then finally he shows her the ring on his left hand and once again all is well. There is a river
Ness in Co. Derry and also a river Ness in Scotland. This song more than likely originated
in Scotland and became localised in the north of Ireland.

Mickey Doherty (*c*.1898–1969) (photograph by Caoimhín Ó Danachair, 1949 courtesy of CBE).

and then as he recalled it was a song of his youth. Mickey recalled *Bonny Brown Jane* to a different air. Both Mickey and his brother Johnny were great fiddlers as well as being excellent storytellers. Mickey told me a story of an occasion when he was on his way to a remote cottage in Co. Donegal, which was as he put it – 'a long way from the steam-roller road'. He took a short-cut across a field and was about half-way across when he spotted a cow at the other end of the field. 'A bull, be God!' The bull looked at Mickey and then began to 'paw' the ground. Mickey took his pack from off his back and unloosened the string and took out his fiddle and bow. He then rosined his bow and put the fiddle under his chin. By this time the bull was charging at full pace. He started playing, as he said himself 'a most melodious and sensuous tune called *The Yellow Heifer*' as he walked slowly towards the cottage. By this time the occupants had opened their door and Mickey kept walking and playing his fiddle and as he entered the kitchen, the man of the house slammed the door closed behind him and bolted it. Just then the bull crashed into the door with its two horns stuck into it good and proper – 'It's a good job that was a musical bull!' says Mickey.

7 The Bonny Bunch of Roses

As I roved out one evening, it being in the charming month of June,
The wild and warbling songsters, their charming notes they did sweetly sing,
'Twas there I espied a wee lass, who seemed to be in grief and woe,
Conversing with young Bonaparte, concerning the Bonny Bunch of Roses O.

Then up steps bold Napoleon, he clasped his mother by the hand,
Saying, 'Mother dear have patience until I am able to take command,'
'Perhaps your ag-ed father, on St Helena his body lies low,
And you might quickly follow after, so beware of the Bonny Bunch of Roses O.'

He took five hundred thousand men and kings likewise to bear his train,
He was so well provided for, that he could sweep the world for gain,
But when he came to Moscow, he was overpowered by frost and snow,
And with Moscow all a-blazing, he lost the Bonny Bunch of Roses O.

Adieu, adieu dear mother, it's now I'm on my dying bed,
I thought I would live to be clever, but now I must droop my youthful head,
And when my bones are a-mouldering and weeping willows over me grow,
The deeds of bold Napoleon will gain the Bonny Bunch of Roses O.

A frequent visitor to the Holmes's céilí-house in the early years of the last century was
Willie Clarke who was from the neighbouring townland of Lisboy. Willie was a fiddler and

singer and Joe learned many tunes and songs from him including this one *The Bonny Bunch of Roses*. Most sources give the meaning of the song title as representing England, Ireland and Scotland and others say *The Bonny Bunch of Roses* refers to the red tunics worn by the British Army in the nineteenth century and in earlier times.

Napoleon Bonaparte appears as a hero, and was regarded with a marked sympathy by the common people of Ireland and Britain. The 1792 publication *The Rights of Man* by Norfolk man Thomas Paine sold over 200,000 copies, which reflected the mood of the people and their desire for a democratic society. Few at that time living in the wake of the French Revolution could see much to praise in the alleged freedom they were living under with its poverty and lack of democracy, and they came to look with considerable envy at the alleged democracy of the French. When exiled on St Helena in the South Atlantic, Napoleon declared that one of the major blunders of his career was that he sailed with his fleet from Toulon on 19 May 1798 for Egypt and not Ireland.

8 The Bonny Wee Lass o' the Glen

It being on a fine summer's morning, alone as I carelessly strayed,
Bright Phoebus the sun was adorning, the beautiful brow of Knocklayd,
I drew nigh to a neat little cottage, a wee lassie bid me come in,
I stood all amazed and said nothing, but gazed on the wee lass o' the glen.

Her cheeks were as red as two roses, the skin of this beautiful maid,
Was whiter by far than the snow that blows over the top of Knocklayd,
She was so endowed in beauty, I cannot express with my pen,
And I'd love to be kissing and courting the bonny wee lass o' the glen.

She dwells at the foot of Knocklayd, in a valley that's fertile and green,
By the side of a murmuring river, that flows through the townland called Breen,
Where the blackbird and thrush loudly whistle and the cuckoo her notes do
     extend,
And with music the whole valley's ringing, to charm the wee lass o' the glen.

'Oh, Jimmy,' she says, 'Do not tease me, your talk, oh, I would you'd give o'er,
Your flattering tongue does not please me, it has deceived numbers before,
Besides I'm too young for to marry, my age it is scarce five and ten.'
And that was the answer I got from the bonny wee lass o' the glen.

So now to conclude these few verses, in praise of the dear girl I love,
May he who created all beauty, shower blessing on her from above,
And if I do gain her favour, I will count myself blessed among men,
And through life I will do my endeavour, to please the wee lass o' the glen.

This is another song which Joe got from his own mother. When Joe sang *The Bonny Wee Lass o' the Glen* in Séamus and Mary Clarke's pub in Ann Street, Ballycastle, Co. Antrim one night back in the 1960s, an old friend and storyteller Andy McKinley told us that this song was composed in the nineteenth century by a local uilleann piper called Johnny Scally in praise of a young girl from the townland of Breen, Glenshesk – one of the nine glens of Antrim. Another young woman from the townland of Breen called Jeannie Close and her husband Paddy McGrath provided much hospitality and a welcome haven for both of us during the 1970s. Paddy and Jeannie lived at Moneyleck, Rasharkin, Co. Antrim and we spent great nights in their home with Jeannie, a sober driver providing transport to other céilí-houses and gatherings.

Joe attended his first Fleadh Cheoils with me during the 1960s. These were county and provincial events held in the counties Cavan and Monaghan in the towns of Cootehill, Ballybay and Clones. The first time Joe attended a Fleadh Cheoil na hÉireann was in Listowel, Co. Kerry in 1972. We shared the Burntwood House Guest House with Paddy and Jeannie McGrath and their family and accordion player Winston Given. We had wonderful music and singing sessions in Stack's and Regan's public houses along with Sarah and Rita Keane, Seán 'ac Dhonncha, Siney Crotty, Denis Murphy and many others. It was suggested, after many late nights and early morning sessions, that an afternoon nap would be advisable. So we all returned to the Burntwood House and retired to our beds. At around 8.00pm the bedroom doors were all rapped urgently by Joe – 'Get up boys and girls, get up quick, it's getting dark!'

9 Brian O'Lynn

Brian O'Lynn was a gentleman born,
He lived at a time when no clothes they were worn,
As fashions went out, of course Brian walked in,
'I'll soon lead the fashions,' says Brian O'Lynn.

Brian O'Lynn had no britches to wear,
He got an old sheepskin and made him a pair,
With the fleshy side out and the woolly side in,
'They'll be pleasant and cool,' says Brian O'Lynn.

Brian O'Lynn had no shirt to his back,
He went to a neighbour and borrowed a sack,
Then he puckered the meal bag in under his chin,
'Sure they'll think it's a scarf,' says Brian O'Lynn.

Brian O'Lynn was hard up for a coat,
So he borrowed the skin of a neighbouring goat,
With the horns sticking out from his oxters, and then,
'Sure they'll take them for pistols,' says Brian O'Lynn.

Brian O'Lynn had no watch to put on,
So he scooped out a turnip to make him one,
Then he placed a young cricket in under the skin,
'Sure they'll think it is ticking,' says Brian O'Lynn.

Brian O'Lynn, went a-courting one night,
He set both the mother and daughter to fight,
To fight for his hand, they both scratched at their skin,
'Sure I'll marry you both,' says Brian O'Lynn.

Brian O'Lynn, his wife and wife's mother,
Were all going home o'er the bridge together,
The bridge it broke down and they all tumbled in,
'We'll go home by water,' says Brian O'Lynn.

In the mid-1960s Joe and I were returning from a session in Patrick and Mary Magill's home at the foot of Slemish Mountain, in the townland of Ballynacaird, Co. Antrim, in the early hours of the morning when we took a wrong turn on the road. We seemed to be driving endlessly on small windy mountain roads and getting nowhere. Our dilemma seemed to prompt Joe to commence singing and the verse he sang was:

Brian O'Lynn, his wife and wife's mother,
Were all going home o'er the bridge together,
The bridge it broke down and they all tumbled in,
'We'll go home by water,' says Brian O'Lynn.

We finally got onto the main Carnlough to Ballymena road and we got our bearings once more. Joe then shortened the road home by singing the whole song from top to bottom as sung by his mother.

Sam Henry published a version of the song in his *Songs of the People* series in 1933 with an interesting note – 'In the old records of the Manor of Cashel (Portglenone, Co. Antrim) we find under the date 18 April 1786 the name of Bryan O'Lynn as a Grand Juror, and on that same day he was appointed an 'Apprizer'. Under the signatures of the Grand Jurors is written:

Bryan O'Lynn was a Scotchman born,
His head it was bald and his beard it was shorn.'

I'm not so sure about the Scotchman born bit, as O'Lynn is very much a common name in the area and the local ancient barony of Loughinsholin records their long association in the locality – Lough-inch-O Fhloinn – the lough and island of the O'Lynns or O'Flynns.

The Revd Baring-Gould published a version of the song in 1890 under the title *Tommy A'Lynn* with an interesting refrain, and the song hero in this instance is from Holland:

Tommy a'Lynn was a Dutchman born,
His head was bald and his chin was shorn
He wore a cap made of rabbit's skin,
With the skin side out and the wool within.
All to my tooth and my link-a-lum-lee,
Tommy a ranter and a rover,
Tommy a bone of my stover,
Brew, screw, rivet the tin,
O a rare old man was Tommy a'Lynn.[4]

Baring-Gould states that this song is alluded to in the *Complaynt of Scotland*, 1549; it is probably the *Ballett of Tomalin*, licensed to be printed in 1557.

The only other printed version with a gibberish refrain I came across was published in Philadelphia by J.H. Johnson on a nineteenth-century broadside ballad:

With my ranting, roaring, hoaring, boaring, screwing,
Gouging, auguring, melliting, chiseling, stokering,
Plastering, gammering, sailoring, wafering,
Capering, tinkering, soldiering, butchering,
With my three-handled, four-ironed gouging pin,
I'm a beautiful creature, says Bryan O'Lynn.[5]

Whatever the pedigree and history of the song, it's been around for a long time and it turns up on broadside ballads and in song collections in Ireland, Britain and North America. As a singer, James Joyce laced his works with references to numerous songs and the song *Brian O'Lynn* occurs frequently throughout *Finnegans Wake*. I heard another Dubliner singing a verse which Joe didn't have. Dominic Behan sang:

Now Brian O'Lynn and the daughter and mother,
Were all lying close in the bed together,
The night it was cold and the blankets were thin,
'Lie close to the wall,' said Brian O'Lynn.[6]

10 The Brown-Haired Girl

Fare-well to my na-tive coun-try, __ since I __ must bid a-dieu, and like-wise to my brown-haired girl __ since I must part __ with you, al-though it is a-gainst __ my mind, that I'm cross-ing o'-er the main, still __ I live in hope for __ to re-turn, to my brown __ -haired girl a-gain.

Farewell to my native country, since I must bid adieu,
And likewise to my brown-haired girl since I must part with you,
Although it is against my mind, that I'm crossing o'er the main,
Still I live in hope for to return, to my brown-haired girl again.

My love she's tall and handsome, her waist it is quite round,
Her cheeks they are like roses red, her hair's a lovely brown,
Her teeth like polished ivory, her breath does smell like thyme,
It was her killing glances, that stole this heart of mine.

Many a pleasant evening by Moyola's banks we spent,
Where bonny woods and plantings that yield me much content,
'Tis there the thrush and blackbird do change their notes so gay,
It never was my intention love, to sail to Amerikay.

One day as I stood musing, I thought my heart would break,
Still thinking of my brown-haired girl, not one word could I speak,
But as I took a notion of crossing o'er the main,
I went unto my brown-haired girl and told her so in plain.

'Oh, Jimmy, lovely Jimmy, are you going to leave me here?
It was for your own sake darling, that I shed many a tear.'
I clasped my darling to my breast, while the crystal tears did flow,
Saying, 'There's not another breathing knows the pain we undergo.'

Our ship she is well-manned love and we are bound for sea,
Our captain he gave orders and him we must obey,
'Aloft, aloft my lively lads, without fear or dread,
There's a south wind rising that will clear us round the head.'

Sailing down Lough Foyle me boys, Magilligan Point we passed,
I never will be happy 'til I wed to my brown-haired lass,
And when we reach the other side we'll drink a flowing glass,
And the toast will be right merrily – here's a health to my brown-haired
    lass.

This is another song from Joe's mother. It would seem that the lad in the song had joined the Navy, or was about to emigrate. He very reluctantly leaves his 'brown-haired girl'. In 1926 William Laverty from Dunaghy, Ballymoney, Co. Antrim provided Sam Henry with three verses of this song for his *Songs of the People* series. Dunaghy is a neighbouring townland to Joe's home in Killyramer and the last verse provided by Laverty was a bit different to the one sung by Joe:

We lifted our anchor and set sail and soon were out of view,
We had a bold sea captain, likewise a jolly crew,
I thought my very heart would break, as Magilligan Point we passed,
And I'm sure it won't be whole again, 'til I see my brown-haired lass.[7]

Another Laverty, and to my knowledge he was no relation to William, was Bobby from Lisnagunogue, Dunseverick, Co. Antrim and he was the source of many fine songs and dance tunes on the fiddle. It was through Alec Elder of Ballymoney that I first came to know Bobby Laverty back in the early 1960s. Alec drove a mobile-shop for McClure's grocery business in Ballymoney and he got to know many musicians, singers and characters in and around the counties Antrim and Derry through his grocery round. Alec played the fiddle and he would often arrange soirees to which I would receive an invitation along with Joe Holmes and sometimes other local musicians. There were many other céilí houses we visited at this time including Jeannie and May McAllister from Liscolman, Co. Antrim. Jeannie and May had a servant 'boy,' Johnny McFadden, who in 1907 came as a young man to work for the McAllisters. Johnny learned the fiddle from Andy Thompson from Loughlynch, Co. Antrim and Johnny in turn taught Jeannie McAllister and the pair of them fiddled and farmed their way through life. On a winter's night sometime in the late 1960s Joe and I called into Hugh McBride's pub at Dunseverick. Well we were in luck because Bobby Laverty was there in full flight. We shared some music and songs and Bobby told us a wonderful local story:

Johnny McFadden and Jeannie McAllister, Liscolman, Co. Antrim, *c.*1968
(photograph by W. 'Speedy' Moore courtesy of CCE).

Do you see them heap of stones out there they call Dunseverick Castle? Well that place at one time way back was a very important place. One of the main roads out of Tara led direct to Dunseverick and I'm told there lived a man there – I think his name was Kane or O'Kane and there are still loads of people with that name around here 'til this day. Well, just like the people here today this boyoh O'Kane was a great fisherman. Well, he had a bit of a wander-lust and he set off in his boat one day for Scotland and sure it's only a stone's-throw from here. It's only about twelve miles from Dunseverick to Campbelltown in Kintyre. Well, from there he headed down Scotland and into England and from there across to France and he didn't quit 'til he landed in the Holy Land. Now didn't he fall in with some fellow fishermen and he was soon fishing along with them on the Sea of Galilee. Well, in time they became great friends and when a wedding came up he got an invitation along with the rest of them. I'm told the wedding was something else and there was lashings of food and drink – barrels of Guinness stout and Bushmills whiskey. Well, our Dunseverick man was the star of the party – telling stories and singing songs to beat the band, when the barman announced that they were clean out of beer. Well, there was consternation all round and what do you think – a fellow with long hair, a beard and flowing white robes stepped out and told the organisers to bring in barrels of water that he was going to turn into wine. Well, this was too much for our Dunseverick man – 'You'll do nothing of the sort,' says O'Kane, 'You'll buy your round like everyone else!'

11 Captain Wedderburn's Courtship

Bring to me some winter fruit that in December grew,
You must bring to me a silk mantle, warp ne'er went through,
A sparrow's horn, when priest was born to wed us into one,
So you and I in bed may lie and I'll lie next the wall.

Oh, what is rounder than a ring, what's higher than a tree?
And what is worse than woman's work, what's deeper than the sea?
The globe is rounder than a ring, Heaven's higher than a tree,
The Devil's worse than woman's work, Hell's deeper than the sea.

My father used to recite a few lines of this ballad, which his father used to sing in the early years of the last century. When I related these to Joe he unfortunately could only recall a fragment of this riddling ballad, which occurs throughout Ireland, Britain and North America. Willie Clarke of Lisboy used to sing a more complete version back in the 1920s, but Joe could only remember these two verses. The theme of riddles and the ingenious lover is an ancient one and it forms the plot of many fairy tales and occurs in the Arabian Nights as well as in Greek collections. The girl poses a group of riddles which her suitor must answer correctly to gain her favour. The *Northern Constitution*, Coleraine, Co. Derry published a fuller version of the classic ballad in the *Songs of the People* series on 12 December 1936. This version was supplied by John Millen from Fish Loughan, Co. Derry,[8] entitled *The Keeper of the Game*.

It's of a merchant's daughter that lived down yonder lane,
She fell in with William Dempsey, the keeper of the game;
Said he unto that fair young maid, 'If it was not for the law,
I would steal you frae your mammy and hae you once for all.'

'It's go away, young man,' said she, 'and do not trouble me,
Seven questions you must answer if you would marry me,
Before I be your lover or leave my father's hall,
Or run away frae my mammy and be yours once for all.'

'What's rounder than a ring? What's higher than a tree?
What's worse than any woman's tongue? What's deeper than the sea?
What tree buds first? What bird sings best? And where does the dew find fall?
Answer me I'll go with you and leave my father's hall.'

'The globe is rounder than a ring, heaven's higher than the tree,
The devil's worse than woman's tongue, hell's deeper than the sea,
The yew buds first, the thrush sings best, the dew on earth finds fall,
So you must come with me this night and leave your father's hall.'

'Go away, young man,' she said, 'and do not trouble me,
Unless three more you answer me, I will not marry thee,
Before I spend with you a night, or leave my father's hall,
Or run away frae my mammy and be yours once for all.'

'It's for my breakfast you must get me a cherry without a stone,
And for my dinner you must have a chicken without a bone,
And for my supper you must have a bird without a gall,
Before I am your sweetheart, or leave my father's hall.'

'Oh, when the cherry's in full bloom, it really has no stone,
And when the chicken's in the egg, it really has no bone,
The dove she is a gentle bird that flies without a gall,
So you must come with me at last and leave your father's hall.'

Now this couple they've got married, I hear the people say,
This couple they've got married and right well they do agree;
He was a clever fellow and he did her heart betray,
And from her mammy this wee lass the keeper stole away.

12 Clough Water

Good friends and comrades, pray pay attention, 'til I sing for you so far away,
I left my home and ag-ed parents, in '56 in the month of May,
To try my fortune I took a notion, for to cross the ocean where the billows roar,
Our top-sails set neatly, she glided sweetly and took me safe to Columbia's
    shore.

And when I landed my friends received me, like Irishmen that are kind and true,
And now I'm happy and contented, all over the billows and life's journey through,
But when I ponder my mind does wander, though far away the Atlantic o'er,
To the fairest flower in Nature's garden, that happy place called the
    shamrock shore.

I oft-times think while in Philadelphia, of the happy singing and scenes of fun,
And on the banks of sweet Clough water, where I oft-times wandered with
    my dog and gun,
But while the ocean keeps in its motion and surges dark on the rocky shore,
I will revere thee with fond emotion, the land of my childhood, old Erin's shore.

So farewell, father and farewell mother and farewell brothers and sisters too,
And to my comrades, both lads and lasses, I kindly send my respects to you,
Should fickle fortune to me prove kindly, I might once more in old Erin dwell,
 Where I hope to meet with a friendly welcome, I'll drop my pen with a word,
    'farewell.'

This is a local song of emigration and the song would seem to indicate that the departure took place around the time of the famine – *'In '56 in the month of May'* (1856). The author is unknown and it is another song from Joe's mother. The Clough River rises in the Antrim hills in the parishes of Ardclinis and Skerry and joins the river Maine at Glarryford, some ten miles from Joe's home at Killyramer. I have included in the appendix a facsimile of this song as it appeared in the *Songs of the People* series in *The Northern Constitution* (see p. 274).[9]

Joe Holmes, *c.*1975 (photograph by John Currie).

13 Come Tender-Hearted Christians

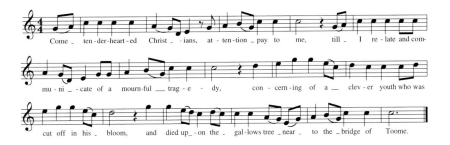

Come tender-hearted Christians, attention pay to me,
Till I relate and communicate of a mournful tragedy,
Concerning of a clever youth who was cut off in his bloom,
And died upon the gallows tree near to the bridge of Toome.

The hero that I speak of was proper tall and straight,
Like to the lofty poplar tree, his body was complete,
His growth was like the tufted fir that does ascend the air,
And waving o'er his shoulders broad, the locks of yellow hair.

In sweet Duneane this youth was born and reared up tenderly,
His parents educated him all by their industry,
Both day and night they sorely toiled all for their family,
Till desolation it came on by cruel perjury.

'Twas first the father's life they took and secondly the son,
The mother tore her old grey locks, she says, 'I am undone,
They took from me my family, my house and all my land,
And in the parish where I was born, I dare not tread upon.'

Farewell unto you sweet Drummaul, if in you I had stayed,
Among the Presbyterians, I'd ne'er have been betrayed,
The gallows tree I'd ne'er have seen, had I remain-ed there,
For Duffin you betrayed me, McErlean you set the snare.

Soon young Roddy was conveyed to Ballymena town,
He was loaded there with irons strong, his bed was the cold ground,
And there young Roddy he must wait until the hour has come,
When a court-martial does arrive for to contrive his doom.

In Ballyscullion I was betrayed and woe unto the man,
Who swore me a Defender and a foe unto the Crown,
Which causes Roddy for to lie beneath the spreading thorn,
He'll sigh and say, 'Alas the day that ever I was born.'

I first heard this ballad in the mid-1960s from Barney Henry, Cloghogue, Co. Antrim and I gave it to Joe. The ballad would appear to be from around the 1798 rebellion period. The date of composition is uncertain as many of the songs about 1798 were actually written long after the events of the rebellion. The Belfast *News Letter* refers to the court-martial, conviction and execution at Toome Bridge, Co. Antrim of one Roger MacCorley on Friday, 28 February 1800. The newspaper also reported that the body was buried under the gallows. Remains believed to be those of the ballad hero were found during the construction of the bridge over the river Bann and were reburied in the graveyard of his native Duneane. MacCorley, it seems, was a member of the Catholic Defenders. Their Protestant counterparts were the Peep o'Day Boys (from 1795 became Orangemen) and represented different sides of the religious controversy. Some Defenders, however, did join the United Irishmen which was a non-sectarian organisation. In counties Antrim and Down the United Irishmen were predominantly Presbyterian and their 'bible' was Paine's *Rights of Man* (1792)[10] and Tone's manifesto of 1791[11] whose objective was 'to unite the whole people of Ireland, to abolish the memory of all past dissensions and to substitute the common name of Irishman in place of the denominations of Protestant, Catholic and Dissenter.'

MacCorley was apparently betrayed by his co-religionists and the lines 'among the Presbyterians, I ne'er would have been betrayed' and 'for Duffin you betrayed me, McErlean you set the snare', are controversial to this day. This was borne out one night in Bellaghy, Co. Derry when Joe and I attended a Fiddlers' Night organised by Brian Toner in the Wolfe Tone Gaelic Athletic Club. Joe and I were asked to sing a few songs and one of them was this old ballad about Roddy MacCorley. When we finished singing the song, a woman rushed over and caught me by the lapels of my jacket and exclaimed – 'What do you mean by singing that song – my name's McErlean!' to which I retorted 'My name's Graham and Watty Graham the United Irishman was hung, drawn and quartered in 1798 and I'm not complaining!' Brian Toner's Fiddlers' Nights in Bellaghy were wonderful occasions of music and fun and Joe Holmes and I made numerous visits over the years. On one such night, sometime in the early 1970s, the poet Seamus Heaney on a home visit appeared at his old GAA Club. Brian Toner, a friend and neighbour managed to persuade

Seamus to give a rendition of an 'aul' poem.' Seamus introduced his choice of poem as a recent one, which was for his Aunt Mary and this was to be its premiere. From memory he recited – *Mossbawn: 1. Sunlight*. This poem has remained one of my favourites and it subsequently appeared in his collection *North* in 1975.

> There was a sunlit absence.
> The helmeted pump in the yard
> heated its iron,
> water honeyed

Back to Roddy MacCorley and to another night, this time in the Fair Hill Bar in Ahoghill, Co. Antrim, where we were to hear another version of the old 1798 ballad sung by Sarah Anne Campbell. In the 1960s the pubs in the North closed at 10.00pm and Sarah Anne kept a shebeen across the road from the pub in her own home. Sarah Anne had a big pot of broth bubbling away on the stove and all hands were dished out with griddle-bread and big bowls of wholesome broth. Then the 'bar' opened and Sarah Anne produced bottles of stout, and various other assortments of beverages and lemonade and tea for the pioneers – members of the *Total Abstinence from Alcohol Society*. Songs were sung, tunes played and much jollification and when the cocks began to crow it was time to head for home. Suddenly Sarah Anne rushed out into her back garden and caught a hen and broke its neck – 'There you are Joe – that will do you for your dinner.' Joe stuffed the hen under his coat jacket and we made for the car with the hen's wings still flapping under his coat!

The ballad form used in this version of Roddy MacCorley clearly borrowed from a much older classic ballad called *Sir James the Ross* (Child 213), which I heard sung by Willie Devlin from Ardboe, Co. Tyrone:

> Of all the northern Scottish chiefs of high and warlike name,
> The bravest was Sir James the Ross a knight of mighty fame,
> His growth was like the tufted fir that crowns the mountain brow,
> And waving o'er his shoulders broad the locks o' yellow flew.[12]

Anna Johnston alias Ethna Carbery (1866–1902) from Belfast composed another song on the Roddy MacCorley theme beginning, 'Oh, see the fleet-foot hosts of men', and is in no way related to this older ballad. Toome, Duneane and Drummaul, Ballyscullion and Ballymena are placenames in the counties Antrim and Derry.[13]

14 The Corncrake Among the Whinny Knowes

Oh, the lass I had the first of all, was handsome, young and fair,
With her I spent some happy hours, upon the banks of Ayr,
With her I spent some happy hours, where yonder burnie flows,
Where the echo mocks the corncrake, amang the whinny knowes.

We loved each other dearly, disputes we seldom had,
As constant as the pendulum, her heart-beat always glad,
We sought for joy and found it, where yonder burnie flows,
Where the echo mocks the corncrake amang the whinny knowes.

Oh, maidens fair and pleasures dames, who pluck the fragrant blooms,
You'll dearly pay for every scent in barbers for perfume,
But rural joy is free to all, where scented clover grows,
And the echo mocks the corncrake amang the whinny knowes.

Oh, the corncrake is now awa', the burn is to the brim,
The whinny knowes are clad with snow that tops the highest hill,
But when cold winter is awa' and summer clears the sky,
We'll welcome back the corncrake that bird of rural joy.

When summer does return again and the leaves are fresh and green,
I'll take my lass for a stroll down by the burnie stream,
With love all in her bright blue eyes and beauty on her brow,
We'll listen to the corncrake amang the whinny knowes.[14]

This is a song which was another favourite of Joe's mother. The song appears in Scottish collections and Robert Ford in his *Vagabond Songs and Ballads of Scotland* has this footnote – 'This is the first and only occasion, I think, on which the corncrake – beautifully feathered, but most unmelodious of birds – has been mixed up in a love song; and the performance, even if it possessed less literary merit – and it has little to boast of – is worth preserving on that account.'[15]

The corncrake, drawing by Michael Viney.

This Scottish song recalls a bird which is now almost extinct in Ireland. The Irish Wild-Bird Conservancy corncrake census of 1995 found only 141 calling males – apparently only the male bird crakes. The corncrakes are distributed over three main areas – north and west Donegal and the Shannon Callows. The corncrake was one of the first birds to suffer with the intensification of Irish farming. In a thirty-year-period the number of corncrakes has fallen from tens of thousands to a few hundred male and female birds.

15 The County Tyrone

My parents oft told me they would try to control me,
They would make me a draper would I stay at home,
But I took a notion for higher promotion,
I would try other parts from the County Tyrone.

I came to Newry, where I fell a-courting,
A bonny wee lass for a wife of my own,
But she was still asking and making inquiry,
'What is your character from the County Tyrone?'

For my character you need never mind it,
For married nor promised I ne'er was to none,
She swore by her conscience she would run all chances,
And travel with me to the County Tyrone.

Early next morning, bright Phoebus adorning,
We straight took our way by the three mile stone,
And the guards did pursue us, but they never came to us,
Till they met with an old man was walking alone.

He told them where he met us, that the guards did pursue us,
And all of our story to him we made known,
There being such trouble, our pace we did double,
And he showed us the road to the County Tyrone.

But we came to the quay, where a vessel was lying,
And there our whole state unto them we made known,
So they threw a plank to us and on board they drew us,
And they told us their vessel was bound for Tyrone.

This maid she lay dying, lamenting and crying,
I offered a cordial that I brought from home,
Which she kindly did mention without a pretension,
And sir, I'll do without it till I go to Tyrone.

Now we're safe landed in our native country,
In spite of her parents I did bring her home,
And my love's name to finish is Miss Janie Innes,
And I bold McGuinness from the County Tyrone.

Another character who frequented the Holmes's céilí-house was Johnny Toland from the nearby townland of Ballyboyland. Joe said Johnny had a 'bag' of songs and this was one of his favourites, which Joe's mother transcribed into her song book. When I compare Johnny's text which he gave to Joe, with the one published in 1926 by Sam Henry for his *Songs of the People* series it is very similar and may indicate that this was Johnny's source. Henry's informant was Dick Gilloway, originally from Magilligan, Co. Derry.

The song appears on numerous broadside ballads during the early and late nineteenth century with many as eleven verses printed. One of the verses which doesn't appear in the *Songs of the People* is particularly interesting:

This eased their trouble, their steps they did double,
They swore if they caught me they'd break all my bones,
They swore if they got me, a prisoner they'd make me,
Transport me to Antigua, hang me in Tyrone.[16]

The inland section of the Newry Canal, constructed between 1731 and 1742, ranks as the earliest summit level canal in Britain and Ireland. It extends from Newry some 18 miles north-westwards to the Upper Bann, just south of Portadown. The ship canal south of Newry was completed in 1850 and this created a continuous navigable waterway between the Irish Sea and Lough Neagh via Carlingford Lough and Newry. Also known as lighters, most barges on the Newry canal were pulled by horses until steam power was introduced towards the end of the nineteenth century.

16 Daniel O'Connell and His Steam Engine

Oh, come all you gay fellows now wants to be men,
And then listen awhile unto what I declare,
Concerning what happened the other evening,
Just as we were all coming home from the fair,
On crossing the moor sure I spied an old woman,
Sat in, in a gap she was milking her cow,
And the song that she sang was *Mo Buachaillin Donn*,
Or some other ditty, I cannot tell now.

I hadn't been long discoursing the old woman,
When a fine jolly tinker by chance came my way,
To rest he sat down for the weather was warm,
'What news honest man', the old woman did say,
'There is no news at all', replied the bold tinker,
'Only one thing I wish that it never had been,
Concerning this man they call Daniel O'Connell,
He's now getting children in Dublin by steam!'

'Oh, his soul to the devil' replied the old woman,
'For he is a rascal and that is for sure,
He's always endeavouring and plotting and planning,
And finding out ways for to punish the poor,
There are good men in Ireland as any in Europe,
And as clever fellows by land or by sea,
And they are as good men in the field of battle,
And I'm very sure they were got the old way.'

'Oh, long life to your courage', replied the bold tinker,
'And long may you reign with youth on your side,
And if all the young girls in Europe were like you,
O'Connell might leave his steam engine aside,
For they are so loyal and strict to their duties,
If a young man looked at them, they'd scratch out his eyes,
And then they will sit like old hags in the corner,
And no one to pray for their sins when they die.'

One night in the early 1970s on our way over to Eddie and Gracie Butcher's in Magilligan, Co. Derry, Joe started singing this song in the car about Daniel O'Connell, but there were gaps here and there. When we arrived at Butcher's the topic soon came round to this song and Eddie recalled bits and pieces as well. Between Joe and Eddie the song was cobbled together and it became a favourite of mine, so much so that on a US tour in 1976 I sang it at a concert in Grand Rapids, Michigan. After the concert a priest came over and said that it was strange that Ireland in her piety should have three adulterers for national monuments in her main thoroughfare: O'Connell Street, Dublin – Charles Stewart Parnell, Lord Nelson (it's gone now) and Daniel O'Connell. The author of this song perhaps knew something of Dan's reputation.

The Thomas Davis Lecture delivered on RTE Radio on 13 April 1975 by Dr Diarmaid Ó Muirithe of UCD on the subject of *O'Connell in Irish Popular Tradition* had this to say: 'All over the country the people told stories of his fabulous virility. Rathkeale, Co. Limerick stands indicted as the only town that didn't provide a woman for his bed. His mistresses were legion and they included Queen Victoria! … These stories are products of the folk-mind. The heroes of old were ever famous for their sexual energy.'

The south Armagh collector Michael J. Murphy, who did Trojan work for the Irish Folklore Commission and latterly for the Department of Irish Folklore, University College Dublin, turned up numerous stories and lore on the O'Connell theme in the Ulster countryside. In 1942 he took down a story from Dromintee, south Armagh farmer Tom Dunne; Murphy gave it the title, *Dan O'Connell: A Son of His Da's*:

Dan O'Connell was a going boy too in his day … Truth or lies the story was told on him. He was fond of the women too. One day when he went back home to Kerry or Cork or wherever it was he lived, he met this lad on the road. Dan was a big man at this time. He asked the lad his name and he told him and he asked him who his Da was and he said he had no father or the father was dead or something. So Dan asked him his mother's name and the lad told him, and Dan reached the lad a golden guinea. – 'Next time I meet you,' says Dan, 'I'll give you another golden guinea.'

The lad walked on, but round the bend of the road he hopped the ditch and away like hell back the way he came, over the ditches and round another bend, hopped out on the road and met Dan again. Dan put his hand in his pocket and reached him the guinea, – 'You're a son of your Da's all right', says he.[17]

DANIEL O'CONNELL

17 The Dark-Eyed Gypsy

There were three gypsies lived in the east,
And they were braw and bonny O,
They sang so sweet at the castle gate,
That they charmed the heart of the lady O.

She gave to them the sparkling wine,
She gave to them the brandy O,
And the gay gold ring that this lady wore,
She gave to the dark-eyed gypsy O.

When the lord of the castle he came home,
And enquired for his lady O,
'She is gone, she is gone,' said the young servant boy,
'She's away with the dark-eyed gypsy O.'

'Come saddle to me my milk white steed,
The bay is ne'er so speedy O,
And I'll ride for a day and a whole long night,
Till I find my own wedded lady O.'

Then Charles he put spurs onto his horse,
And oh, but he rode so speedy O,
Till he fell in with his own wedded love,
Along with the dark-eyed gypsy O.

'Are you going to forsake your house and your land?
Are you going to forsake your children three?'
'I will leave them all for the one I love,
And I'll follow my dark-eyed gypsy O.'

'Last night I lay on a fine feather bed,
My own wedded lord beside me O,
But this night I lie on a cold barn floor,
In the arms of my dark-eyed gypsy O.'

Joe learned this version of the old Scottish ballad from his mother. The events recorded in the ballad are said to have happened in the early seventeenth century. A legend tells about Maybole Castle in Ayrshire, home of John Kennedy, sixth earl of Cassillis. Kennedy's wife, the Lady Jean Hamilton, eloped with Johnny Faa, king of the Gypsies. Johnny Faa and his band of gypsies were caught and hung and the countess was said to have been imprisoned for life in Maybole Castle. The ballad has wide currency and versions have turned up in song collections and broadside ballads in Ireland, Scotland, England as well as North America.

The American folklorist, Alan Lomax, in the first full-length album of folksongs published by the Folk Archives of the Library of Congress, Washington, DC, recorded a version in 1941. The singer was Woody Guthrie (1912–67), who had his version of the ballad from his mother, which she called *The Gypsy Davy*. In 1942 the magazine *Common Ground* published Woody's delightful essay, *Ear Players*, in which he acknowledges his mother's influence:

> When you play music by ear, it don't mean you wiggle your ears while you're playing it. You just use your ears to remember what you hear. You sort of write down a bunch of sounds somewhere in your head and save them for future use. Sometimes you hear a tune and catch some of the words and for a long time you go around with it roaring through your head like a lost steamboat. My mother was an ear musician.

Woody's whole life and creative work are bound up by tradition and by his experiences in folk culture; his early grounding in traditional song expresses the values he absorbed from his mother's singing. A broadside ballad from the nineteenth century with the title *Gipsey Davy* and the printer's imprint of H. De Marsan, New York demonstrates the adaptation process of this old ballad to its New World environment with this verse:

> This lord he was a fine young man,
> And he set this lady crazy,
> So she packed up her duds and away she ran
> Along with the Gipsey Davy.[18]

An Irish nineteenth-century broadside ballad printed *c.*1867 by W. Birmingham of Dublin has this concluding verse:

Then she took the garment that she wore,
And wound it as a head-dress O
Saying, 'I'll eat the grass and drink the dew,
And I'll follow the dark-eyed gipsy O.'[19]

Another great version of this old ballad was collected by Tom Munnelly in the 1960s from the Co. Roscommon traveller, John Reilly. John called it *The Raggle Taggle Gypsy* and Christy Moore made it popular when he recorded it with the group Planxty. Back in the early 1970s, before the formation of Planxty, I received a phone call from Father Tony Meeney, the curate of St Joseph's Parish in Dunloy, Co. Antrim. Father Meeney asked if Joe and I would do support act for a young up-and-coming Dublin singer called Christy Moore, who was booked for a concert in the newly opened St Joseph's Parish Centre in Dunloy. I agreed and Joe and I came to the parochial house before the concert to meet Christy and sort out a programme. Father Meeney introduced us to a rather hairy Christy Moore and his mate Sid Isaacson and both of them were dressed in the hippy gear of the period complete with beads and Afghan goat-skin coats! Father Meeney told us he was just returned from Lourdes and that he had purchased a bottle of VSOP brandy, which he produced out of a duty-free bag. He sat it down on the coffee table with five glasses. He then went off to get soda water and ginger ale, when Christy reached over and pulled the cork out on the bottle with his teeth and poured out four large glasses of brandy. 'Down the hatch – sláinte', says Christy and he and Sid downed their glasses in one gulp. Father Meeney came in from the kitchen and he looked at Joe and me with our large full glasses of brandy and no doubt he held Joe and myself responsible for the half empty bottle! But fair play to him, he never said a word. He just poured out three smaller measures for Christy, Sid and himself!

The poet Robert Browning composed on this theme his poem, *The Flight of the Duchess*, having heard a beggar woman sing a version of *The Dark-Eyed Gypsy* ballad.[20]

18 Dick the Dasher

Oh, Dick the Dash - er is my name, I'm up to ev - er - y - thing that's game, my oc - cu - pa - tion, bless the mark, is what you might call a bar - ber's clerk.

Dick the dasher is my name,
I'm up to everything that's game,
My occupation, bless the mark,
Is what you might call a barber's clerk.

I'm so exact you all will see,
At the neatness of integrity,
Because my friends for me don't feel,
If I don't go out what you'd call genteel.

For many years I bore respect,
Till love destroyed my intellect,
For the daughter of the landlady,
Her unlucky love threw over me.

And for the kindness I received,
I went and asked her mother's leave,
If she'd let her daughter go with me,
Next evening to a shilling spree.

The old duchess she gave consent,
I kept two bob and paid no rent,
I thought I would go and toe and heel,
And something about us so very genteel.

Next day I went to the barrack yard,
To see the soldiers mounted guard,
'Twas then I heard a tune or two,
Some hearty boys my hapins drew.

66

My heart was heavy, my pocket light,
And how could I go to the spree next night?
And how could I disappoint Miss Peel?
And something about her so very genteel.

This put me into a rumbling fuss,
To get more money, a thing I must,
I had no clothes, but what I had on,
And bugger the shirt had I but one.

The shirt was bought on it I found,
Got wrote on it worth half-a-crown,
And to Paddy's Market I did steal,
In my fourpenny dickey, so very genteel.

Miss Peel was there in her evening frock,
Met me in my dickey at eight o'clock,
And when I entered the dancing room,
I hung up my hat in a great perfume.

When the fun and frolic was at its height,
A shawl was stolen from one Miss White,
'Oh, stop the dancing, stop the reel,
And search them all that are un-genteel.'

Now at the thought of being stripped,
Made me into a corner slip,
I saw it was useless for to hide,
For the tail of my dickey it soon was spied.

'Oh, here's the rogue', they all cried out,
'Bolt the door, don't let him out.'
'Do you think that I came here to steal?'
'The bigger the rogue, the more genteel.'

The boys to strip me they began,
They loosed my buttons one by one,
My coat and waistcoat they took off,
And left me shivering in my buff.

The girls did laugh, cried one Miss Hunt,
'Good gracious look at Dickey's front',
Now how do you think that one could feel,
At being search so un-genteel?

And in a moment I was free,
But they found no shawl on me,
I on with my clothes and took up my stick,
And out of the door walked Dandy Dick.

Now before I get my feelings hurt,
I ne'er will court without a shirt,
I'll wait my turn at the fortune wheel,
To bring me to what you would call genteel.

Sarah Heaney at her cottage at Killerfaith, Dungiven, Co. Derry, *c.*1967
(photograph by Len Graham).

Jimmy Currie from Balnamore, Co. Antrim was a cousin of Joe's brother-in-law Dan Currie. Jimmy worked for the 'big' house – Leslie Hill, outside Ballymoney and he was a frequent visitor to Killyramer. This comic song was a favourite and Joe learned it from Jimmy with some help with a few missing verses from Bob McConaghie from Ballymoney. Joe told me that a 'dickey' was a false shirt-front which had no back or sleeves. The only other printed version of this song I have found turns up in a collection from Canada.[21] A nineteenth-century broadside ballad printed by John F. Nugent of Dublin has a different song with the title *A New Song Called – The Dickey Shirts and Jenny Lind Hats*:

> Young ladies beware when courting you go,
> And don't walk with a boy, unless one that you know,
> For the more their necks shaved and oil on their hair,
> Mind look out for their shirts, it's a dickey they wear.[22]

Joe and I heard another version back in the 1960s from fiddler and singer, Michael Kealey from Killerfaith outside Dungiven, Co. Derry. We had gathered for a house-party in Sarah Heaney's cottage. Sarah was also from Killerfaith and kept a great céilí-ing house. That night singers Michael Kealey and Jimmy Kelly were also present. Some twenty years later I was attending a wedding in Co. Clare, when at the reception a man came over to me – 'I have a confession to make to you', says he. 'Do you remember a night in Killerfaith about twenty years ago when you were smoked out of Sarah Heaney's cottage?' 'Remember, I'll never forget it' says I. 'Sarah's old open-fire smoked us all out of her house and Joe and I had to go home.' 'Well,' says your man, 'I was a wee lad at the time and my Da – Jimmy Kelly wouldn't let us into the party, so we got up onto Sarah's thatched roof and blocked the chimney with sods of turf.' 'Go on out of that you wee skitter,' says I, but when I looked up at him he was bigger than me, so I let him off with a caution!

19 Erin's Green Shore

One evening so late as I rambled, by the banks of yon clear purling stream,
I sat down on a bed of primroses and I gently fell into a dream,
I dreamt I beheld a fair female, her equal I ne'er saw before,
And she sighed for the wrongs of her country, as she rambled around Erin's
    Green Shore.

I quickly addressed this fair female, 'my jewel, come tell me your name?
In this country I know you're a stranger, or I would not have asked you that
    same.'
'I'm a daughter of Daniel O'Connell and from England I've lately crossed o'er,
To awaken my brethren in Ireland, as they rambled around Erin's Green Shore.'

Her eyes were like two sparkling diamonds, or the stars of a cold, frosty night,
Her cheeks were like two blooming roses, her teeth like the ivory so white,
She resembled the goddess of freedom and green was the mantle she wore,
Bound round with the shamrock and roses, that grow around Erin's Green
    Shore.

In a transport of joy I awakened and I found it was only a dream,
The beautiful maiden had vanished and I'm sure I'll ne'er see her again,
May the sun of old Erin shine on her, for I'm sure I will ne'er see her more,
May the sons of old Ireland smile on her, as she rambles around Erin's Green
    Shore.

This is another song on the theme of Daniel O'Connell (1775–1847). Joe had this from Willie Clarke of Lisboy. This is an aisling (dream song formula) in which a maiden representing Ireland appears to the poet who sleeps in a tranquil bower, when she advises him of 'the wrongs of her country.' The song has widespread distribution with oral versions collected all over Ireland, Britain and North America. There are also many nineteenth-century broadside ballads in various collections. An Oklahoma version of the song records the title as *Dixie's Green Shore* and renames O'Connell as 'Daniel O'Colon,' but perhaps the most bizarre version of poor Daniel's name was collected in Monongalia County, West Virginia, where he becomes 'Aaron Goconlogue'.[23]

20 Erin's Lovely Home (A)

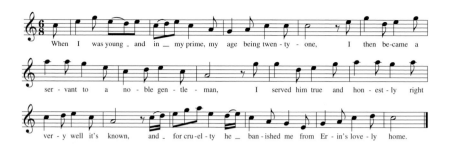

When I was young and in my prime, my age being twenty-one,
I then became a servant to a noble gentleman,
I served him true and honestly right very well it's known,
And for cruelty he banished me from Erin's lovely home.

Now the reason why he banished me, I mean to let you know,
It's true I loved his daughter and she loved me also,
She had a princely fortune and for riches I had none,
For this reason I must go away from Erin's lovely home.

It being her father's garden, where flowers were in full bloom,
It being in her father's garden, in the lovely month of June,
She says, 'My dearest Willie, all along with you I'll roam,
And we'll never fret for those we leave in Erin's lovely home.'

Another song from Joe's mother but unfortunately Joe could only recall three verses. In the fuller version of nine verses published in the *Songs of the People* the song goes on to tell the story of the young man's fate for courting a girl above his station. Sam Henry published the song in his series on 27 September 1924, but he doesn't give the name of his informant. However, he gives his source location as Stranocum, which is a short distance from Killyramer where Joe was born. Here are the other verses as Sam Henry published them:

All you young men I pray draw near that have your liberty,
A sad and dismal story I mean to let you know,
While in a foreign country I now must sigh and moan,
When I think on the days I spent round Erin's lovely home.

That very day I gave consent that proved my overthrow,
And far from her father's dwelling along with her did go;
The night was bright with the moonlight as we set out alone,
We thought we had got safe away from Erin's lovely home.

When we arrived in Belfast all by the break of day,
She said, 'Prepare, my jewel, our passage for to pay.'
Five hundred pounds she counted down, saying, 'That will be your own,
So never fret for those you left round Erin's lovely home.'

Now to my great misfortune, I mean to let you hear,
It was in three days after, her father did appear,
He brought me back to Omagh Jail in the County of Tyrone,
From that I was transported from Erin's lovely home.

When I received my sentence, it grieved my heart full sore,
The parting from my own true love, it grieved me ten times more.
There are seven links upon my chain and every link a year,
Before I can return again to the arms of my dear.

When the coach came to the jail yard to take us all away,
My true love she came to me and thus to me did say,
'Cheer up, my dearest Willie, for you I'll not disown,
Until you do return again to Erin's lovely home.'

21 Erin's Lovely Home (B)

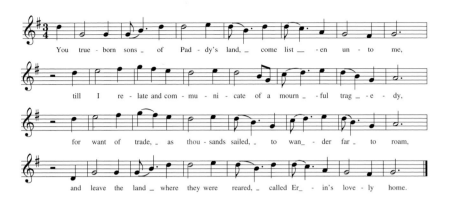

You true-born sons of Paddy's land, come listen unto me,
Till I relate and communicate of a mournful tragedy,
For want of trade, as thousands sailed, to wander far to roam,
And leave the land where they were reared, called Erin's lovely home.

My father being a farming man, reared to industry,
He had two sons of tender age and lovely daughters three,
Our lands too small to maintain us all, some of us had to roam,
And leave the land where they were reared, called Erin's lovely home.

My father sold his second cow and borrowed twenty pounds,
Being in the merry month of May, we sailed from Derry town,
There were thousands more along the shore, all anxious for to roam,
And leave the land where they were reared, called Erin's lovely home.

We were scarcely seven days sailing, when a fever wrecked our crew,
They were falling like the autumn leaves, bidding friends and life adieu,
We raised a prayer to Him above, why did we ever roam?
And leave the land where we were reared, called Erin's lovely home.

Alas, my sister she fell sick, her life was taken away,
It grieves me ten times more to see her body thrown into the sea,
Down in the deep her body lies and rose in a terrible foam,
Her friends may mourn, but she'll never return to Erin's lovely home.

Joe and I learned this song from Martha Mullan who along with her husband Frank owned *The Dolphin* fish and chip shop in Causeway Street, Portrush, Co. Antrim. Martha learned this song from her father Johnny Somers from Magilligan, Co. Derry. The mid-nineteenth-century broadside ballad entitled *The Emigrant's Tragedy* features some verses which haven't survived in the oral tradition in Ireland including the following:

> Forty-seven, I'll ne'er forget, when fever plagued the land,
> And famine with gigantic steps stretched forth its devious hand,
> Which many men, like infants then, unable for to roam,
> In cold death lay to dogs a prey, in Erin's lovely home.
>
> When we had reached America our numbers were but small,
> And fourteen days of quarantine was worse to us than all,
> In this sad state we had to wait, though anxious for to roam,
> In a strange land – a feeble band from Erin's lovely home.[24]

This poignant song of emigration paints a graphic picture of the hardships suffered by the Irish emigrants in the nineteenth century on their voyage to North America on the so-called 'coffin' ships. Voyages from the north of Ireland to North America usually took between seven and nine weeks. A letter sent home from Philadelphia from James Horner in August 1801 to his parents in Bovevagh, Co. Derry describes the hardships that most emigrants encountered on their journey in the era of sailing ships:

> Dear Father and Mother,
> I have taken this opportunity in letting you know I am well at present, thanks be to God for his mercies towards me. I am well and happy since I left you. I was very bad for three weeks at first for we had rough weather that time but I soon got better and was able to eat some of my sea store. We had nine weeks passage sailing and had thirty children died with the smallpox and measles and we had one old woman that died. Do not fret for me being away from you but think that this time will soon be over, that you will see me once more. I believe it was my fortune to come here to a strange land …[25]

Another emigrant's letter in the Public Record Office in Belfast[26] with a date closer to the time of this song, again recalls the plight of passengers arriving from Europe to US and Canadian ports. In this instance Robert Smyth is writing home to his father James Smyth, Moycraig, Co. Antrim on 2 June 1840:

> It may be of some service to you or your friends to know that the European vessels arriving at the different ports in this country this season [1840] are in a dreadful condition with sickness … Many there are … that come into our channel with the smallpox on board … The following vessels at Gross Isle below Quebec at last

account with sickness on board the barque *Independence*, from Liverpool, 270 passengers, 11 deaths and 128 sick of the smallpox. The barque *Nelson Village* from Belfast, 280 passengers, 16 deaths, 30 sick of the smallpox. ... There are daily arriving a great many of my countrymen into this country and on account of the hard times the general cry is ... 'God help them, what is going to become of them?'[27]

22 The Exile of Erin

Oh, Er - in, my coun - try though sad and for_ - sak - en, in _ dreams I do vis - it the sea - beat - en shore, but a - las in the far for - eign land I'll a_ - wak - en, and _ sigh for the lass that will meet me no more; and though cru - el fate will nev - er re_ - place me, in a man - sion of peace, where no per - ils can _ chase me, and _ nev - er a - gain shall my _ broth - ers em_ - brace me, they _ died to de - fend me, or live to de - plore.

Oh, Erin, my country though sad and forsaken,
In dreams I do visit the sea-beaten shore,
But alas in far foreign land I'll awaken,
And sigh for the lass that will meet me no more;
And though cruel fate will never replace me,
In a mansion of peace, where no perils can chase me,
And never again shall my brothers embrace me,
They died to defend me, or live to deplore.

Joe could only remember one verse of this song, but his mother sang a fuller version. This song is attributed to Thomas Campbell (1777–1844), although this is disputed and some say George Nugent Reynolds (1770–1802) was the author. The 'who wrote it?' controversy regarding the authorship of *The Exile of Erin* raged between the Reynolds and Campbell camps for some time during the early nineteenth century. On 30 September 1841, a letter to the Editor of *The Times*, London appeared:

> Dear Sir,
> I wrote *The Exile of Erin* about the end of 1800 or the beginning of 1801. It appeared in the *Morning Chronicle* and in the *Star* newspapers immediately after my writing it, and affixing my name and surname to the composition. Reynolds, the alleged author of my song lived 16 months after its publication with my name, and never claimed the authorship. I ascertained the date of his death – through Lord Nugent, his relation – from the parish register of the place where he lies interred. I remain, Sir, Your obedient servant, T. Campbell, 8 Victoria Square, Pimlico, London.[28]

THE
Exile of Erin.

Toasts and Sentiments.
Let us haste to Kelvin Grove.
Toasts and Sentiments.
Young Donald of Dundee.
Araby's Daughter.

DUBLIN :
Printed for the Booksellers

Title-page of a Dublin Chapbook, *c.*1830.

Thomas Campbell was the author of the song *The Wounded Hussar.*[29] Another of Campbell's compositions found its way into my father's memory bank and he was able to quote large passages of *Lord Ullin's Daughter*, which he said was 'drummed' into him at primary school:

> A chieftain to the Highlands bound cries, 'Boatman, do not tarry!
> And I'll give thee a silver pound to row us o'er the ferry.'
> 'Now who be ye would cross Lochgyle, this dark and stormy water?'
> 'O, I'm the chief of Ulva's isle, and this Lord Ullin's daughter.'

Thomas Campbell was born in Glasgow in July 1777. Because of his association with such Irish exiles as Anthony McCann, who had fled Ireland after the Rebellion of 1798, Campbell was arrested in Edinburgh for high treason. A search of his trunk revealed a copy of his song, 'Ye Mariners of England' which proved him loyal![30]

James Joyce must have been familiar with *The Exile of Erin* as references to this song occur throughout *Finnegans Wake*. I include in the appendix, p. 275, a facsimile copy of a broadside ballad of *The Exile of Erin*, printed by Alex Mayne, High Street, Belfast, *c.*1850, which includes a phonetic Irish language translation of the song.[31]

78

23 The Factory Girl

As I went a-walking one fine summer's morning,
The birds on the bushes did warble and sing,
The lads and the lasses together were sporting,
Going down to the factory their work to begin.

I spied one amongst them, she was fairer than any,
Her skin like the lily that grows in yon dell,
Her cheeks like the red rose, that grows in yon valley,
But she's only a hard-working factory girl.

I step-ped up to her, it was for to view her,
When on me she cast a proud look of disdain,
'Stand off me, stand off me and do not insult me,
For although I'm a poor girl, I think it no shame.'

'I don't mean to harm you, nor yet love to scorn you,
But grant me one favour, pray where do you dwell?'
'I am a poor girl, without home or relations,
And besides I'm a hard-working factory girl.'

'I have lands, I have houses, adorned with ivy,
I have gold in my pocket and silver as well,
And if you'll go with me a lady I'll make you,
So try and say yes, my sweet factory girl.'

'Now greed and temptation rules many a nation,
To many a rich lady, perhaps you'd do well,
Your friends and relations they would all frown upon me,
For I'm only a hard-working factory girl.'

It's true I did love her, but now she won't have me,
And all for her sake I must wander a while,
O'er high hills and valleys, where no one shall know me,
Far away from the sound of the factory bell.

This song is another from Joe's mother and it is one of the most popular songs with singers old and young to the present day at traditional singing festivals and gatherings at home and abroad. Frank Purslow, who edited the Hammond & Gardiner manuscript,[32] published a version collected in Basingstoke, Hants., in 1906. He says that although it is a rather modern-sounding title for a folk song, it probably dates back to the end of the eighteenth century. He also is of the opinion that the song is of Northern Irish origin. In this song we find the signs of a new-found independence for women with the advent of the industrial

Sarah Anne O'Neill, Geordie Hanna and Len Graham performing at the Armagh Folk Club, *c.*1978 (photograph courtesy of John Butler).

Len Graham and Joe Holmes at the Traditional Singing Seminar, Ardmore Hotel, Newry, Co. Down, *c.*1976 (photograph by Geraldine Sweeney).

revolution. The poor girl is pursued by a rich man and she refuses his advances but shows defiant independence which was characteristic of many female workers newly released from the home.

This song was one of the subjects of a lecture given by Seán O'Boyle at a traditional singing seminar in 1977, held in the Ardmore Hotel, Newry, Co. Down. Seán played several audio recordings of various Ulster singers and songs he had collected during the 1950s and 1960s. One example which he played was *The Factory Girl* sung by George Hanna from Co. Tyrone. 'Now,' says Seán, 'I made that recording of George Hanna about 20 years ago – we have another Hanna here today, a younger man called Geordie, who is a nephew of the singer I am just after playing. Geordie, will you please sing for us two verses of *The Factory Girl*.' Geordie Hanna then obliged by singing two verses, as requested. 'Thank you Geordie,' says Seán. 'Now we have another singer here today – her name is Sarah Anne O'Neill and she is a sister of Geordie Hanna and a niece of the first singer – Sarah Anne will you please sing for us two verses of *The Factory Girl*.' Sarah Anne then sang the two verses as requested. 'Now, ladies and gentlemen,' says Seán, 'There you heard three similar, but very different versions of the same song from members of the same family – this to my mind is the very essence of what traditional singing is all about – individuality! Three singers singing the same song, but each doing their own thing with different phrasing and each putting their very own individual stamp on the same song.'

81

24 Farewell Ballymoney

Oh, courting is a pleasure, between my love and I,
And it's down by yonder valley, I will meet her by and by,
It's down by yonder valley, she is my heart's delight,
And it's with you lovely Molly, I could spend till broad daylight.

When going to church last Sunday, my love she passed me by,
I knew her mind was altered, by the roving of her eye,
I knew her mind was altered to a lad of low degree,
Oh, Molly, lovely Molly, your looks have wounded me.

I then took out a bottle and held it in my hand,
Saying, 'Take a glass dear Molly, our courtship's at an end,
So raise a glass dear Molly, drain the bottom dry to me,
For there are ten guineas wagered, that married we ne'er shall be.'

Oh, never court a wee girl with a dark and a roving eye,
Just kiss her and embrace her, don't tell her the reason why,
Just kiss her and embrace her, till you cause her heart to yield,
For a faint-hearted soldier, never gained a battlefield.

Some do court in earnest and some do court in fun,
And I can court the old sweetheart, for to draw the new ones on,
I tell him that I love him, for to keep his mind at ease,
And when his back is turned, I court with who I please.

Farewell to Ballymoney and County Antrim too,
Likewise lovely Molly, I bid a fond adieu,
Amerikay lies far away, across the ocean blue,
And I'm bound for there dear Molly and again I'll ne'er see you.

This song also came from Joe's mother. It appears under variant titles in the north of Ireland and North America. In Ireland the opening line varies from 'When going to mass' and also 'When going to church', depending on the religious denomination to which the singer is affiliated or wherever he or she 'hangs their hat on Sunday'. Joe sang 'church'.

The Irish Folklore Commission in Dublin[33] in the 1930s organised a primary schools' programme. This involved the children in the Republic of Ireland attending national schools being asked to collect folklore, stories or songs from their parents, grandparents or neighbours. This scheme resulted in some fascinating material being collected by the children. A version of this song came from Ballyhaise National School, Co. Cavan in 1938 under the general heading – 'Local Songs' and instead of Joe's *Farewell to Ballymoney*, we have it localised to the Co. Cavan *Farewell unto the Shannon banks*. The famous Ritchie family from Kentucky have a version called *Lovin' Hannah* and the renown folksong collector, Cecil Sharp, who collected songs in the early part of the last century in the Appalachian area of the US, as well as the south of England came across a fragment in the Marylebone Workhouse in 1909.

25 Faughanvale

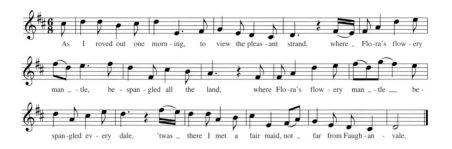

As I roved out one morning, to view the pleasant strand,
Where Flora's flowery mantle, bespangled all the land,
Where Flora's flowery mantle bespangled every dale,
'Twas there I met a fair maid, not far from Faughanvale.

'Good morning to you, fair maid,' I unto her did say,
'Is this the road to Derry? come tell to me, I pray.'
'This is the road to Derry, I will give you honest bail,
And who are you acquainted with, that lives in Faughanvale?'

'Oh, indeed, Miss, I may tell you, my acquaintances are few,
But your beauty's so enticing, I am ensnared by you,
Your beauty's so enticing and your graces are so real,
That I must rue the morning, I passed through Faughanvale.'

She modestly made answer, 'Kind sir, I'm not for you,
I am engaged to a young man, our passage is paid through,
Our ship's for Philadelphia, if it blows a pleasant gale,'
And her words left me lamenting on the shores of Faughanvale.

The small birds in the forest do join in harmony,
In sounding my love's praises, wherever that she be,
In sounding my love's praises, on every hill and dale,
And the happy bells, her praises tell on the banks of Faughanvale.

Now I will walk up to Derry, I'll call in at Sergeant Cole's,
And I'll drink a health to Molly, she's the object of my soul,
And if she proves hard-hearted, until death I will bewail,
Like a broken-hearted lover, on the braes of Faughanvale.

This is another song from Joe's 'steam-roller' days, learnt from a Co. Derry work-mate. There is a completely different song which featured on the 25 February 1939 in the *Songs of the People* under this title. It was composed by a local poet called Thomas Young from the townland of Killywool in *c.*1879. In Joe's song here we have the common theme of unrequited love with the young man doing the sensible thing – he goes into Sergeant Cole's public house and drowns his sorrows!

26 The Flowering Trade

Oh, I hear that the flowering has become a good trade,
The girls in this country their fortune is made,
When they rise in the morning their spirits are low,
And the very first race to the tay-pot they go.

Refrain:
To the tay-pot they go, to the tay-pot they go,
And the very first race to the tay-pot they go.

Then it's down in the ashes their toes they present,
Saying, 'Mother, my head it is likened to rent,
The cordial that drives the disorder away,
Oh, there's nothing to me like a wee drop o' tay'.

Now when they are married they'll do what they can,
To make a good wife and to help a good man.

Joe could only recall a fragment of this song which his mother sang. He told me that the 'flowering' trade mentioned in the song refers to embroidering, which many women-folk worked at as a cottage industry. There was a big demand for linen handkerchiefs, tray cloths, chair backs etc., with hand-embroidered flowers, shamrocks etc.

I was unable to find this song in any collections at home or abroad, but I was delighted to find a reference to the title and first line in an article by Hugh Shields in *Ulster Folklife*.

Hugh's attention had been drawn to a collection of broadside ballads in the library of the Royal Society of Antiquaries of Ireland in Dublin. Of the nearly 200 songs in the collection, more than half have printer's imprints showing Alex Mayne of High Street, Belfast, including the song *The Flowering Trade* which I reproduce in the appendix, p. 276.[34] Hugh dates the broadsides to the mid nineteenth century, but he was unable to find any other source for this song. Hugh Marks of Kilkeel, Co. Down in his reminiscences, songs and stories published in 1961[35] recalled one verse of a song which referred to 'flowerers'. Hugh endorsed Joe's account – that flowering referred to the hand-embroidering cottage industry of the nineteenth and early twentieth centuries:

> Och it's aisy knowin' the flowerers, when they go into town,
> Wi' their long masled shins an' wi' their petticoats hangin' down,
> Wi' their boots half laced an' their piercers[36] by their side,
> And says aul' Mr Crutchley, 'Ye've made yer holes too wide.'

Breda McKinney, in her unpublished MPhil. thesis,[37] recorded some interesting recollections from Co. Donegal-man, Packie Manus Byrne (b.1917). Packie told her about some cottage

The cottage industry of *The Flowering Trade* with the Widow Greer, Wren's Nest, Bryansford, Co. Down, *c.*1910 (photograph courtesy of MAGNI).

industry experiences he witnessed in the early years of the twentieth century, which is in some ways comparable to the waulking song tradition in the west of Scotland, involving women working with tweed. Here's Packie's account of the Co. Donegal women singing as they worked:

> It was really nice when you would get four or five of them together, quilting or something, sewing up and down from top to bottom; they'd probably all be singing in unison. They knew nothing about harmony, but they could make a real good job of the melody, decorations and all. And even the younger girls like my sisters – you'd get three or four of them sitting around and they'd be singing at the top of their voices and working away at the embroidery – the song kind of came naturally.

27 The Gallant Hussar

A damsel possessed of much beauty, as she stood by her own father's gate,
The gallant hussars were on duty, to view them this damsel did wait,
Their horses kept capering and prancing, their accoutrements shone like a star,
From the plains they were nearer advancing, she espied her young gallant
    hussar.

Their pelisses slung o'er their shoulders, so careless they seemed for to ride,
And warlike appeared these young soldiers, with glittering swords by their
    sides,
To barracks so early next morning, this damsel she went in her car,
Because that she loved him sincerely, young Edward, her gallant hussar.

'Twas there to discourse with her soldier, these words she was heard for to say,
Oh, Jane as a heart there's none bolder, to follow her laddie away,
'Oh, fie,' said young Edward, 'be sober and think on the dangers of war,
When the trumpet sounds, I must be ready, so wed not your gallant hussar.'

'For six months on bread and cold water, my parents they made me confine,
Such hard-hearted parents to a daughter and one that was loyal and kind,
But unless they confine me forever and banish you from me afar,
I'll follow my soldier so clever and I'll wed my young gallant hussar.'

Said Edward, 'Your friends you must mind them, or else if you don't you'll
    be done,
They will leave you no portion behind them, so pray do my company shun.'
Said Jane, 'If you be true-hearted, I have gold from my uncle in store,
From this moment we ne'er shall be parted and I'll wed my young gallant hussar.'

As he gazed on each beautiful feature, the tears from his eyes they did flow,
'I will wed with this beautiful creature, to forsake cruel dangers of war,'
So now they're united together, friends think of them near and afar,
Heaven bless them both now and forever, young Jane and her gallant hussar.

Joe was of the opinion that this song, which is another of his mother's songs, dates back to
the Crimean War, but most of broadside ballads date from *c.*1820 and would seem to pre-
date this war by some thirty years. One of the later nineteenth century broadside ballads
has another set of words, under the title, *The Answer to Young Jane and her Gallant Hussar*:

> 'You know that we are not long a-courting,
> And you need not ramble afar,
> I would purchase you out of the army,
> So now bid farewell to the war.'[38]

28 Glenarm Bay

Being on a mild Sep-tem-ber morn, the weath-er it be-ing warm, it was my lot to stray a-long the bay of sweet Glen-arm, the yel-low corn was wav-ing ripe and ev-ery field looked gay, and the blue sea washed the peb ___- bles white, a _ - long _ Glen-arm ___ Bay.

Being on a mild September morn, the weather it being warm,
It was my lot to stray along the bay of sweet Glenarm,
The yellow corn was waving ripe and every field looked gay,
The blue sea washed the pebbles white, along Glenarm Bay.

'Twas there I spied a charming maid, a maid both young and gay,
The sun arose, nor brighter shone than she appeared that day,
I step-ped up to this fair maid and unto her did say,
'What brings you here, so early, dear, along Glenarm Bay?'

She answered me right modestly, 'What makes you ask me so?
There's nothing brings young women here, but what all young men know,
It's the love that stirs a maiden young, she modestly did say,
And a manly man must prove himself, along Glenarm Bay.'

Says I, 'My dear I am sincere, here is my heart and hand,
Young women's frames at first were formed to pierce the hearts of man,
Take pity on your wounded swain and we will name the day,
And heal these wounds, your charms gave me, along Glenarm Bay.'

She says, 'My dear if you're sincere, your flattery I won't protest,
If you but knew the love that's true, flows through my burning breast,
And when old age comes creeping on and our locks are turning grey,
We both will mind the harvest morn, we met along the bay'.

Joe could only recall the first three verses of *Glenarm Bay*, which came from Johnny Toland from Ballyboyland, so I gave him two verses from my family collection to help him complete the song. It is a song that takes me back to my earliest recollections in Glenarm of my maternal grandmother Robinson and my mother singing of their native village. This was one of their favourite songs. My uncle Willie Robinson however had a less sentimental view of the surrounding countryside of his native Glenarm and would sing 'The Black Rock's[39] white with seagull's shite, along Glenarm Bay' instead of 'The blue sea washed the pebbles white, along Glenarm Bay.'

I remember Glenarm as a hive of great characters then including Uncle Willie who had a nickname around the Glens of Antrim and was known as Willie 'The Cat'. My mother told me that this nickname was due to the nocturnal life-style he led before he got married. I heard at a later date from another source that it was nothing of the sort and that it went back to his youth when he played the part of the cat in the local production of the pantomime, *Dick Whittington and His Cat*! Uncle Willie's popularity was evident with the huge turn-out for his funeral in 1974. After the burial family and friends all congregated in Jim McMullan's Pub in Toberwine Street, Glenarm, and many anecdotes were exchanged on his colourful life and exploits in and around the Glens of Antrim in the early years of the twentieth century. The fiddle player and poitín maker, Mickey McIlhatton, known as King of the Glens,[40] came over to me and regaled me with some of his personal memories of Willie 'The Cat'. He then produced from his pocket a strange metal contraption and asked me, 'Do you know what these are Leonard?' I said that I didn't have a clue what they were, and he explained. 'They're spurs for game cocks and your grandfather Johnny Robinson made them for me some fifty years ago. Johnny was the best blacksmith in the Glens of Antrim and beyond. I could have sold them spurs a hundred times over, but I wouldn't part with them – they're tempered steel you know and they're as light as a feather!'

Another character from Glenarm and an old friend of mine was John Rea (1915–83). John was a hammered-dulcimer player and a far-out relative of my own. My maternal grandmother and John's mother were cousins and my mother, as a child, used to visit the neighbouring Rea household at Town Parks with her mother in the 1920s. She said it was a very jolly household with music-making, song and dance a daily occurance. John's father and some of his brothers played various instruments including fiddle and melodeon and my mother recalled John as a wee boy standing on an up-turned butter box, playing the hammer-dulcimer which was set on the kitchen table beside his mother as she worked, dancing from the bake-board to the griddle!

I introduced Joe Holmes to John Rea and they got on like a house on fire, swopping tunes, songs and stories. John was also a fine fiddle player, but the dulcimer was his first love. Some time after Joe died in 1979, a big festival was organised in London called *The Sense of Ireland* and John Rea and I were asked over and we spent a wonderful week together sharing a room in the Tara Hotel. One of the concerts was in the Royal Albert Hall and we were performing along with other musicians and singers from all over Ireland, providing support for the head-line band *The Chieftains*. The hall was filled to capacity

John Rea (1915–83), Town Parks, Glenarm, Co. Antrim, playing the
hammered-dulcimer, *c.*1976 (photograph by Colin Hamilton).

with some 6,000 people in the audience. When John and I came off the stage after our
performance, Donncha Ó Dúlaing from RTE Radio was backstage with a microphone and
tape recorder and he asked John 'were you not nervous John, playing your dulcimer in
front of all those people?' 'Nervous?' says John, 'Damn the fear – I wouldn't give a damn
if the Queen of England, de Valera or the Pope in Rome was in the audience – I just play
tunes on my wee dulcimer!'

When John Rea died in November 1983, his son Alec telephoned to tell me of the sad news and confirm the funeral arrangements. He told me that the Presbyterian clergyman in Glenarm had also recently died and that he had contacted a clergyman in Buckna to perform the funeral service. I decided I had better contact the clergyman to let him know who John Rea was and his status as a traditional musician. So I made the telephone call and stressed the importance of John Rea and his music and gave details of John's broadcasting career on radio and television with the BBC, RTE, and also his appearances on UTV, as well as his albums with Topic Records of London and his many stage and festival appearances, including London's Royal Albert Hall. John's funeral coincided with an Arts Council of Northern Ireland *You and Yours* Tour, which was in nearby Cushendall the previous night. I made contact with Ciarán Carson, who was then the Arts Council's Traditional Arts Officer, and two of the musicians on the tour, Jackie Daly and James Kelly, kindly agreed to play a lament on the accordion and fiddle at the graveside. The clergyman proceeded with the funeral ceremony and when it came to the sermon he chose to give a 'hell-fire and brimstone' oration and had selected all the most malevolent references to dulcimers and the Devil's music from the Old Testament that he could find! The poets Michael Longley and John Montague were standing beside me in the Glenarm Municipal Graveyard and John Montague remarked, 'Thank God I'm a Taig',[41] to which I responded, 'Another sermon like that John and I'll be joining you!'

29 Good Friends and Companions

Good ____ friends and _ com - pan - ions, to ___ - geth - er com - bine, come
Refrain: So here's a health to _ the com - pany and _ one to my lass, let's

fill up your glass - es in _ cho - rus with mine, we will drink and be mer - ry, good _
drink and be mer - ry, all _ out of one glass, let's _ drink and be mer - ry, good _

drinks and re - frain, for we may or might nev - er all _ meet here a - gain.
drinks and re - frain, for we may or might nev - er all _ meet here a - gain.

Good friends and companions, together combine,
Come fill up your glasses in chorus with mine,
We will drink and be merry, good drinks and refrain,
For we may or might never all meet here again.

Refrain:
So here's a health to the company and one to my lass,
Let's drink and be merry, all out of one glass,
Let's drink and be merry, good drinks and refrain,
For we may, or might never all meet here again.

Here's a health to the wee lass that I love so well,
For style and for beauty there's none can excel,
She smiles on my countenance and she sits on my knee,
There is none in this wide world as happy as me.

Our ship lies at anchor, I have seen her in dock,
That she be safe landed without shake or shock,
And when we are sailing to the land of the free,
I will always remember your kindness to me.

I have read that old proverb, I have read it so true,
My love she's as fair as the bright morning dew,
I have read that old proverb, I suppose so have you?
So good friends and companions, I now bid you adieu.

This song today has become the parting anthem for most traditional singing events throughout Ireland. Joe learned it from his neighbour and fellow fiddler Paddy McGinley from the townland of Ballyboyland. The song is also widespread in Scotland with the Stewart family from Blairgowrie, Perthshire singing a version. *The Greig-Duncan Folk Song Collection* has several versions collected in the north-east of Scotland in the early twentieth century under the title *The Emigrant's Farewell to Donside*, which includes a verse of which I have never come across in Ireland:

> Let us drive away sorrows, drown tears in a glass,
> Let every young lover drink a health to his lass,
> Let us drink and be merry, from all hatred refrain,
> For we may and might never all meet here again.[42]

30 Grá mo Chroí[43]

At the foot of Slem-ish moun _-tain, clear _ wa-ter does flow, there _ lives a _ wee lass - ie, far _ whit - er than _ snow, her _ waist small _ and slen - der, for all young men to see, and her name in plain _ I _- rish is _ fair _ grá mo croi.

At the foot of Slemish mountain, clear water does flow,
There lives a wee lassie, far whiter than snow,
Her waist small and slender, for all young men to see,
And her name in plain Irish is fair grá mo chroí.

If I was a scholar and could handle a pen,
I would write my love a letter and to her I would send,
I would write her a letter and seal it with love,
If her heart was a mountain, it might her remove.

If the moon she may darken and show us no light,
And the bright stars of heaven fall down from their height,
That the rocks they may all melt and the mountains remove,
If ever I prove false to the fair one I love.

If I was an emperor and had the care of a crown,
And had I all the money, that's with it laid down,
I would kindly retain it, to the one that I love,
And my mind I'd resign to the high Power above.

If the ships on the ocean may go without sail,
And the smallest of fishes turn into great whales,
In the middle of the ocean may there grow a large tree,
If ever I prove false to my fair grá mo chroí.

Joe's mother sang 'Slemish mountain' in the first line of this song, but Jimmy Kealey, a fiddler and singer from Ballymoney and a regular visitor to Killyramer, sang 'Newry mountain'. Kealey was Sam Henry's informant for this and other items for his *Songs of the People* series. Another printed source in Colm Ó Lochlainn's *Irish Street Ballads* also has 'Newry mountain', which originated from a W. McKimmin of Newry and sent to P.W. Joyce in 1875. So I fear Antrim has to concede to Down on this one. Jimmy Kealey of Union Street, Ballymoney was one of the best known fiddlers in north Antrim in the first half of the twentieth century and he broadcast regularly on local BBC radio. Jimmy's son Gerry was a fine musician too on the accordion and he often accompanied Joe and I on our musical rambles. Jimmy Kealey also sometimes performed on radio and in concert with Sam Henry. Joe told me that Jimmy taught fiddle to several young pupils in the locality and one young lad who Jimmy thought was getting a bit too big for his boots, asked Jimmy one time what he thought of his fiddle playing, 'Well,' says Jimmy, 'If you put in what you left out and left out what you put in – you would be a damn good wee fiddler!'

31 The Green Brier Bush

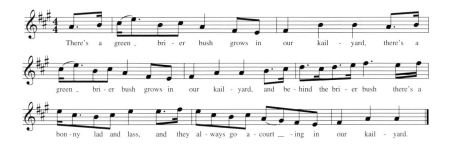

There's a green brier bush grows in our kail-yard,
There's a green brier bush grows in our kail-yard,
And behind the brier bush there's a bonny lad and lass,
And they always go a-courting in our kail-yard.

This is another of Joe's fragmentary recollections, which he heard sung by Johnny Toland. A 'Kail-yard' is a kitchen vegetable garden.

Robert Burns, known as the national bard of Scotland, submitted a re-worked version to James Johnson's *Scots Musical Museum* in 1796, under the title *There Grows A Bonie Brier-Bush*, with the comment that the older version of the song 'is very rude.' I was hoping that the 'rude' version would turn up in Burn's collection of bawdy pieces *The Merry Muses of Caledonia*, but to no avail. Then I came across another fragment collected by Hamish Henderson and Peter Kennedy in the 1950s from the singer and settled traveller from Aberdeen, Jeannie Robertson, called *The Cuckoo's Nest*, which may be the song Burns was referring to:

There is a thorn bush in oor kail-yard,
There is a thorn bush in oor kail-yard,
At the back of the thorn bush there stands a lad and lass,
But they're busy, busy hairing at the cuckoo's nest.[44]

32 Green Broom

There was an old man and he lived in the east,
He lived by the cutting of broom, green broom.
He'd one lazy son and his name it was John,
He would lie in his bed until noon, gay noon,
He would lie in his bed until noon.

The old man arose and he put on his clothes,
He cursed and he foamed through the room, gay room,
If Jack would not rise and go sharpen his knives,
And get off to the woods to cut broom, green broom,
And get off to the woods to cut broom.

Then Jack he arose and he put on his clothes,
He cursed and he foamed through the room, gay room,
'I'm of good noble blood and my learning is good,
And must I be a cutter of broom, green broom,
And must I be a cutter of broom.'

Then Jack he arose, to the green wood he goes,
And he cuts a large bundle of broom, green broom,
And Jack travelled on till he passed many towns,
Till he came to a castle of fame, gay fame,
Till he came to a castle of fame.

A lady she sat at her window so high,
And on hearing Jack crying, 'Brooms, green brooms',
She rang the bell and to her maid she called,
'Go fetch me that lad who cries, broom, green broom,
Go fetch me that lad who cries broom'.

Then in Jack he came and up stairs he goes,
And he enters the lady's room, gay room,
'You're a clever young blade, Jack leave off your trade,
And marry a lady in her bloom, gay bloom,
Yes, marry a lady in her bloom'.

Then Jack he consents and to church they went,
And he married this lady in her bloom, gay bloom,
And Jack blessed the day, he travelled that way,
There's an art in the cutting of broom, gay broom,
There's an art in the cutting of broom.

The oldest printed version of this song seems to be from 1720, when it appeared as *The Jolly Broom-Man* or *The Unhappy Boy Turned Thrifty* in D'Urfey's wonderfully titled song collection *Pills to Purge Melancholy*. The storyline in D'Urfey's text is close to what Joe sang with the exception that Joe's version had a happy conclusion of marriage, whereas in D'Urfey there's no marriage, but Jack takes on an apprentice to teach him the 'art' of the cutting of broom!

Joe's version again came from Johnny Toland and Joe thought it may have come via the travelling community who at one time used to peddle their tin-ware, hand-made brooms and other goods from door-to-door around the Irish countryside.

33 Here I Am Amongst You

Here I am amongst you and I'm here because I'm here,
And I'm only twelve months older, than I was this time last year,
Righ rah, with me tour righ rah, with me tour I oor I ah,
Righ de dom with me tour I ah, with me tour I oor I ah.

Oh, never throw a brick at a drowning man, when you're near to a grocer's store,
Just throw him a cake of Sunlight soap, let him wash himself ashore,
Righ rah, with me tour righ rah, etc.

Oh, the more a man has, the more a man wants, the same I don't think true,
For I never met a man with one black eye, that wished that he had two.
Righ rah, with me tour righ rah, etc.

Oh, it's early to bed and early to arise, the same I don't think true,
For how in the Hell can a man go to bed, when he has none to go to.
Righ rah, with me tour righ rah, etc.

Joe and I learned this wee nonsense song from Paddy Joe Kelly from Rocktown in Co.
Derry. Paddy Joe was a jolly wee man who specialised in comic songs. Kevin Conneff of
the group *The Chieftains* got the song from us and recorded it with an additional verse,
which he wrote himself:

> Oh, I think that I have said enough,
> Someone show me the door,
> I'll take a bow and leave you now,
> And I won't come back no more.

When Joe and I would sing it we would follow it with a polka called *My Love Nell* which we lilted. Joe had learned this dance tune as a boy from his older brother Harry, who also played the fiddle and who had emigrated to Canada in the 1920s. Joe recalled a fragment of a song to this air:

> Oh, my love Nell is a charming girl,
> From the county Down came she,
> But I weeped and I wailed,
> When the big ship sailed,
> For the shores of Amerikay.

34 India's Burning Sands

In blithe and bon - ny Scot - land, where the blue - bells they do grow, there dwells a love - ly maid - en fair, down in yon val - ley low, and all day long she herds her sheep, by the love - ly banks of Clyde, al - though her lot in life is low, she is called the vil - lage pride.

In blithe and bonny Scotland, where the bluebells they do grow,
There dwells a lovely maiden fair, down in yon valley low,
And all day long she herds her sheep, by the lovely banks of Clyde,
Although her lot in life is low, she is called the village pride.

An officer from Paisley town, went out to fowl one day,
And wandered through these lonesome shades, where Mary's cottage lay,
And often he came back that way, each time a visit paid,
His flattering tongue soon won the heart of that sweet village maid.

A long and loving look he took upon that form so fair,
And he wondered much so bright a flower should grow and flourish there,
And oft they would together walk through many a hill and dale,
Yet never deemed how love could steal, those gentle hours away.

At length he came one morning fair, his face was dark with woe,
'Oh, Mary dear, it's' Henry says, 'from you I now must go,
The young recruits have got the rout and I to duty yield,
I must forsake your lowland glens for India's burning field.'

'Oh, Henry, lovely Henry, how can you from me part?
But take me as your wedded-wife, you know you've won my heart,
Where green woods grow and valleys low, you were my heart's desire,
And as your servant I will go, disguised in man's attire.'

He brought her on to Paisley town and much they wondered there,
To see that young recruit that looked so gentle, slight and fair,
The ladies all admired her as she stood there on parade,
But little they knew a soldier's cloak concealed a lovely maid.

They soon crossed o'er the raging seas, to India's burning lands,
No pen can tell what Mary bore through India's trackless sands,
But as she fought, her strength gave out, her woe she strove to hide,
By smiling when she turned around to Henry by her side.

She saw her lover was cut down, a spear had pierced his side,
And from his post he never flinched, but where he stood he died,
She raised him from his bleeding gore and in her arms him pressed,
But as she strove to quench his wounds, a ball passed through her breast.

And as those couple lived in life, in death they loved the same,
And as their fond hearts' blood ran cold, it mixed in one red stream.
True love like this is hard to find, it is so true and strong.
She left her friends in the lowland glen, gone, never to return.

Another song Joe had from his mother and more than likely came from Scotland. It is a very full version of the song with its 'female soldier in disguise' motif. Most of the folk song collections in Ireland, Britain or North America will contain one or more songs on this theme, whereby the girl dresses up as a soldier or sailor in order to rejoin her lover in service on land or on sea. It would appear that they both were killed in action fighting in India. The conflict referred to appears to be the First Indian War of Independence, or the 'Indian Mutiny', which would date this song from around 1857.

35 Johnny Doyle

I am a wee damsel, entangled in love,
My case I'll make known to the heavens above,
A-making my thoughts known, I count it no toil,
For to wander this wide world o'er, with young Johnny Doyle.

There's one thing that grieves me and I must confess,
I go to meeting and my true-love goes to mass,
But for to go to mass with him, I would count it no toil,
For to kneel at the altar, with young Johnny Doyle.

It being on a Wednesday evening, we were making of the plan,
That me and my Johnny were going to take a walk,
My waiting-maid was listening, as plain as you can see,
And she went unto my mother and told her on me.

My mother she conveyed me to a room, that was on high,
Where no-one could hear me, nor pity my sad cry,
She bundled up my clothes and told me to be gone,
For she knew in her fond heart, I loved this young man.

A horse and side-saddle, my father did provide,
With four and twenty horsemen to ride by my side,
Five hundred bright guineas, my father did provide,
The day that I was to be Sammy Moore's bride.

Folding down the clothes, he found she was dead,
And Johnny Doyle's handkerchief tied round her head,
Folding down the clothes, he found she was dead,
And a fountain of tears over her he did shed.

This is another song Joe had from his mother, but he could only recall five verses. Sam Henry in his *Songs of the People* column published eleven verses in 1926, but the most complete Irish text seems to be the Kilwarlin, Co. Down 1845 MS of John Hume in the National Library, Dublin which has fourteen stanzas.

The song tells the sad tale of parental disapproval of a mixed religion/class match. The parents forced the young girl to marry Sammy Moore and not her Catholic lover, Johnny Doyle. In the last verse, when Sammy Moore goes to her bedchamber he finds the young girl dead, with Johnny Doyle's handkerchief tied round her head. I have included the last verse from the Henry collection as verse 6.

Johnny Doyle must have emigrated for in Sam Henry's *Songs of the People* we find an interesting account of good fortune from the 'Worth of an Old Song':

There were notices in the newspapers recently about a couple of humble folk in Co. Down who had come in for a large fortune which had been left by an American dollar millionaire, Mr Jefferson Doyle. An interesting little story is told of the way in which the recipients were traced as the nearest relatives of the rich man. There is a well-known Irish song – known as well to the Irish in America as to the Irish at home – which begins 'I'd range the world over with you, Johnny Doyle.' The millionaire died without anyone to inherit his money, and it occurred to his lawyer that perhaps there might be a clue in the 'Johnny Doyle' of the song. He accordingly wrote to Dr Grattan Flood, the well-known Irish musician, for the text and information about the origin of the song. Dr Flood was able to supply exactly what he wanted and this was particularly valuable, because the Johnny Doyle in the ballad was not merely a real person, but the father of Mr Jefferson Doyle. The song perpetuated the memory of the elopement of Johnny Doyle about a century ago from Rathfriland, Co. Down, to the United States, and there are still Doyles of the family in this place and they have now come into a goodly heritage through the words of the song.[45]

36 Johnny and Molly

Said John-ny to Mol-ly, 'I am now _ going to _ leave _ you, and do not be griev - ed at _ my going a _ - way, for the more we are part _ - ed, we'll _ al-ways be true _ - heart _ - ed, and a - gain I'll re _ - turn in the _ sweet _ month of May.'

Said Johnny to Molly, 'I am now going to leave you,
And do not be griev-ed at my going away,
For the more we are parted, we'll always be true-hearted,
And again I'll return in the sweet month of May.'

Said Molly to Johnny, 'Oh, I will mourn for you,
And I will be griev-ed at your going away,
For you know very well that your absence does grieve me,
I'm afraid you would die in some strange country.'

'I'll dress myself up like a neat little sea-boy,
Amidst of all dangers, I will stand your friend,
And when that the lofty high winds are a-blowing,
My dear I'll be with you, to plough the rough main.'

'Your delicate fingers our ropes could not handle,
Your lily-white feet love, our decks could not stand,
Nor the cold nights of winter, you ne'er could endure them,
So stay at home darling, to the seas do not go.'

Her two little arms, round his neck she entwined them,
And the clear, crystal tears from her eyes down did flow,
And her lily-white hands on the deck she kept wringing,
Crying, 'Oh, my belov-ed will I ne'er see you more?'

Come all ye pretty fair maids, that's inclined to marry,
Oh, ne'er place your affection too much upon one,
For first they will court you and then they'll deceive you,
They will leave you, as I'm left to mourn when they're gone.

This is yet another from Joe's mother's song-bag and another one with the 'female in disguise' motif. Here the girl wants to dress up and join her sailor lover and go to sea. However, in this case the young man manages to dissuade her by declaring that:

Your delicate fingers our ropes could not handle,
Your lily-white feet love, our decks could not stand,
Nor the cold nights of winter you ne'er could endure them,
So stay at home darling, to the seas do not go.

When Joe and I sang this song one night in McConnell's of Bellanaleck in Co. Fermanagh, Sandy McConnell followed it with a fragment of a variant of the same song to another air. Sandy was the father of the renowned flute player and singer Cathal McConnell.

Fleadh Cheoil na hÉireann, Ennis, Co. Clare, 1977. L-R: Len Graham, Jackie Devenney,
Ciarán Carson, ? , Roísín White, Cathal McConnell, Frank Harte and Joe Holmes
(photograph courtesy of Roísín White).

Cross Keys public house, Toome Bridge, Co. Antrim, *c*.1973:
Joe Holmes, Len Graham with Dermy Diamond, Dianna Skillen, Eugene 'Spooly' Kelly,
John Parkinson, Gerry McCartney, Andy Dickson and others unidentified
(photograph courtesy of NITB).

It was while attending the All-Ireland Fleadh Cheoil of 1964, which was held in Clones, Co. Monaghan, that I met Cathal for the first time. He and I were kindred song spirits and he invited me to visit his home and his father Sandy, who was very interested in traditional song, music and folklore. A few weeks later I arrived there at Bellanaleck near Enniskillen, where a McConnell céilí was in full swing. The McConnell home was a traditional home, but there seemed to be an endless flow of visitors coming and going with endless cups of tea and sandwiches being prepared by Cathal's mother Mary and his sister Maura, while tunes filled the air. Over the years I was to visit the McConnell home many, many times and it became a musical home from home for me. I brought Joe Holmes with me to Bellanaleck on several occasions and he was an instant hit with the McConnell's and their many visitors. On one of our visits in the autumn of 1974, we brought two bottles of Mickey McIlhatton's poitín and as Sandy was at that time the only non-pioneer in the house, we drank each others' health. Shortly after this visit we received the sad news of Sandy's passing and Cormac (his eldest son) told me at the funeral that Sandy had asked his wife Mary to hide McIlhatton's other full untouched bottle of poitín for a special occasion. Little did he think that the special occasion would turn out to be his own wake. Cathal, at the age of thirty, was to take his first drink of alcohol at his father's wake, and it was McIlhatton's poitín that was used for the christening!

37 John Reilly the Sailor

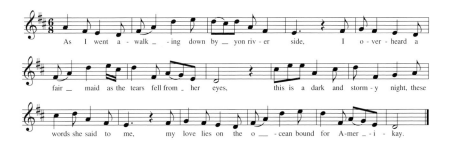

As I went a-walk _ -ing down by _ yon riv - er side, I o - ver - heard a fair _ maid as the tears fell from _ her eyes, this is a dark and storm - y night, these words she said to me, my love lies on the o _ - cean bound for A-mer _ - i - kay.

As I went a-walking down by yon river side,
I overheard a fair maid as the tears fell from her eyes,
This is a dark and stormy night, these words she said to me,
My love he's on the ocean bound for Amerikay.

My love he is a sailor bold, his age is scarce sixteen,
He is the finest young man that ever you have seen,
My father he has riches great, but Reilly he is poor,
And because I love my sailor lad, he cannot me endure.

John Reilly is my true-love's name, he was born near the Drain,
My mother took me by the hand, these words to me she said,
'If you think more of Reilly, you must leave this country,
Your father says he'll have his life, or shun his company.'

'Oh, mother, dear mother don't be severe, where will I send my love?
My very heart lies in his breast as constant as a dove.'
'Oh, daughter, dear I'm not severe, here is five hundred pounds.
Send Reilly to Americay, to purchase there some ground.'

And when she got the money, to Reilly she did run,
'This very night to have your life, my father charged the gun,
Here is five hundred pounds in gold, my mother sent to you,
To sail off to Amerikay and I'll quickly follow you.'

So early the next morning, my love he sailed away,
And as he set his foot on board, these words to me did say,
'Here is a token of true-love you may break it in two,
You have my heart and have my ring until I find out you.'

'Twas scarcely three years after, she was walking on the shore.
When Reilly he came back again and stole his love away,
The ship was wrecked all hands were lost, the father grieved full sore,
He found Reilly in her arms all drown-ed on the shore.

And on her breast a letter found, it was all stained with blood,
Saying, 'Cruel was my father, he tried to shoot my love,
Now let this be a warning to all fair maids, I pray,
To never let the lad you love sail to Amerikay.'

Paddy 'Stump' McCloskey from Carnamenagh, Co. Antrim, a contributor to the *Songs of the People* series, was a regular visitor to the Holmes's céilí-house. Sometimes he was accompanied by his two nieces, who lived close-by to Killyramer in the townland of Dunaghy. This song came from them and Joe said the singing in unison of the McCloskey sisters was a real treat. Joe's mother transcribed the words of this song into her song book.

The song is widespread and versions appear in collections and on broadside ballads found in Ireland, Britain and North America. The 'broken-token' motif features once again, but with her father's disapproval, we have yet another sad ending when the young couple are drowned in a ship wreck en route to the US. In Joe's version John Reilly is from the 'Drain', which I have been unable to identify, although there is a small village called Drain's Bay just north of Larne, Co. Antrim. Two Canadian texts locate Reilly in 'the town of Bray'.[46] The English folk song collector George B. Gardiner collected a version of this song in 1907 from Robert Giles, in Portsmouth Workhouse and in that version young Reilly 'lives down by the quay'.[47]

38 The Jolly Ploughboy

And like the jol-ly plough-boy, she whis-tles and she sings, and at night she does re-turn a-gain, with the dew on all her wings, with the dew all on her wings, with the dew all on her wings, and at night she does re-turn a-gain, with the dew all on her wings.

And like the jolly ploughboy, she whistles and she sings,
And at night she does return again, with the dew all on her wings,
With the dew all on her wings, with the dew all on her wings,
And at night she does return again, with the dew all on her wings.

Joe could only recall one verse of this song, which his mother only sang in snatches. The Co. Fermanagh singer Paddy Tunney sang a fuller version and *The Johnstons* group recorded and popularised this in the early 1970s. Also a version of the song was in the Butcher family repertory. There are many copies of it on nineteenth-century broadside ballads with one of them printed by J.O. Bebbington, 26 Goulden Street, Manchester, *c.*1850 and which I include in the appendix, p. 277, as a facsimile copy entitled *The Lark in the Morning.*[48] It includes some 'rustic' verses, which I haven't heard sung in the oral tradition in Ireland:

And as they return from the wake in the town,
The meadows being mown and the grass cut down,
We chanced to tumble all on the new mown hay,
Its kiss me now or never, the maiden did say.

When twenty weeks were over and past,
Her mamma asked her the reason, why she thickened in the waist,
'It was the pretty ploughboy,' the damsel did say,
'That caused me to tumble on the new mown hay.'

Come all you pretty maidens, wherever you be,
You may trust a ploughboy to any degree,
They're used so much to ploughing, their seed for to sow,
That all who employ them are sure to find it grow.

Joe Holmes, *c.*1975 (photograph by John Currie).

Mentioning Paddy Tunney above, reminded me of an Ulster traditional singing concert in which Joe and I were asked to perform at in the early 1970s. The event was the Éigse na Trionóide in Trinity College, Dublin and the organiser asked if I could bring Joe and also pick up Geordie Hanna, the Tyrone singer in Derrytresk on our way to Dublin. We arrived in Dublin, but we were a couple of hours too early for our performance, so I took the two lads to Mulligan's Pub in Poolbeg Street to wet our whistles before the show. Our visit to Dublin coincided with a rugby match between Ireland and Wales at Landsdowne Road and the pub was crowded with Welshmen. I noticed a man at a table sitting on his own who was reading the *Irish Times* and I asked him if he would mind if we joined him. He told us to come ahead and sit down, so I settled Joe and Geordie and went over to the bar to get our drinks. Our man continued reading his *Irish Times* and taking the occasional sip from his pint of Guinness. He had about three-quarters of a pint left in his glass, when this big

Outside Slattery's public house, Capel Street, Dublin Folk Festival 1975.
Frank Harte, Joe Holmes and Len Graham (photograph courtesy of Frank Harte).

fellow a Welshman I think, reached over and lifted our man's pint and downed it in one gulp. Our man reaches round for his Guinness and finds the glass empty and gives us a look that would wither you! I pointed over to the big fellow with his back to us, who had scoffed his pint.

'Ah,' says your man, 'A pint of Guinness never reared me – Paddy, pull me another pint, when you get a minute.' He then turned round to us, folded up his *Irish Times* and says, 'Where are ye lads from?' 'We're from the North', says I. 'Down for the match?' 'No,' says I, 'We're giving a concert in Trinity College this afternoon.' 'Are ye be God. Well you know I love the North; I go up there brave and often. I love to go up to McArt's Fort, you know it's up the Cave Hill near Belfast. Wolfe Tone met all those great Northern men in 1792 – McCracken, Neilson, Hope and all those guys. What time did you say your concert started?' I looked at my watch, 'Two o'clock,' says I. 'We'd better get round there now.' 'Very good, I'll be round to hear you when I finish my pint.' So we set off for Trinity College and Paddy Tunney was the other northern singer booked for the concert. Well we all went up on the stage together and we were told to do twenty minute sets, with Joe and myself doing some duet and solo singing. Joe and I opened the show, then Geordie and Paddy Tunney. Paddy had just started and was giving a big long introduction to his first song, when who should walk up the hall and sit himself down in the front row, but your man we were after meeting in Mulligan's pub. He waved up at us and we all, except Paddy, waved back. Paddy sang his first song and then started into a big long introduction for his second song. The next thing we knew, our 'friend' in the front row jumps to his feet and shouts – 'Arrah me arse, you black northern bastards!' and with that he stormed out of the hall. Paddy gave us all a quizzical look, but fair play to him he finished his introduction and ended the first half with a bit of a dance. The organiser came rushing over to us as we left the stage. 'Do you know that awful man?' 'Not really,' says I. 'We are only after meeting him in Mulligan's pub.' 'He's barred from here' says our perturbed organiser. 'I don't know how he got in. We had a nuclear physicist over from Cambridge University last month – giving a public lecture – and your man gave him similar treatment. He told him he knew F*** all about physics!'

Frank Harte very kindly gave accommodation in his home at Chapelizod to Geordie, Joe and myself. I was provided with a settee for a bed and Joe and Geordie were given a double bed. Frank and I overheard Geordie addressing Joe, 'Who does your laundry Joe?' By this time Joe had stripped down to his long-johns. 'My mother died about fifteen years ago Geordie and I do all my own laundry now,' says Joe. 'Joe Holmes,' says Geordie, 'you're a regimental man!'

Next morning we were seated down for breakfast and Stella, Frank's wife, was serving us up with the full Irish breakfast or 'tightner'. She told us she was having some difficulty with her dog – a big hairy bitch which was almost as big as an Irish wolfhound. Stella had borrowed a big dog of the same breed, but he wasn't showing any interest in Stella's bitch. I told her that Geordie had lots of experience with greyhounds. So Stella then turned to Geordie for advice, but Geordie wasn't very forthcoming with his knowledge of dogs. Later when we were travelling into Dublin in my car, Geordie from the back seat says, 'You know boys I could have given Stella some good advice, but it wasn't the sort of conversation I wanted to have with a woman over breakfast!'

39 Laurel Hill

When war had oppressed every nation with horror,
Wellington he ventured his life o'er the main,
To pull down French tyrants and make them surrender,
For the sake of old Ireland, I ventured the same,
I left those green hills, where I courted with Nancy,
She said, 'Jimmy dear, you'll be true to me still,
Till you gain that great victory and return from man's slaughter,
I'll mourn round the valleys of sweet Laurel Hill.'

When we landed in Spain, we were almost exhausted,
Being tossed by the winds and the billows so high,
Pursuing our foes over yon snowy white mountains,
Where many a bold hero was obliged for to die.
At last we survived in the hottest of battles,
O'er yon snowy mountains, we fought with great skill,
While thousands lay bleeding and gore all around me,
I smiled at all danger far from sweet Laurel Hill.

Our leaders were brave and we were stout-hearted,
France, Spain and Holland knew what we could do,
We pulled down French batteries with the great guns of Britain.
Caused orphans to mourn on distressed Waterloo,
So now the war's over and we all are returning,
From the dangers of war, for to rest for awhile,
And we gave them three cheers as we sailed for old Ireland,
And that long-looked-for valley and beautiful isle.

When we arrived by the side of yon harbour,
I spied my fair maid by the side of yon hill,
She was viewing the trout in yon lovely Bann water,
Still adding more beauty to grace Laurel Hill,
She appeared unto me like one all dressed in mourning,
I asked her the reason she roamed the Bann shore,
'My Jimmy is a soldier and he's ne'er returning,
Alas, oh my Jimmy I'll n'er see him more.'

'He has left me to mourn under these wild lonely mountains,
Where the fox and the otter do sport with free will,
Where the trout seeks its mate in yon lovely Bann water,
But, I can't find my Jimmy all around Laurel Hill.'
'Oh, it's I am your Jimmy, your long-looked-for soldier,
Although my tongue is altered and I'm in disguise,
Don't you mind on Kyle's brae, as oft times we courted,
When the bugles loud blast called me off in surprise.'

She fell into his arms like one pale and silly,
The tears falling from her like dew from the thorn,
Her eyes they bewitched everyone that beheld her,
As she welcomed her long-looked-for soldier's return.
So now to conclude, I will sing Wellington's praises,
That undaunted hero and an Irishman still,
His praises will be sung when kings are all forgotten,
And shall ring round the valleys of sweet Laurel Hill.

This is one of the great Ulster songs associated with the Battle of Waterloo (1815). On
hearing it for the first time sung by Eddie Butcher on a radio programme in and around

1967, and as soon as the programme was over, I jumped into my car and made a bee-line for Magilligan where Eddie lived. About one hour after the radio programme was over, I was knocking the front door of the Butcher home in the townland of Aughil, 'Are you the man that was singing on the wireless?' 'I am,' says Eddie and that was the beginning of another wonderful and enriching song friendship. We sang many songs for each other on that first encounter and Eddie's wife Gracie produced tea and sandwiches to revive the two song fanatics. At the end of the night, I asked if it would be all right if I brought a friend over with me on my next visit and they agreed that he was more than welcome. The friend was Joe Holmes and over the ensuing years, until Joe's death in 1978 and Eddie's death in 1980, I paid him a visit almost weekly. Many singers, musicians and devotees crossed the ever-welcoming Butcher threshold along with Joe and me for nights of endless songs.

One of the first songs Eddie asked me for the words of was the *Murlough Shore* which incidentally was the same song that introduced me and Joe Holmes. I obliged him on my next visit. Hugh Shields' wonderful book *Shamrock, Rose and Thistle*, on the songs of Magilligan with mainly Eddie's repertory, was published in 1981. Eddie had supplied Hugh with a version of *Moorlough Shore*. I smiled on reading the following comment from Hugh: 'In 1966 Eddie Butcher could sing me only three lines of *Moorlough Shore* … But three years later, Eddie, silently attentive, was able – by what means I could not discover – to sing a five verse version!'[49] Eddie sometimes played a little game with Hugh over the years and if Hugh wrote asking about such and such a song, Eddie would ask me or other singers from the locality had they the words. Eddie wouldn't be long putting an air to it. There were many other songs that passed back and forth between us. After Eddie died and I was over in the Butcher's home, Eddie and Gracie's son Billy came over to me, 'Is that your handwriting?' 'It is,' says I. 'I found that in my father's waistcoat pocket and he was learning it just before he died.' The song was *Bonny Portmore* and I had provided a text, but didn't have the melody. Eddie, it seems, was getting it ready for Hugh's next visit!

On one of the early visits to the Butcher's, Eddie sang Joe and I a wonderful five-verse version of the Waterloo song *Laurel Hill*. After he finished, Joe threw back his head and sang another verse which Eddie didn't have, to a different air. Joe told us he often heard it sung in his own home by a neighbour – a man called Willie Clarke, who sang and played the fiddle. He told us Willie was long since dead, but his son-in-law, John Johnson, was a singer and accordion-player and that he had a sweet shop in Ballymoney.

Some days later, Joe and I called on John in his shop in Castle Street, bought a quarter pound of brandy ball sweets and came away with the song. John also told us that the author of the song was a Coleraine man called Jim Richmond, who fought at Waterloo and the girl was Nancy Weir also from Coleraine. The theme of the returning unrecognised lover is a common motif, although Eddie's version omits this part of the song story.

When Eddie sang *Laurel Hill* at Féile na Bóinne in Drogheda in 1976 it was quite a hit and one of the audience, Mary McGrath of the famous Curragh of Kildare horse-breeding family, was so impressed that she named a very expensive thoroughbred foal at the National Stud *Laurel Hill*, in honour of the song. Eddie often wondered did it ever win any big races – like Lord Lurgan's *Master McGrath*, the greyhound which won the Waterloo

Cup three times in the nineteenth century. Then he threw his head back and there and then broke into the ballad in anticipation of a big win!

> Lord Lurgan stepped forward and he said, 'Gentlemen,
> If there's any among you has money to spend,
> For you nobles of England I don't care a straw,
> Here's five thousand to one upon Master McGrath.'

The above mentioned Féile ne Bóinne of 1976 has iconic status in recent folk memory as a landmark event in the folk singing calendar. It was the first of many traditional singing festivals where Seán Corcoran and Helen Brennan, and others of the Féile na Bóinne Committee, brought together singers from all over Ireland. Following the Drogheda event singing festivals sprung up in Belleek, Co. Fermanagh, Downpatrick, Co. Down, Newry, Co. Down, Portrush, Co. Antrim, Forkhill, Co. Armagh, Inishowen, Co. Donegal, Derrytresk, Co. Tyrone, Rosslare, Co. Wexford, etc. The first Féile na Bóinne was memorable and when Eddie Butcher arrived home to Magilligan he was inspired to put pen to paper and gave us some of his memories of a great weekend and within days of the event he was singing his new song to me in his kitchen:

The Drogheda Song

On the first day of October, on a Friday being the day,
We started off for Drogheda, a long and tedious way,
We passed through towns and villages, passed manys a green field,
But our hearts were all contented with Devenney at the wheel.

I sat beside Devenney for to watch him drive along,
To pass the time he sometimes sang a lively little song,
We had three other passengers and they were full of life,
There was Joseph Holmes and Leonard Graham, accompanied by my wife.

Now on the road to Drogheda, you never were alone,
For Leonard Graham and Joseph Holmes sometimes sang a song,
They then sang one together which was a lovely song,
And their voices rang through Antrim as the car she jogged along.

When we landed in Drogheda, the car came to a stand,
From Dublin, Cork and Galway they came out to shake our hands,
They shook our hands tenderly, they shook our hands so rare,
Then we got another welcome from the boys of Co. Clare.

When we entered in the festival, sure everything looked grand,
Tom Munnelly seemed for to be the boss with a big book in his hand,
'Twas he who called the singers all, he called them one by one,
It would have made your aul' heart tremble, for to hear them sing their song.

Dr Shields, sure he was there with his attractive wife,
They both came up from Dublin, for to spend a glorious night,
I was glad for to see them there, their company for to share,
Search the north and south of Ireland, you'll not find a better pair.

Well the time came round for us to go, the truth to you I'll tell,
They all came out from the hotel to bid us all farewell,
Devenney started up the car all ready for to start,
I thought that day my heart would break, when parting with Frank Harte.

But now that we are home again, we have nothing to regret,
The time we spent in Drogheda, I never will forget,
Long life unto Seán Corcoran, the man who asked us there,
And with his generosity, on us he did not spare.

Now I will end as I began, the truth to you I'll tell,
In praise of Jackie Devenney for he's a skillful man,
He took us there and brought us back and done his work so well,
Search the whole United Kingdom and there's no-one can compare.[50]

40 The Lily of the West

Come all you Nova Scotia lads and listen unto me,
I have been a rover all my life, but now I'm quit the sea,
I've sailed the stormy ocean, but the place that I love best,
It's sunny California, the lily of the west.

When I was young and foolish, I went unto the States,
My name being on the drummers, Philadelphia, I was engaged,
I led a wild and reckless life, so you can guess the rest,
And I'm off to California, the lily of the west.

The snow-clad hills of Picta are too severe for me,
The burning plains of Africa, I never want to see,
Give me the girl that I love best and that is my request,
And I'm off to California, the lily of the west.

You talk of Manitoba and the Isle of Nois so gay,
Likewise to Colorado, don't heed what people say,
If you want to gain a fortune lads, I'm afraid you'll be oppressed,
Then push to California, the lily of the west.

Farewell my friends and rivals, no longer can I stay,
I'll think of all your kindness, when I am far away,
The train is at the station and I must do my best,
So I'm off to California, the lily of the west.

There are many versions of this song found in Ireland, Britain and North America. This is another from Joe's mother. A very different version appears in the *Songs of the People*, collected in 1934 from Maggie Brownlow of Cloyfin, Co. Derry. Maggie's version, in common with some of the nineteenth-century broadside ballads, includes the lover's jealousy resulting in a dagger being stuck in the rival's breast which is ruled by the judge as a crime of passion:

> I stepped up to my rival with dagger in my hand,
> I dragged him from my false love and boldly bid him stand,
> Being mad with desperation, I pierced my rival's breast,
> For I was betrayed by Flora, the lily of the west.
>
> I had to stand my trial and boldly did I plead,
> The cause in my indictment, that shortly had me freed.
> This beauty bright I did adore, the judge did her address,
> Saying, 'Go, you faithless Flora, the lily of the west.'

The closest text to Joe's turns up in Canada in the Helen Creighton Collection. Creighton collected several Canadian versions of *The Lily of the West* between the 1930s and the 1950s. Two versions turned up with a similar text to Joe's song from Harold Hilshie from Pope's Harbour and Luther Fulton from Pembroke, both in Nova Scotia.[51]

41 The Load of Kail Plants

Oh, _____ sweet Bal - ly - mon - ey of fame and re - nown, I went to the fair, be - ing held in that town, on the fifth day of May in the year for - ty - five, a ver - y fine day for the bees for to hive. Oh, I be - ing young my for - tune to ad - vance, I went to the fair with a load of kail plants, I went up the main street be - fore Rob - in - son's mart, I low - ered my cart with a proud beat - ing heart.

Oh, sweet Ballymoney of fame and renown,
I went to the fair, being held in that town,
On the fifth day of May in the year forty-five,
A very fine day for the bees for to hive.
Oh, I being young, my fortune to advance,
I went to the fair with a load of kail plants,
I went up the main street before Robinson's mart,
I lowered my cart with a proud beating heart.

Oh, the boys from Loughguile, likewise Armoy,
They all gathered round me, my plants for to buy,
I addressed them with words, both proper and plain,
When I said forever, they all said, 'Amen'.
There was pamphrey and Dutch and curleys so sweet,
And rousing drum-heads that grow up like leek,
There was cow-kail, pull-early boys, eat while you're able,
And pickle for dressing a gentleman's table.

Now my plants are all sold and I wish them long life,
I've nothing to do, but look out for a wife,
The lady I view, I'll mark all of her points,
For I don't want a wife, that is stiff at the joints.
The first that I viewed, she wore a silk gown,
With long yellow locks and her hair hanging down,
Says I to myself, me girl, you're a swizzer,
And I stood her a drink, where they give the big measure.

Oh, then we set off on a kind of a walk,
Me and my girl we began for to talk,
She hemmed and hawed in gentle reflection,
But I soon won her over with kindly affection.
And then I presumed for to kiss this fair dame,
And then I presumed for to ask her, her name,
'Well indeed then kind sir, my name is McCloy,
I'm the peat cadger's daughter from the town of Armoy.'

'*In the year forty-five …*' in this song would seem to indicate that it dates back to 1845. Sam Henry published the song in 1924 in his *Songs of the People* column and gave his source as Mary Clarke and the author as a man by the name of Dempsey.

The song lists a catalogue of different types of Kail (cabbage), an unusual topic for a song of courtship!

The Mullaghbawn, Co. Armagh fiddler, Josephine Keegan, told me that her father, Joe Keegan, a flute-player, played this song air as a jig, which he learned when working in Scotland in the early years of the last century. He had some snippets of words to the tune including '*I wish I was back home in Dalry*'. I recall hearing Belle Stewart, the Scottish settled traveller from Blairgowrie in Perthshire, sing the song *Geordie Weir* to this same air with the first line – 'I wish I was back aince mair in Dalry' (that is, once more). I would say this is the same song Joe Keegan heard. Paddy Tunney, the Co. Fermanagh singer, also sang *The Rollicking Boys of Tandragee* to the same jig tune.

42 Long Cookstown

It's three long quarters I spent a-weaving and for my wages, I was paid down,
And for to buy a new suit of clothing, I made my way unto long Cookstown,
As I walked up through long Cookstown, oh, Nancy Whiskey I chanced to smell,
Say I to myself, I'll call and taste you, it's three long quarters I loved you well.

I step-ped into an ale-house tavern, I begged their pardon for making free,
But Nancy met me in every corner, 'You're heartily welcome, young man,'
     says she,
When I awoke all in the morning, I found myself in a strange bed,
I strove to rise, but I was not able, for Nancy Whiskey ran through my head.

Then I called onto the landlady, to see what reckoning I had to pay,
There's fifteen shillings for ale and brandy and after that, you may go or stay.
I put my hand into my pocket, that was the money I did pay down,
On looking back into my small purse, all remained was one bare half-crown.

I put my head out of a window, a smiling damsel I chanced to spy,
With her I spent my two and two pence and all remained was the fourpenny boy,
So I'll go home and I'll join my weaving, my little shuttle I'll steer awhile,
And I will earn more pocket money, for Nancy Whiskey did me beguile.

In Joe's time during the first half of the twentieth century, Ballymoney and district was a hive of industry with the various stages of the flax process from the growing of the crop, to the harvesting. The flax had to be pulled and not cut and then carted to the dams for steeping and when retted was thrown out, beet by beet, by men standing up to their waists in putrid water, for the flax-water couldn't be run-off, as it would contaminate and kill the fish in the rivers. The wet flax was then carted to grass fields and spread to dry – when this was achieved it was taken to the flax mill to be cleaned. This was done by passing the flax straw through rollers to break up the fibre; it was then made into stricks by children or junior workers. Stricks were small handfuls that the scutcher could easily manipulate. He would hold it over the stock and turn it round and round, whilst the rotating wooden blades would open it up and the cleaned strick was neatly dressed by the scutcher and ready for the next stage of its many processes. Joe had experience of all of the aforementioned processes, but it was to the scutching that he spent, as he said himself, the best years of his life. The scutchers often got serious injury to their hands and fingers, but Joe was fortunate, especially as a fiddler, that he didn't incur any injury during his scutching career. However, the dusty atmosphere of the flax mill was very unhealthy and he did suffer some respiratory problems in his latter years.

An early nineteenth-century survey of Co. Antrim[52] gives detailed information on the trades in the area including much information on trades to do with the linen industry. The Revd John Dubourdieu, rector of Annahilt, Co. Down, was commissioned by the Dublin Society to conduct a statistical survey of Co. Antrim which detailed fairly comprehensively statistics and information regarding the parish of Ballintoy. It records 7 flax-scutchers and 288 weavers, but does not specify if these were weavers of flax or wool. As it also contains a reference to 20 tailors, I think we can safely assume that both linen and woollen cloths were woven. For the dancers it records 4 fiddlers/pipers, and displaying the importance of the horse in the nineteenth century, 17 blacksmiths were employed in the parish. Other occupations recorded are 21 salmon-fishers, 25 shoe-makers, 5 thatchers, 7 wheel-wrights, 5 rabbit-hunters, 16 huxters, 3 letters of blood and some other bizarre details – 49 bastards, 10 blind, 2 dumb, 9 insane, 33 poor and to keep the lid on the whole lot – 118 yeomen! The Revd Dubourdieu observed and recorded all this in the parish of Ballintoy in the year 1803 and some years later again in the Co. Antrim Ordnance Survey Memoirs of the 1830s[53] we find a corn mill at Killyramer, flax mills at nearby Ballyboylands and the Topp as well as 23 linen weavers in the town of Ballymoney. So flax and linen had a long association with the area and of course it was a major, labour intensive industry throughout all of Ulster.

'Long Cookstown', as it is called in this song, consists practically of one long street, a mile and a half in length. It is one of the Plantation towns, laid out in 1609 and called after its founder, Alan Cooke.

Joe Greer, Cookstown whistle-player and character, gave us an old local saying: 'Long hungry Cookstown, where the dogs bark all night and the stones are all chained!' *Long Cookstown* is a localised version of the song *Nancy Whiskey* and it turns up with different locations mentioned. Besides Cookstown, Dublin, Glasgow, London and Longford also feature. Tommy Makem sang me a Co. Armagh version he has from his mother Sarah:

I am a weaver, a Darkley weaver, I am a rash and rakish blade,

And to buy me a suit of clothing, into Keady my way I made,
Well I came in by the Keady Monument and Nancy Whiskey I chanced to spy,
I was tempted to go and try her, for seven years now I have been dry.

The hero of the *Long Cookstown* song is a weaver, one of the many trades associated with the linen industry.

43 Lovely Armoy

Draw near my kind friends and relations, I am going to take my farewell,
I'm bound for a far distant nation, no longer in Armoy to dwell,
I'm leaving that sweet little village, wherein I was raised as a boy,
But sadly it grieves me for to leave you and part from you lovely Armoy.

By the banks of yon bonny Bush water, where the fishes swim neatly and fair,
By those banks I have often times wandered, in an evening when free from
     all care,
By those banks I have often times wandered, in an evening when free from
     employ,
No wonder it grieves me to leave you and part from you lovely Armoy.

I'm taking my leave off this evening, bright Phoebus declines from my view,
And I take my last walk round the garden, where the flowers are all sparkled
     with dew,
With banks of blown roses all around me, there the fair maid oft met me
     with joy,
No wonder it grieves me to leave you and part from you lovely Armoy.

We kissed and shook hands and then parted, I started my course without fail,
Till I came to the city of Belfast, where our good ship lay ready to sail,
Strict orders were given to board her, my pen I no longer employ,
No wonder it grieves me to leave you, I'll be far from you, lovely Armoy.

Lovely Armoy was another of Joe's mother's songs and the village of Armoy, in Co. Antrim held special affection for Joe. He often reminisced about the dances held in Molloy's Hall in Armoy from the 1930s right up to the late 1950s. Joe was a member of the Molloy Céilí Band which played reels, mazurkas, hornpipes, lancers, highland schottisches, quadrilles and all the old-style dances until they were finally ousted by the modern influx of the Show-Bands and Country and Western music. When a branch of Comhaltas Ceoltóirí Éireann was formed in Ballycastle, Co. Antrim in the mid-1960s, some of the original members of the old Molloy Céilí Band, became founder members, including Danny Molloy and Joe Holmes. A colourful Armoy character was fiddler Seán 'The Shadow' McLaughlin, who won the senior All-Ireland Fiddle competition at Fleádh Cheoil na hÉireann in Longford in 1957. Seán was a rather flamboyant 'artist' who fancied himself as a bit of a 'Michelangelo'. Joe and I visited his Armoy council-house dwelling one time and were amazed to see Seán had modeled his kitchen ceiling on the Vatican's Sistine Chapel. Joe immediately reverentially removed his cap! Also the glittering array of shinning horse-brasses around the fire-place nearly took the light out of our eyes. Yes, Seán was somewhat eccentric and when he was dying he requested that he be buried, dressed in a white tuxedo, with a red dicky-bow and a half pint of Bushmill's whiskey in his inside pocket. As far as I know his wish was granted!

44 Maggie Picken

Mag - gie Pick - en on the shore, gath - er - ing win - kles off Cul - more, she

lifted her leg and gave a roar, what the dev - il ails ye? Mag - gie Pick - en on the shore,

she had daugh - ters three or four, wish - ing she had man - y more, what the dev - il ails ye?

Lilt

Maggie Picken on the shore, gathering winkles off Culmore,
She lifted her leg and gave a roar, what the devil ails ye?
Maggie Picken on the shore, she had daughters three or four,
Wishing she had many more, what the devil ails ye?

Me mother sent me to the well, better she had gone hersel',
I missed me foot and in I fell, what the devil ails ye?
Me mother sent me to the burn, with a scrubber and a churn,
I missed me foot and nearly drowned, what the devil ails ye?

This is a dance tune to which my mother danced and also sang some snatches of nonsense words as well. It was a very popular dance with verses and versions found all over Ulster. The dance tune carries the words of one of Robert Burns's songs – *Whistle o'er the lave o't*. Authorship of the melody was claimed by an Irishman called John O'Keefe and it was performed in the opera *The Poor Soldier*, which was produced in Covent Garden in 1783.[54] However, Robert Burns disputed this and claimed the tune was composed by Dumfries fiddler John Bruce about the year 1750.[55]

John Campbell of Mullaghbawn, Co. Armagh provided me with two other verses:

Maggie Picken on the shore, one behind and two before,
Maggie said she'd pick no more, gathering up her flagstones,
Maggie Picken went to town, she was walking up and down,
Went into a shop and bought a gown – now she's in the fashion.

Maggie Picken had a pig, hoking in the pratie rig,
Now there are no spuds to dig in Maggie Picken's garden,
Maggie Picken had a dog, sent him out to catch a frog,
Now the frog is in the dog and Maggie Picken's barking!

Elspeth Barnes from Ballyurnanellan, Co. Down gave me another two verses with the girl's name changed to Katie Bairdie:

Katie Bairdie had a cow, black and white about the brow,
Open the gate and let her through, Katie Bairdie's cow,
Katie Bairdie had a pig, hoking up the pratie rig,
Take a stick and give her a crig, Katie Bairdie's pig.

Katie Bairdie had a cat, she could catch both mouse and rat,
Wasn't that a clever cat, Katie Bairdie's pussy,
Katie Bairdie is my wife, she could use both fork and knife,
Wasn't she the handy wife, Katie is my darling.

John Fyfe of Belfast gave me some verses which he learned from his grandmother Letitia Marshall from Donemana, Co. Tyrone, of which I quote one verse:

Maggie Picken's big romance, started at the harvest dance,
Didn't think she had a chance, Maggie Pickens courting,
Maggie Picken always said, she didn't think she'd ever wed,
She's in love with little Ted, now Maggie's wed to Teddy.

45 A Maid in a Flowery Garden

There was a maid in a flow-er-y gar - den, as a young squire — came ri-ding by, he

step-ped up to her and as — he viewed her, he said, 'Fair maid would you — fan - cy I?'

There was a maid in a flowery garden,
As a young squire came riding by,
He step-ped up to her and as he viewed her,
He said, 'Fair maid would you fancy I?'

'Oh, no kind sir, I am a poor servant,
A servant maid of low degree,
Some other female might suit you better,
As I'm not fit love, your bride to be.'

'Do you see yon castle, just over yonder?
It's all surrounded by lilies fine,
And more than that sure I will give you,
If you'll come this night and say, "You'll be mine."'

'Oh, what care I for your rings or your diamonds,
Oh, what care I for your castle and gold to me,
For it's seven years since I had a sweetheart,
And if he's living he'll return to me.'

'If it's seven years since you had a sweetheart,
Perhaps he's dead in some far-off land,
Take my advice you're a noble lady,
And wait no longer on any man.'

He took her up on his back behind him,
And off to church sure this couple flew,
And now they are married and live in splendour,
And bless the day that they ne'er did rue.

This is another of Joe's mother's songs. The *Songs of the People* calls it *The Broken Ring* and this published version includes the all important 'broken token' motif, which Joe didn't sing:

He pulled his hand out of his pocket,
His lily-white fingers were thin and small,
He showed her the ring was broke between them,
And when she saw it, down she did fall.

This song is widespread and versions have been collected in Ireland, Britain and North America.

46 The Maid of Erin's Isle

The sun does set down in the west, when its daily journey's o'er,
The small birds they have sought their nests, as night draws o'er the shore,
With ruby wine I'll fill my glass and banish care awhile,
And I'll drink a health to my sweetheart she's the maid of Erin's Isle.

When I'm in my love's company, my mind it is content,
And for to gain her favour, my inclination's bent,
And should I chance to gain this maid, kind fortune would on me smile,
She's a lovely fair, none can compare, with the maid of Erin's Isle.

Her eyes they shine like any star, that in the sky does shine,
Her lovely hair in ringlets fair, her form is all divine,
Her cheeks they are a rosy red and her heart it knows no guile,
She's a lovely fair, my sweet cailín, the maid of Erin's Isle.

Oft have I roamed with you Mary, o'er Boyden's flowery vale,
Where little lambs do sport and play, through grove and quiet dale,
But look ye down, ye Powers above and on our union smile,
For while I've life, I'll swear I'll love, the maid of Erin's Isle.

Now to conclude and finish, I will end as I began,
A blessing on you Mary, you are my loved fair one,
With ruby wine I'll fill my glass, I'll banish care awhile,
And I'll drink a health to the bonny wee lass she's the maid of Erin's Isle.

Johnny Toland of Ballyboyland sang this song with an extra last verse, which doesn't appear in the *Songs of the People* in 1924. Outside of this publication, I have been unable to locate this song in any other Irish, British or North American folk song collections. However, there are several early nineteenth-century copies of broadside ballads[56] which only print three stanzas and instead of the name of 'Boyden' they print 'boyhood.'

47 The Maid of Mourne Shore

I am a rambling Irishman, I have rambled up and down,
Still looking for my equal, but that I ne'er can find,
I ne'er saw one I could call my own, till I came to Mourne shore,
'Twas there I met a charming girl and she has my heart in store.

The first place that I saw my love, it was in Kilkeel town,
I viewed her mild behaviour, as she walked up and down,
She was brighter than the Queen of May and for beauty she has more,
She is the darling of my heart and she dwells on Mourne shore.

The next place that I met my love it was on Mourne strand,
I step-ped up unto her and I gave to her my hand,
I put my arm around her waist and I gave her kisses three,
And said I, 'My charming Mourne girl, will you pad the road with me?'

'For to pad the road with you young man, I am a year too young,
And besides oh, all you Lurgan lads have a false and flattering tongue.'
But the eventide was coming down and she could no longer stand,
And she fell into my arms, on the banks of Mourne strand.

But when she came unto herself and saw what she had done,
She wrung her hands and tore her hair, saying, 'Forever I'm undone,
Will you marry me my Lurgan lad? As you promised me before,
And my father will divide his land on the banks of Mourne shore.'

'I will tell you, as you told me, I am a year too young,
And besides all you Mourne girls have a false and flattering tongue,
But if ever I live to come to age, my vows I will make stand,
And I'll marry you my Mourne girl, on the banks of Mourne strand.'

This is no doubt a song which originated in Co. Down. However I came across the song on three occasions in Co. Antrim. The *Songs of the People* printed five stanzas in 1934 from a Bushmills, Co. Antrim source and Hugh Marks collected four verses from Mark McCashin of Ballykilbeg, Co. Down, which he published in 1961.[57] Here we have a six-verse version from Joe, learned again from Johnny Toland of Ballyboyland.

48 Mary of the Wild Moor

It being on a cold winter's night,
And the wind blew across the bleak moor,
There poor Mary came with her child wandering,
Way back to her own father's door.

'Oh, father pray do let me in,
Arise and open your own door,
Or the child in my bosom will die in the cold,
By the wind that blows across the wild moor.'

Her father was deaf to her cry,
Not a voice or sound reached his ear,
But the watch-dog did bark and the village bell tolled,
And the wind blew across the wild moor.

Now how must her father have felt,
When he opened the door in the morn,
And found Mary dead and her child yet alive,
Fondly clasped in its dead mother's arms.

Wild and frantic he tore his grey hair,
As unnerved he gazed out the door,
There by the moon, she had perished and died,
By the wind that blows across the wild moor.

Now her father in grief pinned away,
And the child to its mother went soon,
And no one lives there until this day,
And the cottage to ruins is gone.

But the villagers point out the spot,
And the willows bend over the door,
There poor Mary died a gay little bride,
By the winds that blew across the wild moor.

This song has widespread currency and features in folk song collections in Ireland, Britain and North America, as well as appearing on several nineteenth-century broadside ballad collections.[58]

Sarah Makem of Keady, Co. Armagh recorded for the BBC in 1952 another song with a similar theme called *The Forsaken Mother and Child*. Joe's mother was the source of *Mary of the Wild Moor*.

49 Molly Bán Lavery

Come all you gallant fowlers that handle a gun,
Never you go out a-fowling, by the set of the sun,
For it might happen you as it happened to me,
For to shoot your true lover, beneath an oak tree.

Refrain:
With her apron tied around her, I took her for a swan,
But oh and alas, I shot poor Molly Bán.

This song has received much attention from scholars and folk song collectors over the years and it appears frequently in collections published in Ireland, Britain and North America. Joe could only recall a fragment of this song, which his mother sang. The song appeared in the *Songs of the People* series in *The Northern Constitution*, Coleraine on the 16 January 1926 and it came from Hugh Clarke who was from Croaghan, Macosquin, Co. Derry as follows, and entitled *Molly Bawn Lowry*:

I will tell you a story that happened of late,
About Molly Bawn Lowry, that beautiful maid,
She being going to her uncle's when a shower came on,
She went under a hawthorn the shower to shun.

Refrain:
With her apron pinned around her, I took her for a swan,
And oh and alas, it was my own Molly Bawn.

It's when he ran up and found she was dead,
A well full of tears for his true love he shed.
He ran home to his father with his gun in his hand,
Crying, 'Father, dear father, I have shot Molly Bawn.'

His old father jumped up, his head being grey:
'Stay at home in your country, do not run away,
Stay at home in your country, let your trial come on,
For before you be condemned I will lose all my land.'
At the day of the trial Molly's ghost did appear,
Crying, 'Uncle, dear uncle, James Reynolds is clear.'

Now the girls of this country they are all glad for to hear,
It's Molly Bawn Lowry the flower of Glenkeer,
For if all the young girls were placed in one row,
Molly Bawn she would appear as white as the snow.

Now come all you sharp shooters that handle a gun,
Beware of sharp shooting at the setting of the sun,
For it might happen with you as it happened with me,
For to shoot your own true love right under a tree.

In its most complete form, the *Molly Bán* plot contains the following elements. As the sun is setting, Molly Bán Lavery makes her way home from her uncle's when a sudden shower of rain comes on. A green bush is her only shelter and huddling beneath it, Molly covers herself with her white apron. Meanwhile her lover, James Reynolds, has been hunting all day with his dog. Upon returning home with his gun in hand, he is attracted to a patch of whiteness showing among the green leaves of a bush. In the twilight of the evening, he supposes this must be the whiteness of a swan's feathers. He raises his gun and shoots and runs to claim his quarry, when to his horror he finds his lover Molly lying dead. In at least seven Irish variants the full name of the girl is given as Molly Bán Lavery and the hunter/lover is named as James Reynolds.

In the John Hume MS of 1845 of *Songs and Ballads in use in the Province of Ulster*,[59] collected in and around Kilwarlin, Co. Down, we find an eight-stanza version. The bird in this version is a 'cran' probably a crane and not a swan. The last verse gives a Co. Antrim location for Molly Bán Lavery's origin:

In Lisburn she was born and in Lurgan educated,
But oh, in Kilwarlin poor Molley was defeated!
With her apron being about her she was taken for a cran,
But oh and alas, it was poor Molley Bann!

My paternal great-grandmother was a Lavery from Aghagallan, Co. Antrim and my father once told me that the Laverys were so numerous around that area, they all had to have family nick-names to distinguish the different branches of the clan Ó Labhradha. When performing at a concert in Aghagallan some years back I enquired about the Laverys and indeed they are still there in plenty and one of the family branches to this day retains the family nick-name of 'Bán'.

50 The Murlough Shore

You _ hills and _ dales and _ flower-y vales, that _ lie _ round _ Mur-lough shore, you _ whins that _ grow o-ver Mar-tin's Hill, will I e _-ver _ see you more. Where the prim-rose _ grow _ and the _ vi-o-let too, and the trout and the salm _-on _ play, till with line and _ hook, de _ - light I took, for to spend _ my _ youth-ful _ days.

You hills and dales and flowery vales,
That lie round Murlough shore,
You whins that grow over Martin's Hill,
Will I never see you more.
Where the primrose grow and the violet too,
And the trout and salmon play,
Till with line and hook, delight I took,
To spend my youthful days.

Last night I went to see my love,
For to hear what she would say,
That she might take some pity on me,
For I was going away,
She says, 'I love a sailor lad,
He's the boy I do adore,
So take that for your answer now,
And trouble me no more.'

'Perhaps your sailor laddies lost,
Whilst crossing o'er the main,
Or has he found another love,
And won't return again?'
'Well if my sailor laddies lost,
No other I'll ever enjoy,

For ever since I saw his face,
I loved my sailor boy.'

Our good ship lies at Warrenpoint,
Right ready for to sail,
May the wind that blows me, favour her,
With a good and pleasant gale,
Had I ten hundred pounds in gold,
Or ten times as much more,
I would leave it all to the girl I love,
That dwell near Murlough shore.

Farewell unto Lord Antrim's grove,
Where stands the bleaching green,
Where the linen webs lie clean and white,
And the crystal streams run still,
Where manys a pleasant hour I've spent,
But now alas they're o'er,
Since the girl I loved has vanished,
Far, far from the Murlough shore.

This is the song which brought Joe Holmes and I together. I sang it at an Antrim and Derry Fiddlers' night in Dunminning, Co. Antrim, in the early 1960s and Joe asked me for the song words. Joe's grandmother sang it to a different air to the one I had from my grandmother. Eddie Butcher of Magilligan, Co. Derry also got the song words from me. Hugh Marks collected a similar set of words under a different title, *Walmsley's Shady Groves*, from Willie McDonald of Ballymartin, Co. Down and published it in 1961.[60]

John McGettigan the Co. Donegal singer recorded a version of the song, which was issued on a 78rpm record in 1937 and this is the version that Sarah and Rita Keane from Co. Galway sing.

51 My Charming Blue-Eyed Mary

As I roved out one summer's day,
For to view the flowers springing,
I met a fair maid on my way,
And she was sweetly singing.

I saluted this pretty fair maid,
She being so young and early,
She appeared to me like Venus bright,
My charming blue-eyed Mary.

'Where are you going my pretty fair maid?
Where are you going so early?'
'For to milk my cows, kind sir,' she said,
'And then to mind my dairy.'

'Will you go with me you pretty fair maid?
Forsake your cows and dairy,
And come along with me,' he said,
'My charming blue-eyed Mary.'

It being on a bank we both sat down,
Where the flowers were spring fairly,
It was there I kissed the ruby lips,
Of charming blue-eyed Mary.

He gave to her a gay gold ring,
These words as he passed were spoken,
He gave to her a gay gold ring,
To wear it as a token.

Now six long weeks had passed and gone,
No lover came to Mary,
But often times she viewed her ring.
As she stood in her dairy.

Being passing o'er yon flowery fields,
Next Monday morning early,
A young seaman came a-courting her,
'Is this my blue-eyed Mary?'

'Come along with me you pretty fair maid,
Forsake your cows and dairy,
And come and be a captain's bride,
My charming blue-eyed Mary.'

She gave consent and with him she went,
Forsook her cows and dairy,
And he made her his bonny bride,
My charming blue-eyed Mary.

Here we have the 'love token' motif once again. In some cases it's a diamond ring, but in Joe's mother's version it's a gold ring. The period of separation in Joe's version is 'six long weeks,' whereas some nineteenth-century broadside ballads give 'six months' (see appendix, p. 278),[61] and include a verse which Joe didn't have:

Then since you have got your will of me,
Kind sir pray do not leave me,
For if I'd prove with child by you,
My parents they would slight me.

52 My Father's Servant Boy

You lovers all, both great and small, attend unto my theme,
There is none on earth can pity me, but those that feel my pain,
I live between Dungannon and the town of Aughnacloy,
But now I'm in Amerikay with my father's servant boy.

Where is the man who will or can a farmer's son despise,
His bread to win, he does begin before the sun does rise,
My love and I are Adam's seed, I never will deny,
There is none on earth I love as well as my father's servant boy.

My parents wished to have me wed unto a gentleman,
And in the church we were to meet and join in wedlock bands,
The night before I strolled from them unto a village nigh,
Where there I met my own true love, my father's servant boy.

I took my love along with me I could do nothing more,
I bid adieu to all my friends and to the Shamrock Shore,
To Belfast town we both went down, where the *Achates* did lie,
And in that ship I sailed away with my father's servant boy.

When we reached the other side our money was all gone,
Sometime we were supported by a friendly Irishman,
Till a gentleman from Ireland did give us both employ,
Two pounds a week I do receive with my father's servant boy.

I left my parents lonesome in sorrow they did weep,
Day and night condoling, without a wink of sleep,
Until I sent a letter to the town of Aughnacloy,
Saying, 'I am in Amerikay with my father's servant boy.'

They sent an answer straight to me to Philadelphia town,
Saying, if I would come home again, I would get five hundred pounds,
But I was joined in wedlock, which crowned my life with joy,
And until I die, I'll ne'er deny, my father's servant boy.

This was the news that I did send from Philadelphia town,
That where they were worth a shilling, I was worth a pound,
With pleasure and contentment I never will deny,
I am living in Amerikay with my father's servant boy.

And as this couple lived in life, in death they loved the same,
And as their fond heart's blood ran cold, it mixed in one red stream,
True love like this is hard to find, it is so true and strong,
She left her friends in the lowland glen, gone, never to return.

Here we have once again parental disapproval of their daughter's choice of a lover. The parents want her married to a 'gentleman,' but she wants only her 'father's servant boy.' Joe's mother named the emigration ship as the *Achates*. Sam Henry's *Songs of the People* in 1927 called it the *Ackythere*, whilst some nineteenth-century broadside ballads[62] settle for the *Avey*. They all name the Irish port of departure as Belfast and the US port of arrival as Philadelphia.

53 My Love is on the Ocean

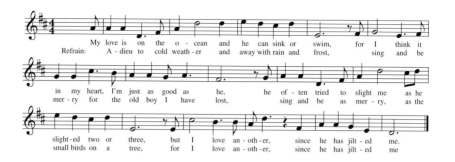

My love is on the ocean and he can sink or swim,
For I think it in my heart, I'm just as good as he,
He often tried to slight me as he slighted two or three,
But I love another, since he has jilted me.

Refrain:
Adieu to cold weather and away with rain and frost,
Sing and be merry for the old boy I have lost,
Sing and be merry, as the small birds on a tree,
For I love another, since he has jilted me.

The next place that I met him, 'twas in a shady grove,
He came stepping up to me and offered me a rose,
He thought I would accept it, but I proudly let him see,
That I loved another, since he had jilted me.

His mother she's a lady and of a high degree,
I hear she's rather indignant and rather hard to please,
She oft times talks about me her tongue is never done,
'Go home and tell your mother that I don't want her son.'

This song from Joe's mother seems to be related to one published in the *Songs of the People* in 1933 called *Farewell He*:

It is fare thee well, cold winter, it is fare thee well, cold frost,
There is nothing I have gained, but a lover I have lost,
I will sing and I'll be merry and I'll clap my hands with glee,
And I'll rest me when I'm weary, let him go then, farewell he.

Again, on a similar theme *Let Him Go, Let Him Tarry*, gives the same advice to the jilted lover:

Farewell to cold winter, summer come at last,
Nothing have I gained, but my true love I have lost,
I'll sing and I'll be happy like the birds upon the tree,
But since he deceived me I care no more for he.

The texts of both songs above are, however, very different to what Joe sang.

Versions of *My Love is on the Ocean* turn up in a few North American collections – two by Ozarks collectors Vance Randolph and Max Hunter and another by E.E. Gardner and G.J. Chickering who discovered it in 1931 in a manuscript book of Mrs Peter Miller, who heard it sung about 1895 in Connor's Lumber Camp, West Branch, Michigan. This Michigan version includes an additional verse which Joe's mother didn't have:

Many the pleasant evenings together we have went,
Many the pleasant evenings together we have spent.
His talk was rather tender, and his watch was rather slow;
Many the time I told him to take his hat and go.[63]

54 My Parents Reared Me Tenderly

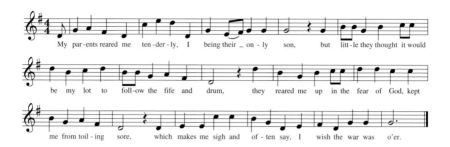

My parents reared me tenderly, I being their only son,
But little they thought it would be my lot to follow the fife and drum,
They reared me up in fear of God, kept me from toiling sore,
Which makes me sigh and often say, I wish that the wars were o'er.

For to improve my learning, I went to school a while,
And by my own industry, I went in decent style,
Strong liquor being in my head, as I strolled through Glasgow Green,
I with Joe Barber did enlist, to go and serve the queen.

When I had learnt my exercises, 'twas then I did inquire,
If I would have my liberty, when five years would expire?
The answer that they gave to me, it grieved my heart full sore,
I would not have my liberty for twenty years or more.

I took the second bounty, I fear it is for life,
To cross the briny ocean, the gun to be my wife,
And since it's so that I must go and leave my native shore,
Oh, love, don't mourn, for I'll return when the cruel wars are o'er.

Joe learned this song from John McAfee from Armoy, Co. Antrim, who played for pence on the streets at the various fairs and market days in the North Antrim towns during the early years of the twentieth century. John would often call into the Holmes's household en route to and from such events and he was a most welcome guest with his music, song and good company. Sam Henry collected this song from John McAfee at the Dervock Fair in

John McAfee photographed by Sam Henry at Dervock Fair, Co. Antrim in 1932
(photograph courtesy of John Moulden).

October 1932 and it appeared in the *Songs of the People* column on the 5 November 1932
along with John's photograph which was one of the few photographs to appear in the
series.

Kenneth Peacock collected a version of this song in Newfoundland in the 1960s,
which has a verse I haven't come across in the oral tradition in Ireland:

> It was early day one morning I asked him one request:
> Would I be free and at liberty when my ten long years were passed?
> And this reply he made to me which grieved my heart full sore,
> That I should go and serve the queen for twenty-one years or more.[64]

55 My Willie O

Oh, Ma-ry dear the cocks are crow-ing _____ don't you think it's _ time for _ me to _ go? I must leave you _ here most _ brok-en-heart-ed, _____ for I'm on-ly the _ ghost of your Wil-lie O.

> Oh, Mary dear the cocks are crowing,
> Don't you think it's time for me to go?
> I must leave you here most broken-hearted,
> For I'm only the ghost of your Willie O.

Unfortunately, Joe could only remember one verse of his mother's song, sometimes referred to as *The Lover's Ghost*. A number of lyrical folk songs present the situation of two lovers disturbed by the early crowing of a cock. Perhaps the origin of these songs is found in this supernatural ballad of the lover returned from the dead. As a popular broadside ballad of about 1850, it would seem that this version borrows from the older night-visit theme of the ballad *Sweet William's Ghost* (Child 77). In the older ballad William comes straight from the grave to ask Margaret to release him from his 'plighted troth'. Professor Bertrand Bronson of Princeton University however classifies the ballad *My Willie O* as *The Grey Cock* (Child 248). I first came across the ballad *My Willie O* in my youth-hostelling days in the early 1960s, when I heard Jimmy McGinley from Ros Ghoill, Co. Donegal sing a fairly full version, but without Joe's all important 'cock crowing' verse:

> My Willie sails on board the tender,
> And where to find him I do not know,
> Seven long years I've been constantly waiting,
> Since he crossed the bay of Biscay-O.
>
> One night as Mary lay a-sleeping,
> A knock came to her bedroom door,
> Saying, 'Arise, arise, you lovely Mary,
> Till you get one glimpse of your Willie-O.'

Young Mary rose, put on her clothing,
And out of her bedroom she did go,
It's there she saw her Willie standing,
And his two cheeks as white as snow.

Saying, 'Willie dear, where are those blushes?
The blushes you had long years ago?'
'Oh! Mary dear, the cold clay has changed them,
I am only the ghost of your Willie-O.'

'Oh, Mary dear the morning is coming,
Don't you think it's time for me to go?
I am leaving you quite broken-hearted,
For to cross the bay of Biscay-O.'

'Oh, if I had all the gold and silver,
And all the money in Mexico,
I would grant it all to the King of Erin,
For to bring me back my Willie O.'[65]

Robbie Haldane from Belfast kindly sent me another Co. Donegal version of the ballad he collected from Dan 'Bartley' McGlynn of Largnalore. Dan gave the 'ghost' a name-change. In his version of the ballad, he calls him '*Danny O*,' but again the 'cock crowing' verse is missing.

The nineteenth-century broadside ballad printed by W. Birmingham of Dublin in *c.*1850[66] gives the 'cock crowing' verse and also includes a verse which I have never come across in the oral tradition:

Although my body lies in the West Indies,
My ghost shall guard you to and fro,
So farewell jewel, since we are for parting,
Since I'm no more your Willy O.

56 The Nobleman's Wedding

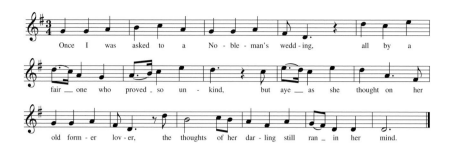

Once I was asked to a Nobleman's wedding,
All by a fair one who proved so unkind,
But aye as she thought on her old former lover,
The thoughts of her darling still ran in her mind.

When supper was over and all things were completed,
It fell each young man's lot to sing a love song,
It happened to fall on her own former lover,
To sing those few verses that won't keep you long.

Oh, manys the lord was seven years from his lady,
And manys the lord he ne'er came back again,
But I was only one year away from my darling,
When an inconstant lover to me she became.

'How can you sit at another young man's table?
Or how can you drink of another young man's wine?
Or how can you lie in the arms of another?
And you that was so long a true-lover of mine.'

The bride she being seated at the head of the table,
And every word she remembered right well,
To bear it in mind this maid she was not able,
And down at the groom's feet she instantly fell.

'There is one request I'll ask unto me if you'll grant it,
The first and the last love perhaps it may be,
Only this one night to stay with my dear mother,
The rest of my time love I'll spend it with thee.'

The request it was asked and immediately granted,
Sighing and sobbing this fair one went to bed,
And early the next morning the young groom he awoken,
He went to her bed-chamber and found that she was dead.

He lifted her up from her soft and downy pillow,
He carried her out into the garden so green,
With sheets and fine pillows he soon did surround her,
Still thinking that his young bride might come to life again.

Oh, Sally, lovely Sally, when you and I were courting,
You vowed and declared that you loved no one but me,
But them that depends upon a fair female's folly,
Their heart it will decay like the bark on the tree.

All around my hat I will wear a weeping willow,
All around my hat until death does come to me,
And if anybody asks me why I wear this willow,
It is all for my true-love that I never more will see.

This was one of Joe's favourite songs from his mother. Hugh Shields suggests that it dates from the eighteenth century and says it has gained more applause in Ireland than any similar song. Certainly, versions have been collected all over Ireland, Britain and North America. Seosamh (Joe) Ó hÉanaí (1919–84) sang six verses for Peter Kennedy in 1959. Joe told Kennedy that he had learned it from his father, Patrick Heaney, at home in Cárna, Connemara, Co. Galway, just before he died in 1937:

> I heard him singing that since I was knee high but only picked up bits of it. There's more of it than that. He sang at night. He'd go through them one after the other. Never stop singing. Never. He was always singing or humming. Always. Never stopped. I was ten years old when he died. I had very few of them learned. He was a small farmer, that's all. Very small. The land there is hopeless. It is hard to believe that anyone can exist there.

George Petrie (1790–1866) sent William Allingham (1824–89) a set of words for *The Nobleman's Wedding* which John Philpot Curran (1750–1817) had taken down from his nursery-maid. This version includes the 'broken-token' motif, which seldom occurs in the oral tradition in Ireland. John Kennedy from Cullybackey, Co. Antrim sings:

> Where is the ring that I gave you when we parted?
> Where is that ring of gold, oh return it again,
> I gave it to you as a true-lover's token,
> Return it to me as a false-hearted one.

From J.P. Curran:

> Here is the token of gold that was broken,
> Seven long years, love, I have kept it for your sake,
> You gave it to me as a true-lover's token,
> No longer with me now it shall remain.[67]

Greig-Duncan:

> Oh this is the piece of gold, love, when we parted,
> That ye gave unto me and I gave to you;
> Ye gave unto me a true lover's token,
> And I gave unto you a true lover's vow.

57 The Old Oak Tree

Oh, dark the night, cold blew the wind and heavy fell the rain.
When young Betsy left her parents home, ne'er to return again,
She threw a shawl around her head, not fearing rain nor cold,
And left her widowed mother's side, for love had made her bold.

The night being ten by the clock, beneath the old oak tree,
The young squire, her own true-love, that with him she would be,
She heeded not the pouring rain, nor yet the thunder's roar,
But held her shawl around her head and walked quickly from the door.

In morning when daylight came, when she did not return,
And her friends did wonder as to why Betsy thus did roam,
At length her mother all distressed, with cries and actions wild,
Saying, 'I'll ramble the country o'er and o'er till I find my only child.'

For three dreary weeks she spent in grief, searching the country round,
But her journey proved of no avail for Betsy ne'er was found,
She wrung her hands and tore her hair and bitterly she cried,
In sorrow and grief, no more to roam, with broken-heart she died.

Near to the scene of all the woe, the owner of these grounds,
Squire McCollum went out to hunt that way with all his hounds,
Over hills and dales they hotly rode with gallant company,
Till as by chance, the fox they lost, beneath the old oak tree.

The pack of hounds did yelp and sniff and tear up the clay,
And with whip and horn could not drive the hounds away,
Then the gentlemen all gathered round and called for pick and spade,
They dug the ground and there they found the missing murdered maid.

Her cheeks that once were red, were black with wounds and blows,
And from her side fresh blood gushed forth and trickled through her clothes,
'I've done the deed,' McCollum cried, 'My soul is fit for Hell,
Pray hide her body from my sight and the truth to you I'll tell.'

'It's true I courted Betsy long, but her I caused such pain,
I won her by my evil ways it is my grief and shame,
With this knife my dinner took, I plunged into her breast,
This is my sad and doleful tale, I need not tell the rest.'

'For I am guilty and I must die a death of sin and shame,'
He took a pistol from his belt and fired it through his brain,
And he was buried where he fell, no Christian grave got he,
None could be found to bless the ground, beneath the old oak tree.

Some versions of this murder ballad are more grisly than this version from Joe's mother. I recall hearing Mary Ann Carolan from Co. Louth in the mid-1970s giving a particularly blood-curdling account of the poor girl's body being found: 'To see the worms eat through her eyes, that once were blue and bright.' Joe's mother sang this ballad, but tastefully had omitted this detail. The broadside ballad scholar, Malcolm Laws, suggests that this ballad is of Irish origin, but as to where or when the ghastly event took place, if it took place at all, is anyone's guess. The villain of the piece in Joe's version is given as McCollum, but I have heard him named as McCullough. In the *Songs of the People* he is called Squire Cowan, whilst a Newfoundland version gives McCallion.

58 Once I Loved

Once I loved with fond affection, all his thoughts they were on me,
Until a dark girl did persuade him, then he thought no more of me,
Now he's happy with another one that has bright gold in store,
'Twas he who caused my heart to ponder, I'm left alone because I'm poor.

Refrain:
Go and leave me if you wish it, never let me cross your mind,
And if you think I'm so unworthy, go and leave me never mind.

Some young men will kiss and court you and they tell you they'll prove true,
But if you leave them for a moment they'll be biding you adieu,
When I left my mother's cottage, little I thought he'd prove untrue,
But some fair maidens love sincerely, loving them that don't love you.

Manys a night with him I rambled, manys an hour with him I spent,
I thought his heart was mine forever, but love I found was only lent,
Many a night when you were sleeping taking of your sweet repose,
When I poor girl lies broken-hearted, listening to the wind that blows.

My heart has failed me and you know it, a heart that only beats for thee,
However could I tell another, tales of love I've told to thee,
So farewell friends and kind relations, farewell to you my false young man,
'Twas you that caused my pain and sorrow, never to return to home again.

The county and provincial weekend Fleadhs were a focal and favourite meeting point for
singers in the 1960s. Many of the best sessions were impromptu ones, but more often than
not they were monopolised by great instrumental playing. So the singers would take
themselves off to quieter corners to feast on their annual outing with singers from other
counties and provinces. The best sessions of all were those where musicians sympathetic to

Keane's Cottage, Caherlistrane, Co. Galway, 1968, before the 'Northern Wing' was added (photograph by David Dillon).

song were in the same company as singers. And so it was at one memorable night at the 1967 Connacht Fleadh Cheoil in Ballinasloe in Co. Galway. Rumour had it on the Saturday evening that a 'special' session was to happen upstairs in the Pillar Bar. Special usually meant that some of the traditional elders and masters would be there. I made my way there as word began to circulate around the town and soon the room was packed to capacity. Among the gathering there was Willie Clancy, the renowned Co. Clare uilleann-piper, Paddy Taylor, the Co. Limerick flute-player – it was an unforgettable night with great humour, music and singing. Willie called for a song from Seán 'Ac Donnacha, the sean-nós singer from Cárna in Connemara, whose song was followed by a song from two sisters – Sarah and Rita Keane from Caherlistrane, Co. Galway. Later when all the masters had made their contributions, I ventured a song or two myself and this led to a conversation about songs with the Keane sisters and their young niece Dolores and I was invited to come and stay with them. First I headed to Spanish Point in Co. Clare and camped there for a few days and recorded some music and songs from Willie Clancy. On my way home I decided to take the Keane's up on their invitation and headed for Caherlistrane to spend a few days with them before heading home to the North. My visit coincided with a busy time on the farm and all hands were engaged in saving the potato crop. So I was handed a basket and along with the family we gathered and bagged spuds until sundown. After dinner, the accordions, fiddle, whistles etc., were produced and the fun began with sets danced in the kitchen and songs sung.

Féile na Bóinne: singers gathered outside Farrard House, Clogher Head, Drogheda, Co. Louth, 1977 (photograph by Joe Dowdall by courtesy of ITMA).
Front L-R: Treasa Ní Mhiolláin, Peadar Ó Cathain, Dolores Keane, Len Graham, Landlady of Ferrard House, Frank Harte, Joe Holmes, Phil Callery.
Back L-R: Nioclás Toibín, Marie McCabe, John Slattery, Sinéad Cahir, Ciaran Carson, Doreen Davy, Róisín White, Darach Ó Cathain, Máirín Mhéiní Ní Chongaile, Tim Lyons, Josie Sheáin Jack MacDonncha, John Rodgers, Jackie Devenney, Tony O'Halloran, Mary McGrath, ? , Dot Callery, Virginia Blankenhorn, Joe John Mac Con Iomaire.

I was to return again many times over the years to Sarah and Rita's home and its generous hospitality. Later they would extend their traditional thatched home and add 'The Northern Wing' to facilitate the northerners such as Joe Holmes, David Dillon, Cathal McConnell, Winston Given, Brian Cousins and many others who would come down with me from time to time. It was on our way home from one of these visits to Keane's that Joe struck up a song in the car . The song was *Once I Loved*, which was one of the songs Sarah and Rita had sung the night before. I congratulated Joe on this great feat of memory, only to be informed that he already knew it as it was one of his mother's songs.

The song is widespread and versions occur on nineteenth-century broadsides and in several collections in Ireland, Scotland, England and North America. A poignant song conclusion was collected in Springdale, Arkansas by Max Hunter in 1960:

So, if he's gone, just let him wander, I hope I never shall cross his path,
For in his heart he loves another and in my grave, I'd rather be,
There's just three things that love, I ask thee, my shroud, my coffin and my grave,
And when I'm dead, love come and see me and kiss the girl you once betrayed.[68]

59 The Parting Glass

A man may drink and not be drunk,
A man may fight and not be slain,
A man may court a pretty girl,
And perhaps be welcome back again,
But since it has so ordered been,
Be a time to rise and a time to fall,
Come fill to me the parting glass,
Good night and joy be with you all.

If I had money for to spend,
I would spend it in good company,
And for all the harm that I have done,
I hope its pardoned I will be,
What I have done for want of it,
To memory I can't recall,
So fill to me the parting glass,
Good night and joy be with you all.

My dearest dear, the time draws near,
When here no longer I can stay,
There's not a comrade I leave behind,
But is griev-ed that I'm going away,
For since it has so ordered been,
What is once past can't be recalled,
So fill to me the parting glass,
Good night and joy be with you all.

When home on holidays from Canada in the late 1960s, after forty years in exile, Tommy McQueston, originally from Killyramer, reminded Joe of this song which was one they both learned from Willie Clarke from Lisboy. The melody speeded up serves as a very popular highland schottische called *The Peacock's Feather*.[69] Several musicians, including Frankie Gavin the Co. Galway fiddler, learned this tune from Joe. *The Parting Glass* was the last song Joe and I sang together in Derry's Guild Hall a few nights before he died in January 1978.

60 The Plains of Waterloo

A fair maid went a-walking down by the banks of Clyde,
The tears came rolling down her cheeks, as she pass-ed by my side,
I remarked her heaving bosom as these words came kind and true,
'I fear, I fear my Willie's slain on the plains of Waterloo.'

'What kind of clothes did your Willie wear, this stranger did reply?'
'He wore a Heiland bonnet with a feather standing high,
A broad-sword hanging by his side and his tartan plaid hung true,
Those were the clothes that my Willie wore on the plains of Waterloo.'

'I was your Willie's comrade, I saw your Willie die,
By bullet wounds he did receive before he down did lie,
He caught me by the hand, saying, some Frenchman pierced me through,
'Twas I who closed your Willie's eyes on the Plains of Waterloo.'

'Oh Willie, dearest Willie,' that she could say no more,
She fell into the soldiers arms, glad tidings to him bore,
He opened up his overcoat for to show his wounds so true,
Saying, 'I am your dearest Willie returned from Waterloo.'

There are two versions of *The Plains of Waterloo* published in the *Songs of the People*, which differ from this one. There are also several nineteenth-century broadside ballads with this title, one of which is this one Joe learned from Willie Clarke of Lisboy, Co. Antrim. Three versions of this song were collected, one in Michigan and two in Newfoundland in the 1930s and 1950s. The only other version similar to Joe's in the oral tradition that I have

167

been able to locate was sung by Willie Scott, the Scottish borders shepherd, which he called *Bloody Waterloo*. Willie's concluding verse gives a happy ending:

> 'Stand up, stand up, my fair maid, my dearest, do not frown,'
> And flingin off his grey coat, his tartans they hung down;
> 'Now since we've met we ne'er shall pairt, till death shall us divide,
> And hand in hand in wedlock bands alang the banks o Clyde'.[70]

In 1952 Kenneth Peacock collected a five-verse version of the song from Mrs John Fogarty of Joe Batt's Arm, Newfoundland, which included this last verse:

> 'If I had some eagle's wings I would surmount on high,
> I would fly to lonely Waterloo where my true love do lie;
> I would light upon his bosom my love for to renew,
> I would kiss my darling's pale cold lips on lonely Waterloo'.[71]

61 The Quaker's Wife

The Quak - er's wife she baked a scone, and John _ - ny danced when it was on,

mer - ri - ly danced the Quak - er's wife, and mer - ri - ly danced the Quak - er.

> The Quaker's wife she baked a scone,
> And Johnny danced when it was on,
> Merrily danced the Quaker's wife,
> And merrily danced the Quaker.

I took Joe to meet Denis Murphy in the Sliabh Luachra area of Co. Kerry in the early 1970s and they also met and shared some tunes together at the Fleadh Ceoil na hÉireann in Listowel in 1972. I was surprised by how many tunes they had in common, in spite of the three-hundred-odd miles separating Antrim and Kerry. Most of Denis's dance tunes came from his teacher and mentor Pádraig O'Keeffe and many tunes he played were of Scottish origin, although in some cases the names were changed. I recall the following tunes being played in Sliabh Luachra sometimes under other titles: *Johnny Cope, Niel Gow's Farewell to Whisky, The Cock of the North, Green Grow the Rushes O, The Muckin' O' Geordie's Byre, The Quaker's Wife* etc. Joe had an extra part for *The Quaker's Wife* and some words which Denis didn't have. The Greig-Duncan Folk Song Collection from the north-east of Scotland has another fragment of *The Quaker's Wife* collected in 1905:

> Merrily danced the Quaker's wife
> An' merrily danced the Quaker,
> Merrily danced the Quaker's wife
> An' sae did Willie Wauker.
>
> Merrily danced the Quaker's wife
> An' a' her bairns about her,
> To ilka ana she gaed a cakie
> An' the Quaker gae the multre.[72]

Another reference to the song turns up in Australia, when a certain Sir Henry Brown Hayes, a wealthy Irishman, was transported to New South Wales for abducting a rich young lady of Cork. This lady was a Quaker and a fragment of a song relating to the incident was published in 1859 under the title *Sir Henry Hayes, True Stories of the Early Days of Australia*, by John Lang:

> Sir Henry kissed behind the bush,
> Sir Henry kissed the Quaker,
> And if he did, and if he did,
> I'm sure he didn't ate her.[73]

The only related Irish text I found appears in James Duffy's *The Dublin Comic Songster* published in 1845 under the title *The White Quaker*, sung to the air of *Merrily Kissed the Quaker*. There are seven verses in that version opening with:

> This life I find is a life of woe, of wickedness and troubles,
> And verily I say unto you, I'll never be free from hobbles;
> I sometimes lived quite snug and warm, I was other times a raker,
> Till I got in a hobble the length of my arm, by going to turn Quaker.[74]

George Thomson's 1799 edition of *Select Collection of Original Scottish Airs* includes Robert Burns's song *Am I, My Chloris Fair* to which Burns specified that it should be sung to the air of *The Quaker's Wife*:

> Thine am I, my Chloris fair, well thou may'st discover;
> Every pulse along my veins, tells the ardent Lover.
> To thy bosom lay my heart, there to throb and languish;
> Tho' Despair had wrung its core, that would heal its anguish.[75]

62 The Rambling Boys of Pleasure

You ram-bling boys of _ pleas __ - ure, give _ ear un _-to _ these lines I _ write, I
own I _ am _ a ro - ver and in ram-bling I _ take great _ de - light, I
placed my mind on a hand-some girl _ and oft - en times _ she does _ me slight, my
mind is nev - er ____ eas ____ -y, on - ly when my _ dar _-ling is in my sight.

You rambling boys of pleasure, give ear unto these lines I write,
I own I am a rover and in rambling I take great delight,
I placed my mind on a handsome girl and often times she does me slight,
My mind is never easy, only when my darling is in my sight.

Down by yon flowery gardens, where me and my true-love do meet,
I took her in my arms and unto her I gave kisses sweet;
She bid me to take love easy, just as the leaves fall from yon tree,
But I being young and foolish, my own true-love's ways I could not agree.

The second time I saw my love, I vowed her path was surely mine,
But as the weather changes, my darling girl she changed her mind;
Gold is the root of evil, it only bears a glittering hue,
Causes many a lad and lass to part, may their heart and mind be ever so true.

I wish I was in Belfast town and my true love along with me,
I would get sweethearts plenty, to keep me in good company,
With money in my pocket and a flowing bowl on every side,
Hard fortune ne'er would daunt me, while I'd be young in this world wide.

The poet W.B. Yeats heard an old peasant woman sing a version of this song in Ballisadare,
Co. Sligo sometime in the late nineteenth century. Yeats described his lines as 'an attempt
to reconstruct an old song from three lines imperfectly remembered' when he published in

1889 his own literary adaptation of this traditional song – his famous poem/song *Down by the Salley Gardens*.[76]

Helen Creighton, the Canadian folk song collector, came across two versions of the song in the 1950s.[77] Interestingly, one of her sources, Angelo Dornan, had Co. Antrim connections. Most of his songs came down to him through his family and particularly from his great grandfather, who emigrated from Ballymoney to New Brunswick in the 1840s. This was a popular song with the nineteenth-century broadside ballad printers and ballad-singers and the ballad sheets show mostly Dublin as the desired place to be with his true love, but sometimes America appears. Angelo Dornan sang Dublin, but Joe's mother preferred to be a bit nearer home in Belfast. Joe sang: 'Down by yon flowery gardens', but most ballad sheets print: 'Sally's garden', which ties in with the Yeats's version. Another connection with the 'sally gardens' theme are the basket-weavers of old who used this term for their willow plantations. This would seem to derive from *saileách*, the Irish for the sally tree or common white willow. By coincidence another version of *The Rambling Boys of Pleasure* was collected by Sean O'Boyle and Peter Kennedy in the 1950s for the BBC survey on the musical traditions of these islands.[78] The singer was Robert Cinnamond from Aghadolgan, Co. Antrim and Robert was one of the last of the Co. Antrim basket-weavers, a trade which employed many people in the flat low-lying area along the shores of Lough Neagh between Lurgan and Antrim. Acres of willow or sally were grown here up until the 1950s and baskets were made to cater for the transportation of distilled water, sulphuric acid, whiskey and other products, which at that time were transported in glass carboys requiring protective basket covers. Robert sang *The Rambling Boys of Pleasure* to a different air to Joe and there were also some differences in their song texts. An extra verse appears on some broadside ballads (see appendix, p. 279),[79] which I haven't heard sung in the oral tradition:

> There is one thing more that grieves me, that to be called a runaway,
> To leave where I was bred and born, oh, Cupid won't you set me free,
> To leave my love behind me, alack and alas what shall I do,
> Must I become a rover into the land I never knew.

In 1957 Hamish Henderson of the School of Scottish Studies collected *Sally's Garden* from Jock and Jimmy McShannon, Machrihanish, Kintyre, Argylshire. This song in places bears some resemblance to *The Rambling Boys of Pleasure*:

> For it's down in Sally's garden, where me and my true love did meet,
> I fondled her with caresses and I gave to her kisses sweet.[80]

In the last verse Joe Holmes sang – 'flowing bowel,' which of course is an Irish colloquialism for bowl. I recall back in the 1960s Cathal McConnell giving the concertina-player Packy Russell in Doolin, Co. Clare the reel *The Flowing Bowl*. On the following Christmas, Cathal's mother showed me Packy's Christmas card: 'A Happy Christmas Cathal – keep playing *The Flowing Bowel* – Packy'!

Talking about 'bowls' or 'bowels' in the vernacular, Joe told me a story about an old woman living near him who had a visit from her clergyman. At the time of the story, ordinary country-folk used to drink their tea out of a bowl. The old woman offered the clergyman tea and he accepted and it was duly served in a bowl. Well the old woman had a wee pet pig – the runt of the litter and she was feeding it in the kitchen. Well, it came over and started to scratch at the clergyman's trouser leg. 'I think the wee pig knows me', says the clergyman. 'Oh, no not at all your Reverence,' says the old woman, 'But I think he knows its ain (own) wee bowel!'

63 The Rambling Irishman

I am a rambling Irishman, in Ulster I was born in,
Many's a happy hour I spent on the banks of bonny Lough Erne;
For to live poor I could not endure, like others in my station,
To Amerikay I sailed away and left this Irish nation.

Refrain:
Right tan tin ah, tan tin ah, right tan tin an ah tin an-a-dee.

The night before I went away, I spent it with my darling,
From 3 o'clock in the afternoon, till the break of day next morning;
And when that we were going to part, we linked in each others arms,
You may be sure and very sure it wounded both our charms.

The very first night I slept on board, I dreamt about my Nancy,
I dreamt I had her in my arms and well she pleased my fancy;
But when I woke out of my dreams and found my bosom empty,
You may be sure and very sure that I lay discontented.

Now when we arrived at the other side, we were both stout and healthy,
We cast our anchor in the bay, going down through Philadelphy;
So let every lass link with her lad, blue jackets and white trousers,
Let every lad link with his lass, blue petticoats and white flounces.

Coming home from Mickey McIlhatton's at Skerry West, Co. Antrim one night back in the 1960s, Joe went over snatches of this song. It was one that his old neighbour, singer and fellow fiddler, Willie Clarke used to sing. Joe was having difficulty recalling the whole song. Some days later, Joe told me he had made some enquiries and confirmed that Willie's daughter Mary, now McQueston, who had moved in the 1930s to Belfast was still alive and there was a good chance she may know the song and he handed me her address. Within a week, I was knocking the front door of Mary's house in the York Street district of Belfast and sure enough she was able to sing me her father's song. This became a great favourite of Joe and myself and on one of our visits to the Keanes of Caherlistrane, Co. Galway we sang it and Dolores fell in love with the song and learned it from us. On the first *De Dannan* album of 1975 Dolores sang with band accompaniment – *The Rambling Irishman* – which has since become a classic. Other recordings of this followed by *The Boys of the Lough*, Dick Gaughan and many others, making it a very popular song at home and abroad. Eddie Butcher sang me a couple of verses of *The Rambling Irishman*, but I think with his phenomenal memory he had learned it from hearing Joe and I singing it. Another version of *The Rambling Irishman* came to me from Julie Henigan from Springfield, Missouri. Julie kindly sent me a copy of an archive recording of the Ozarks singer Bertha Lauderdale. Bertha called the song *New York Bay*[81] and she was recorded in 1961 by folk song collector Max Hunter. Max, unfamiliar with the Irish place-names, in his transcriptions of the recordings of Bertha's songs, he interpreted one song *The Limerick Races* as *The Lemory Graces* and in *New York Bay* the banks of sweet Lough Erne became the banks of sweet Lauairen!

> I'm an Irishman from Monaghan, in the north country I was born in,
> It was many the pleasant hour I spent, on the banks of sweet Lauairen,
> But to be poor I could not endure, as others in my station,
> And with a heart full sore, I quit the shore of the once loved Irish nation.
>
> *Refrain*:
> Laddly-tie-ri-are, laddly-tie-ri-a-a, laddly-tie-i-air-o-laddie.

I am grateful to Dr Michael O'Leary of Boston College for drawing my attention to a three-stanza fragment of the song which is attributed to the bard, Jerry Monaghan, who along with other families residing 'on the banks of the Lough Erne' emigrated about the year 1790.

> On the fourth of June, in the afternoon, we sailed from Londonderry;
> Early next day we put to sea to cross the tedious ferry:
> We hoisted sail with a pleasant gale, as Phoebus was arising,
> Bound for New York, in America, in the grand brig *Eliza*.
>
> A British fleet we chanced to meet, on the twenty-fourth of August;
> A man-of-war came bearing down with crowded sails upon us.
> Brave Knight, being true to all his crew, advanced unto the captain,
> And when he made a bow to him, showed America's protection.[82]

Apparently the vessel *Eliza* was commanded by Captain Knight which entered Delaware Bay and not New York as stated in this version of the song and proceeded to the port of New Castle. Some of them crossed the Allegheny Mountains and settled in Fayette County, not far from present day Connellsville, Pennsylvania and presumably some ventured further afield into the Appalachians, the Ozarks and beyond.

Yet another song was pointed out to me by James Foley of Omagh. James showed me a copy of a song attributed to a nineteenth-century song-smith called James Devine from Loughash, Donemana, Co. Tyrone. This song has similarities to *The Rambling Irishman* and Devine called it *The Banks of Sweet Glenmornan*. John Moulden, who has extensively researched the Sam Henry Collection, kindly sent me a transcript of the song. Sam Henry was absent from the editorship of the *Songs of the People* series from mid-1928 until late 1932 and during this period there were three other contributors to the series, including William Devine from Coleraine. William Devine published *The Banks of Sweet Glenmornan* in the *Songs of the People* series as No. 334 in the *Northern Constitution* newspaper, Coleraine in 1930. You will note from the first verse how James Devine must have been familiar with the older song *The Rambling Irishman*:

> I'm an Irishman from sweet Strabane, a North countryman born,
> Many a pleasant day I spent on the banks of sweet Glenmornan.
> For to live poor I could not endure; like another of my station,
> I took my way to Americay and I left the Irish nation.

The Ozark highlands of Missouri and Arkansas is a region west of the Appalachian Mountains and like the Appalachian region it was heavily settled by the Scotch-Irish in the eighteenth and nineteenth centuries. Because of the large number of Scotch-Irish travelling south from Pennsylvania in the late eighteenth century, the valley route soon came to be known simply as the 'Irish Road'.

There were several waves of emigration from Ireland to North America. The pre-famine migrants from Ulster were predominantly Presbyterians, who became known as the Scotch-Irish. The term 'Scotch-Irish' significantly only became popular after 1850: before that they were usually referred to as Irish (sometimes wild Irish).[83] *The Rambling Irishman* song would appear to pre-date the Irish famine during and after which the majority of emigrants were mainly Catholic. In Ireland the Ulster Presbyterians experienced a number of problems that made their lives difficult. As Presbyterians in an Anglican state, most of them faced religious hostility from the government. Like the Catholic population they were subject to penal laws barring them from higher education and the professions and forcing them to pay tithes to the Church of Ireland. From the 1680s until the American Revolution temporarily cut off shipping, at least 250,000 sailed to North America. After the Revolution an even larger wave crossed, perhaps 500,000 more, peaking in the period between the Napoleonic wars and the Great Famine. Philadelphia was their pre-eminent port of entry, but they settled all along the Eastern seaboard, from Nova Scotia to Georgia. John Dunlap, who was born in Strabane, Co. Tyrone in 1746, the son of a saddler, is said to have served his apprenticeship as a printer in Gray's Printing Shop, Main Street, Strabane, which is preserved as a museum by the National Trust. He emigrated to Philadelphia, and as printer to Congress in 1776 he issued the American Declaration of Independence. He is also remembered as the founder of the first daily newspaper in the US, the *Pennsylvania Packet*. In 1789 he wrote to his brother-in-law Robert Rutherford in Strabane:

> Dear Brother,
> We are told the Parliament of Ireland means to lay restrictions on those who want to come from that country to this … the young men of Ireland who wish to be free and happy should leave it and come here as quick as possible. There is no place in the world where a man meets so rich a reward for good conduct and industry as in America … I am, dear Sir, your affectionate brother, John Dunlap.

The renowned English folklorist Cecil Sharp, who collected extensively in the Southern Appalachian region of the US in the early twentieth century, is recorded in 1917 in conversation with J. Russell Smith at Knoxville, Tennessee. Sharp had just returned from the mountains, joyful over a book full of new ballads, copied down as people had sung them to him.

> 'These missionaries with their schools!' he exclaimed indignantly. 'I'd like to build a wall around these mountains and let the mountain people alone. The only distinctive culture in America is here. These people live. They sustain themselves on the meanest food. They are not interested in eating, but they have time to sing ballads.'[84]

Gray's Printing Shop, Main Street, Strabane, Co. Tyrone, where John Dunlap is said to have served his apprenticeship.

64 The Ride in the Creel

Young Molly she went up the street,
Some fresh fish for to buy,
And a wee town clerk he heard her feet,
And followed her by and by.

Refrain:
Ricky do dom da, do dom da, ricky dicky do dom da.

Saying, 'Molly, lovely Molly,
For you I'm almost dead,
Your aul' da locks the door at night,
And the keys lie under his head.'

No rest, no rest could the aul' wife get,
With dreams running in her mind,
'I'll lay my life,' said the good aul' wife,
'I'll rise and look myself.'

Some help, some help my good aul' man,
Some help I ask of thee,
And get you to the chimney top,
And gie the creel a haul.

The man he got to the chimney top,
And he gie the creel a haul,
And he broke three ribs in the aul' woman's side,
And her head came agin the wall.

178

Now all good folk I'll tell to thee,
This is the end of me reel,
And any aul' woman that's jealous of her daughter,
She's welcome to a ride in the creel.

Joe heard this from Jimmy Currie of Balnamore, Co. Antrim. Jimmy in the early 1970s moved to live with Joe's sister Nancy and her husband Dan Currie at Dunluce, Co. Antrim. I'm grateful for Jimmy's help with filling in the gaps in the song which Joe couldn't remember. Another fine, full version of this old ballad is sung by John Kennedy from Cullybackey, Co. Antrim. Over the years Joe and I spent many memorable nights in John's company at house and pub sessions, fleadhs and gatherings. John is also a gifted musician and teacher and passed on his love for his native tradition to generations of young people from all denominations during troubled times in Ulster.

At one of the Fleadhs held in Clones, Co. Monaghan in the 1960s, we met Packie Manus Byrne from Corkermore, Co. Donegal for the first time. He was a traditional singer, musician and storyteller. Packie over the course of the weekend regaled us with many songs, ballads, tunes and well-told lies. He sang us a Donegal version of *The Ride in the Creel*, as well as many other great songs, ballads and stories. On one of our visits to the Keane's of Caherlistrane, Co. Galway, Mary Keane, the mother of Sarah and Rita and grandmother of Dolores, sang us another wonderful full version of this ballad. Over the years I heard several variants of this ballad throughout Ireland and Scotland and it tells the risqué tale with its trick for entering the girl's bedchamber.

179

65 The Roving Sea Captain

Oh, there was a sea captain got married of late,
To a handsome young lady, he gained her estate,
But he was only married, when he's called away,
For he was a sailor, who sailed the salt sea.

Refrain:
With me crooken die arrow, the rose of the Yarrow,
With young Captain Darragh, it's tarry high ho.

There was a young squire, who lived close by,
And on this young lady he cast a glad eye,
'Oh lady, dear lady', the squire he did say,
'I need your affection, be kind, I do pray.'

He took her in his arms and did her embrace,
He says, 'My dear lady, don't think this amiss,
Your husband, the captain, is now gone from home,
I'll keep you in company until he returns.'

To bed the young squire and lady did go,
The cook and the coachman they followed also,
The housemaid and butler they did the same,
And the footman he lay in the garret with Jane.

Oh, nine months went over and soon did pass,
The roving sea captain, he came home at last,
He took her in his arms and did her embrace,
He says, 'My dear lady, you're thick in the waist.'

'It is nothing, but fat,' the lady did say,
'Would you have me starve, since you went away?
The colic, the colic, it's the colic,' she cried,
'I'm bad with the colic and I think I will die.'

Oh, he sent for a doctor and when he came there,
He ordered the housemaid a drink to prepare.
'Oh colic, oh colic,' came from the next room,
'I'm bad with the colic – I cannot come soon.'

The doctor went for her pulse it for to feel,
She says, 'I am sick from the neck to the heel,'
The doctor said little, but then shook his head,
Saying, 'You'll be alright when you go to your bed.'

They sent for the midwife and when she did come,
She delivered this lady with a darling young son,
The cook and the housemaid she delivered the same,
And Jane in the garret, she ended the game.

Come all ye sea captains, take a warning from this,
Don't go a-blaming should your wife go amiss,
For when you're at sea, they'll get what they want,
And the maids and the mistress got the blanket carrant!

The Cross Keys Pub, near Toomebridge, Co. Antrim was a favourite haunt of Joe and myself. Willie McKeever, a local fiddler, singer and character, was a regular and many memorable nights were spent in his company. The sessions were mostly in the Cross Keys Pub, but sometimes a big night would be arranged in Willie and his sister Lizzie's home. Willie favoured what he called – 'blackguard' songs and the *Roving Sea Captain* was one such song. On the way home one night (or was it morning?), Joe started singing and to my delight it was a version of the *Roving Sea Captain*, which he had heard from Johnny Toland of Ballyboyland.

D.K. Wilgus, who edited the Josiah H. Combs's 1920s folk song collection of the Southern United States, interpreted an expression in the song 'the blanket carrant' as 'to bear a child'.[85] However, Hamish Henderson of the School of Scottish Studies, University of Edinburgh had a different interpretation. In the 1950s Hamish collected a version of the song from Willie Mathieson, a farm servant from Turriff, Aberdeenshire. Hamish informed him that in the *Concise Scots Dictionary*, the meaning of carrant is given as (a) 'an expedition, a sudden journey', or (b) 'revel, an escapade, an uproar', and (c) French – courante, 'a dance'. Hamish concluded that the best interpretation he could come up with for a – 'blanket carrant' was – 'a dance under the blankets!'[86]

66 Sandy and Paddy

An uncle of mine he's an old-fashioned chap,
He sits all the day by the fire,
Talking of nations at home or abroad,
Till you'd think that he never would tire,
He says that old England, the land of the free,
Her flag flies o'er manys the mile,
But the victory is made by the Hieland Brigade,
Or the sons of the Emerald Isle.

Refrain:
If it was nae for Sandy and Paddy,
Where would old England be,
She would nae be where she is today,

Nor Englishmen would nae be free,
Some other nation on earth,
Very soon would be her daddy,
Old England's rose would be trod by her foes,
If it was nae for Sandy and Paddy.

Now in time of peace when there's nothing to do,
Old Sandy and Pat may sing dumb,
But the cry will arise, when trouble breaks out,
For Sandy and Pat for to come.
Then the battle is fought and the victory is won,
And the flag flies again o'er the main,
But there's many an Irish and braw Hieland lad,
Who will ne'er see his country again.
Refrain

Harry Holmes, Joe's older brother, brought this song home from the First World War in 1918 and taught it to Joe. He also presented the twelve-year-old Joe with his first fiddle, which is currently being played by my son Macdara. Harry only sang two verses with refrain but I was able to give Joe another verse from a ballad-sheet my father had bought in the 1920s from a ballad-singer at the Aul' Lammas Fair in Ballycastle, Co. Antrim.

In the not so distant past, the ballad-singer would appear, full-throated in song, at fairs or markets, race-courses, sporting events etc. These were usually members of the travelling community or 'the itinerant class' as the law would classify them. Some of the great carriers of traditional music and song were travellers including Margaret Barry, the Dohertys, Cashs, Dorans, Fureys, Keenans, Reillys etc. Their influence on the music and song tradition can be heard in Ireland and beyond to this day, often performed by those from outside the travelling community. The tradition of the ballad-singer singing and selling their ballads carried on well into the twentieth century and indeed I bought a ballad from a young traveller girl at the Aul' Lammas Fair in Ballycastle for one shilling in the early 1960s. The song, which I still have on file, was *The Blue Hills of Antrim*.

The ballad-sheet of *Sandy and Paddy* printed a first line which differed from Joe's as, 'John Bull he is an old-fashioned chap'. The extra verse supplied via the ballad-sheet dates the song to the period of the Crimean War:

When we fought the Russians in the year fifty-four,
The brave Inniskillings were seen,
Doing their duty like heroes they were,
In defence of their country and Queen,

Ballad-singer at Cushendun, Co. Antrim, c.1910 (photograph courtesy of ITMA)
(In 1995 Cahal Dallat of Ballycastle, Co. Antrim identified the ballad-singer
for me as Roger McMahon from ?).

> The famed Connaught Rangers so true as they were,
> Were always the first at the call,
> To conquer or die for the country they love,
> With the bayonet, the rifle and ball.[87]

Traveller Felix Doran (*c*.1915–72), uilleann piper, at the Aul' Lammas Fair, Ballycastle, Co. Antrim, *c*.1952 (photograph by George Pickow courtesy of Getty Images).

It is worth noting that the first-ever Victoria Cross was awarded during the Crimean War to a Co. Armagh man called Charles Lucas from Druminargale, Poyntzpass. In 1854 Lucas, a twenty-year-old mate, was serving on the HMS *Hecla* in the Baltic when a Russian shell landed without exploding on the *Hecla*'s upper deck with its fuse still hissing. Young Lucas, with what was described as 'great coolness and presence of mind', ran forward, picked up the shell and threw it overboard where it exploded on hitting the water. No-one was killed or injured in the incident and in recognition of his bravery he received the very first VC from Queen Victoria in 1857. To mark the one-hundred-and-fiftieth anniversary of the Victoria Cross in 2006 the British Royal Mail issued commemorative stamps depicting six VC recipients – soldiers, sailors and airmen from all ranks. The 64p stamp featured a portrait of Charles Lucas.

67 The Sea-Apprentice

When first I went a sea-apprentice bound,
I sailed the salt seas all round and round,
I had scarcely sailed a voyage but one,
When I fell in love with my charming Anne.

I went to my captain both stout and bold,
And unto him, my secret told,
'I love a young lass as I love my life,
What would I do if she were my wife?'

The captain said, 'You're a foolish boy,
For to court a girl that you'll ne'er enjoy,
For she'll have sweethearts when you're at sea,
And she'll be married before you'll be free.'

'Well I don't know, but I'll go and try,
For she might fancy an apprentice boy,
And she might alter her mind for me,
And wait on me until I'd be free.'

I bought her ribbons and I bought her gloves,
These things to prove of a heart that loved,
She accepted all and she was not shy,
And she vowed she'd wait on her apprentice boy.

When my ship is anchored and my work is o'er,
I'll steer my barque for sweet Erin's shore,
In my native country my love I'll enjoy,
And she'll welcome home her apprentice boy.

Now come all young sea-apprentices, where'er you be,
Never slight your true-love when you're at sea,
Just love her as you love your life,
And she'll consent to become your wife.

Joe's mother sang these seven verses and the song appeared in the *Songs of the People* on 22 January 1938 with just five verses. Paddy 'Stump' McCloskey of Carnamenagh, Co. Antrim, who was a regular visitor to Killyramer, also sang a shorter version to the air we usually associate with the song *The Doffin' Mistress*. I asked Joe why Paddy McCloskey was nick-named 'Stump' and he told me it referred to stump speeches, which were popular at balls, lint-pulling and harvest dances etc. Along with songs, recitations, 'stump' speeches were very popular party pieces. Paddy McCloskey, besides playing the fiddle and singing, also had several stump speeches in his repertoire, including Robert Emmet's (1778–1803) speech from the dock, when condemned to death: 'Let no man write my epitaph … When my country takes her place among the nations of the earth, then, and not till then, let my epitaph be written.'

Kenneth Peacock collected a version of *The Sea-Apprentice* in Newfoundland in the 1960s with two verses Joe didn't sing:

Our ship is ready and fit for sea,
And tomorrow morning she sails away.
To rise a dance we all did agree,
And I'll ask my true love to dance with me.

'To dance with you, love, I will agree,
And wait on you, love, till you are free,
When all my pleasure and all my joy,
Is to roll in the arms of my 'prentice boy.'[88]

189

68 Seventeen Come Sunday

'Where do you live my bonny wee lass?
Where do you live my honey?'
Right modestly, she answered me,
'In a wee house wea me mammy.'

Refrain:
With me tor I ah, right fal ah do ah da,
Tor I ant tin and-dee.

Her shoes were black and her stockings white,
And her buckles they shone all silver,
She had a dark and a roving eye,
And her hair hung over her shoulder.

'When I go down to your wee house,
When the moon is shining clearly,
Will you open the door and let me in?
And the aul' wife she'll no hear me.'

So I went down to her wee house,
When the moon was shining clearly,
She opened the door and she let me in,
And the aul' doll didna hear me.

'Oh, soldier, soldier will you marry me?
For now it's now or never,
For if you do not marry me,
My heart is broke for ever.'

'Come over the burn my bonny wee lass,
Come over the burn my honey,
Till I get a kiss from your sweet lips,
In spite of your aul' mammy.'

I have heard several versions of this song over the years and it is a particular favourite with the travelling community. Interestingly, Peter Kennedy includes a Cornish language version *Pelea Era Why Moaz, Moes Fettow Teag? (Where Are You Going To, My Pretty Maid?)*, which he recorded in 1950 from Dicky Lashbrook of Launceston.[89] A Cornish language version sung in 1698 was printed by William Pryce of Sherborne, Dorset in 1790. Some collectors connect this song with the *Trooper and Maid* (Child 299) and others make no connection whatsoever. Certainly, when I compare the three texts Child published there are similarities to many of the Irish versions I have heard from Sarah Makem, Séamus Ennis and others, which include the verse:

'And when will you return again,
Or when will we get married?'
'When cockle-shells make silver bells,
That's the time we'll marry.'[90]

This corresponds with Child in all three variants he publishes: (Specimen 'A')

'O when will we twa meet again?
Or when will you me marry?'
'When cockle-shells grow siller bells,
I winna langer tarry.'[91]

The signature tune of a popular BBC radio programme broadcast each Sunday in the mid-1950s called *As I Roved Out* featured Sarah Makem from Keady, Co. Armagh singing her version of this song, which included the verse with 'cockle-shells make silver bells'. This programme presented field recordings of the musical traditions of these islands. Neither Joe's mother's version nor the two versions published in the *Songs of the People* in 1926 and 1939 contained this verse, but otherwise, they would seem to derive from the older source. The song also gained widespread popularity by numerous printings of broadside ballads during the nineteenth century.

69 The Shamrock Sod No More

I never will forget the sorrows of that day,
Being bound across the ocean, our good ship sailed away,
I left my friends on Derry quay, my love on Carrick shore,
For right well I knew I was doomed to tread, the shamrock sod no more.

Right well I knew when I left home, what my sad fate would be,
Still gazing on my comrade boys, they seemed to flee from me,
I watched them till my eyes grew dim, until my heart grew sore,
For right well I knew I was doomed to tread, the shamrock sod no more.

Oh where, oh where, is the trusty heart I once could call my own,
I took my last farewell of her, that day I sailed from home,
It was not her wealth that won my heart, down by yon western main,
It's the constant smile of my favourite girl, that filled my heart with pain.

Oh, if I was a little bird, I would light on my love's breast,
Or if I was a nightingale, I would sing my love to rest,
Or had I the wings of an angel bright, my love I would guard on sea,
For the reason that I love my girl, is because my girl loves me.

It's when I am on my winding sheets, no one to pity me,
It's when I'm on my winding sheets, my thoughts will be of thee,
When I must eat the strangers' bread and bear the strangers' scorn,
It makes me sigh when I'm far from thee, sweet isle where I was born.

Johnny Toland sang this song of emigration, which Joe learned. It would appear to date back to the time of the Famine according to John Ord. Ord, in his *The Bothy Songs and Ballads*, states that the song was written by William Kennedy, who was one of the Scottish *Whistle-Binkie* group of poets. Kennedy apparently was, for some time, British Consul in Texas in the mid-nineteenth century.

This song reminds me and brings back happy memories of the 1960s and 1970s in Sarah Anne and John O'Neill's at Derrytresk, Co. Tyrone. Sarah Anne and her brother, Geordie Hanna often asked Joe to sing this song at Sarah Anne's 'big nights'. Musicians and singers from all over the north would gather in Sarah Anne's for marathons of music, song, good fun and to experience the warmth of the O'Neills' celebrated hospitality. Sarah Anne subsequently learned this song and often sings it and talks of Joe with fond affection.

For the Scoil Éigse in the week prior to the 1976 All-Ireland Fleadh Cheoil in Buncrana, Co. Donegal, Sarah Anne, Geordie, Joe and I were asked to do some Ulster singing workshops for the students attending the traditional singing classes. At one of these afternoon singing sessions, Tom Glackin, father of fiddle player Paddy Glackin, announced that a special bus excursion was being organised for the students, teachers and guest performers to visit the great Co. Donegal fiddler, Johnny Doherty. The bus was booked for 10.00a.m. on Thursday and all interested were to put their names down on the list. Well, we of course put our names down to meet once again our old friend Johnny. On the Thursday morning we arrived at the college in good time and Tom Glackin came over to Joe and myself with bad news. The bus was over-booked and would I mind taking my car to Carrick. I agreed and some ten minutes later Tom came back to ask me if I would mind taking another passenger. The passenger turned out to be a nun in her full pre-Vatican II habit and who had just returned from the missions in Africa. We set off for Carrick and our new friend regaled us with wonderful stories of her time in Africa with some hair-raising accounts of the voodoo! We eventually arrived in Carrick and Johnny Doherty at the time was residing at the Golden Gate public house. We had a wonderful session with Johnny in great form and loving every minute of the attention and praise from his young and not so young, captive audience. Well one thing lead to another – tunes were played, songs were sung, stories told and it came time for our departure from Johnny and a long drive back to Buncrana with our guest traveller. It was around 1.00a.m. when we left Carrick and coming into Glenties, I suddenly realised that I was nearly out of petrol. I pulled up outside the Highland's Hotel and the place was in darkness. There were petrol pumps outside the hotel, so I rang the door bell. After some time and no sign of life I asked our passenger, the nun, if she would mind stepping out of the car and I then resumed ringing the hotel door bell when a chink of light appeared at one of the upstairs windows. Shortly after that the front door of the hotel opened and we were obliged with a fill of petrol – the power of prayer! We headed north again and finally arrived in Buncrana at around 3a.m. and the big gate into the convent was locked. There was nothing else for it I had to give our friend the nun a leg-up over the wall of the convent and she assured us that she had a front door key. Off she went laughing to herself and blessing us for a most enjoyable and memorable day, night and morning!

70 Slieve Gallen Braes

As I went a-walking one morning in May,
To view yon fair valleys and mountains so gay,
I was thinking of those flowers all doomed to decay,
That bloom around you bonny, bonny Slieve Gallen Braes.

Oft, oft of a morning with my dog and my gun,
I roamed through the glens for past-time and fun,
But those days they are all over and I must go away,
So farewell unto you bonny, bonny Slieve Gallen Braes.

Our Isle it so green and our cottage was so gay,
Our children were well cloth-ed and our wives they drank strong tay,
But alas those days are all over and we must go away,
So farewell unto you bonny, bonny Slieve Gallen Braes.

How oft of an evening when the sun is in the west,
I walked hand in hand with the one that I love best,
But those tyrannizing landlords, they would not let us stay,
So farewell unto you bonny, bonny Slieve Gallen Braes.

It's not for the want of employment at home,
That caused the sons of old Erin to roam,
But the rents are getting higher and I'll no longer pay,
So farewell unto you bonny, bonny Slieve Gallen Braes.

Farewell unto old Erin and all our childhood scenes,
To the townland of Lissan and the cross of Ballinascreen,
For those days are all over and we are far away,
So farewell unto you bonny, bonny Slieve Gallen Braes.

This is one of my mother-in-law, Eithne Ui Uallacháin's favourite songs. When her father, Michael Devlin from The Loup, Co. Derry, took up a teaching post in Cullyhanna, Co. Armagh in the early twentieth century this song accompanied him and it was sung at his wedding in Cullyhanna to Violet McPhelimy in 1910.

One night in Conway's Pub in Cookstown, Co. Tyrone in the late 1960s Joe Greer sang a verse that I hadn't heard before:

> Farewell unto old Erin and all our childhood scenes,
> To the townland of Lissan and the cross of Ballinascreen,
> For those days are now all over and we are far away,
> So farewell unto you bonny, bonny Slieve Gallen Braes.

Johnny Loughran (1927–87) from Pomeroy, Co. Tyrone
(pencil sketch by Eamonn O'Doherty courtesy of ITMA).

With that Joe Holmes threw back his head and sang a verse that no-one in the bar had heard before:

> Our Isle it is so green and our cottage was so gay,
> Our children were well-cloth-ed and our wives they drank strong tay,
> But alas those days are all over and we must go away,
> So farewell unto you bonny, bonny Slieve Gallen Braes.

This song reminds me of another night spent in a mountainy area of Co. Tyrone back in the mid-1960s. Johnny Loughran, the blind fiddler from Pomeroy, had told me of a big night coming up near Rouskey and he got his friend John McCann to send me directions. I loaded up the Rover 90 with Joe, Paddy McGinley (fiddle), Alec Elder (fiddle), Sammy Wade (uilleann pipes) and Gerry Kealey (accordion) and we set off for the mountains of Pomeroy. Johnny was telling no lies – it was a big night and tunes were flaked out and songs sung until the dawn chorus told us it was time to go home. When we came out to the car, to my horror a fog had come down and I had the job to drive us down from the mountain onto a broad road with white lines and 'cats-eyes'. We set off very slowly and after driving for about an hour and with no sign of a broad road or white lines I noticed some lights coming from a cottage just off the road. I stopped the car and asked Gerry, the most sensible of my passengers, to ask directions and find out if we were far from the main Omagh to Cookstown road. Gerry dutifully took the torch and made his way over to the cottage. After about ten minutes he returned. 'They couldn't give directions. It was a chicken deep-litter house!' We took off again and after what seemed like hours of trying to keep the car between the ditches on a very narrow road, suddenly, a large mountain hare appeared on the road in front of the car. Dazzled by the lights, he zig-zagged slowly up the road, with the car crawling behind him. From the back seat, Sammy says, 'I'll catch him and throw him over the hedge.' Too late! He opened the back door of the Rover and it being hinged the opposite to every other type of car, the door caught on the ditch and the next thing the door was torn clean off its hinges. Anyway, the hare took off and we retrieved the car door and tied it back onto the car and eventually we reached the main road and the luxury of white lines and 'cats-eyes.' When we were within sight of Ballymoney with a clear road and no fog, Joe began to sing *Slieve Gallen Braes*, a song which had been sung the night before and we all joined in. You could hear the din as we drove through Macfinn in Graham's old motor car!

71　The Son of a Gamble-eer

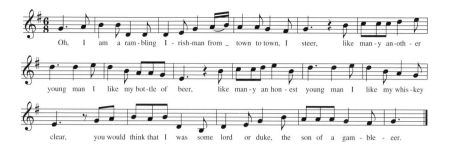

Oh, I am a rambling Irishman from town to town, I steer,
Like many another young man I like my bottle of beer,
Like many an honest young man I like my whiskey clear,
You would think that I was some lord or duke, the son of a gamble-eer.

This old coat that is on my back, I got in the pawn store,
And when it does get wet, me boys, I hang it on the floor,
And when it does get dry again, likewise I put it on,
You'd think I was some lord or duke, not the son of an honest man.

Now this old hat upon my head, I paid two pence for it,
On Sundays when I put it on I cut it very fast,
On Sunday when I put it on I cut it very grand,
You'd think I was some lord or duke, not the son of an honest man.

Now these old shoes upon my feet, they came from the Crimea War,
I got them from an old soldier, who died of wounds and scars,
The soles they leave the uppers and the heels look back to sea,
And the toes they stare me in the face, it's a relic of poverty.

Now if I had a keg of rum and sugar fifty pound,
If I had a tub to put it in and a stick to rumble it round,
I'd drink a health to all in the room, good health and good cheer,
You would think that I was some lord or duke, the son of a gamble-eer.

Mickey McIlhatton (*c.*1899–1975), *The King of the Glens* (courtesy of Eamon Stinson).

The 'King of the Glens' Mickey McIlhatton was the best known and respected poitín maker in the Glens of Antrim. Joe and I were frequent visitors to Mickey's home and enjoyed his kind hospitality and shared many memorable nights of music-making and good fun during the 1960s until his death in 1975. The reference in this song to 'I like my whiskey clear', appealed to Mickey and he often requested this song from Joe. Mickey was a shepherd for most of his life with two 'interruptions'. The first was in the 1920s when he spent two years as a political prisoner on the prison ship *Argenta* in Larne Lough. While interned Mickey made some life-long friends and learned Irish in the 'Dawson Bates College'. This was the name the internees gave their classes after the then Minister of Home Affairs. The Commandant in charge of the prison ship was Captain William Gallagher and Mickey and Gallagher became firm friends. Years later Mickey would invite the Captain up to the Glens for some of the best game shooting in the country. Mickey told us that the Captain always insisted on these shooting expeditions that Mickey walk ahead. Mickey said he could never work out what his reason was for this. When William Gallagher died he did not forget his old friend from the Glens and left Mickey a small legacy. Mickey's second 'interruption' was in the 1960s when he spent four months in Crumlin Road Jail for making poitín. When he was released in 1968 he received a hero's welcome on his arrival at the All-Ireland Fleadh Cheoil in Clones, Co. Monaghan. Mickey surprised us all in the late 1960s, shortly before his seventieth birthday, when he married Mary McDonnell, a local woman a few years his junior. My uncle 'Willie the Cat' met Mickey in Waterfoot not long after the wedding. 'Congratulations and long life to you Mickey and your new wife,' says my uncle. 'Thanks very much Willie,' says Mickey, 'I'm just in the village fixing up a house down here – it's a bit remote up at Skerry West and we want to be near the school-house when the children come along!'

The song *The Son of a Gamble-eer* must have been in vogue in James Joyce's youth in Dublin in the late nineteenth century and early twentieth century, as it's another song which makes several appearances in *Finnegans Wake*. The song also occurs in some early American collections, including one by Carl Sandburg from Chicago, published in 1927, which has this verse:

> I once was tall and handsome, and was so very neat;
> They thought I was too good to live, most good enough to eat;
> But now I'm old my coat is torn, and poverty holds me fast.
> And every girl turns up her nose as I go wandering past.[92]

Another song on a different theme of sheep and cattle droving turns up in an Australian collection under the title *The Ramble-eer*, which contains a similar chorus:

> For I am a ramble-eer, a rollicking ramble-eer,
> I'm a roving rake of poverty, and son-of-a-gun for beer.[93]

72 The Strands of Magilligan

I'm a stranger in this country from Amerikay I came,
Very few in this country can tell me my name,
And I'm here among strangers I will tarry a while,
For the sake of my darling I'll go many the long mile.

On the strands of Magilligan divides in three parts,
Where young men and maidens go to meet their sweethearts,
They will take no denial they will follow and sing,
And the sound of the fiddle oh, it makes my heart ring.

At the top of the cliff where the castle does stand,
It is well built with ivy, down to the back strand,
It is well built with ivy and diamonds shine bright,
It's a pilot for sailors on a dark stormy night.

There the strands of Magilligan, where the wild birds do fly,
And there is one all amongst them and she does fly high,
If I had her in my arms, one night on the strand,
I would kindly subdue her by the squeeze of my hand.

Then it's down in yon nunnery, I will spend all my life,
I'll never will marry, nor be any man's wife,
For it's single and true-hearted, it's here I'll remain,
And I never will marry till my love comes again.

Joe learned this version of the song from his mother. It bears some striking similarities to the English folk song *The Streams of Lovely Nancy* which appeared on numerous printed broadside ballads during the nineteenth century:

> O the streams of lovely Nancy divided in three parts,
> Where young men and maidens do meet their sweethearts,
> For drinking good liquor makes my heart to sing,
> And the noise in the valleys makes the rocks for to ring.

This is the first verse as it appears on a *c.*1820 ballad sheet (see appendix, p. 280).[94] When we examine verse three we find a reference to 'my galligan'. This might well be a corruption of Magilligan in which case *The Strands of Magilligan* may be the origin of *The Streams of Lovely Nancy*?

> Upon younder high mountain where wild fowls do fly,
> There is one amongst them that flies very high,
> If I had her on my galligan or all night on the strand,
> O how soon I would tame her by the slight of my hand.[95]

However, A.L. Lloyd remarks that regarding *The Streams of Lovely Nancy* certain details of its setting are reminiscent of *The Castle of Love and Grace*, a 'parabolic' representation of the Virgin in the fourteenth-century poem, *Cursor Mundi*, and could be a relic of a hymn to Mary.[96] Yet another broadside ballad with the title *The American Stranger* from *c.*1850 has a first verse similar to what Joe's mother sang for *The Strands of Magilligan*:

> I am a poor stranger, from America I came.
> There's no one does know me, nor can tell me my name;
> I am a poor stranger, I'll tarry a while,
> I have rambled for my darling for many a long mile.[97]

Whatever its origin and meaning might be, the Irish version of the song turns up several times in Co. Antrim and of course in the Magilligan area of Co. Derry.

73 The Sweet Bann Water

A - way, a — - way I can stay no _ lon-ger, the _ sweet Bann _ wat-er I mean _ to _ cross, o'er

high _ _ hills and _ lof _ - ty moun-tains, to _ spend a _ night with my own _ wee _ lass, though the

night being dark as _ dun _ _ -geon and _ not a star there _ did _ ap - -pear, I _

would be _ guid-ed with _ out a stum-ble, in _ to the _ arms _ of my _ _ _ dear.

Away, away I can stay no longer, the sweet Bann water I mean to cross,
O'er high hills and lofty mountains, to spend a night with my own wee lass,
Though the night being dark as dungeon and not a star there did appear,
I would be guided without a stumble, into the arms of my dear.

Slowly I crept up to my love's window and slowly knelt down upon a stone,
And through a pane I gently whispered, 'Oh, Mary darling are you at home?'
She raised her head from off her pillow and slowly uncovered her snow-
    white breasts,
Saying, 'Who is this at my window, disturbing me off my night's rest?'

'It is your Johnny, your pride young Johnny, oh, arise up darling and let me in,
For I am tired of my long journey and besides I'm wet love unto the skin,'
Then slowly, slowly the door she opened and slowly, slowly I crept in,
And there we lay in each other's arms, till the long night was nearly in.

'Oh, go away and ask your mother if she is willing my bride you'll be,
If she says no come back and tell me, 'tis the last night I'll trouble thee,'
'I need not go, nor ask my mother, for tales of love she can't endure,'
She will bid me go and court another, then I whispered in her ear.

'Oh, go away and ask your father if he is willing my bride you'll be,
If he says no come back and tell me, 'tis the last night I'll trouble thee,'
'I need not go nor ask my father for he's in his chamber all at his ease,
In his right hand he holds a letter, which reads much to your displease.'

'What makes them speak so ill of me love, a loyal lover to you I've been,
A loyal lover and a constant sweetheart, true to you I have ever been,
For I can climb as high a tree and I can rob as high a nest,
And I can pluck a sweeter flower, but not the flower that I love best.'

For after dawning, there comes a morning and after morning there comes a day,
And after one love there comes another, we need not hold them that will away,
When I sit down all at my leisure and my foolish folly I think on,
On placing my fond affection all on a maid so hard to win.

Another of Joe's mother's songs. It sometimes occurs with the 'cock crowing' motif. This seems to put the song into *The Lover's Ghost or The Grey Cock* (Child 248) category although this is disputed by some ballad scholars. There are many variants of this song found throughout Ireland, Britain and North America. One version collected in Birmingham in 1951 from Cecilia Costello, who was of Irish descent, transfers the song story from the river Bann to the river Thames:[98]

> I must be going, no longer staying,
> The burning Thames I have to cross,
> Oh, I must be guided without a stumble,
> Into the arms of my dear lass.

The version published in the *Songs of the People* on 25 September 1937 was supplied by Valentine Crawford from Bushmills, Co. Antrim, and included the 'cock crowing' verse, which Joe's mother didn't sing:

> When this long night was almost ended,
> And drawing nigh to the break of day,
> She says, 'My darling, the cocks are crowing,
> It's now full time you were going away.'[99]

The Butcher family of Magilligan Co. Derry sang a version which includes the 'cock crowing' motif and has a particularly fine concluding verse:

But I'll go off to the wild mountains,
Where I'll see nothing but the wild deer,
Nor I'll eat nothing but the wild herbs,
And I'll drink nothing but my true-love's tears.[1]

This Co. Derry verse has a near cousin, collected in 1939 by Anne and Frank Warner from Rebecca King Jones from Crab Tree Creek, North Carolina. When the Warner's played her voice back to her, so she could hear how she sounded, Rebecca said, 'Well! I didn't know my voice was so purty. It was a plum gift from the Lord to give me this voice. That's a talent the Lord gives you.'

I'll go with you in some lonesome valley,
Although my meat may be pretty berries,
And the water that I drink be the morning dew.[2]

74 The Trip O'er the Mountain

One night as the moon did illumine the sky, when I first took a notion to marry,
I drew to my stick and away I did strike, you'd have thought I'd been in a hurry,
When I came to that bend where I oft times had been, my heart took a leap
     when my charmer I seen,
I lifted the latch and I bid her, 'Good e'en, will you venture with me over the
     mountain?'

'What notion is this has come into your head? I'm glad for to see you so merry,
It is twelve by the clock, I should be in my bed, speak low or me mammy will
     hear you,'
'I'm using no magic, no scheme nor no spell, I've a true honest heart and I
     love you right well,
And if you'll refuse me, I bid my farewell, I'll retrace my steps over the
     mountain.'

'If I was to make an elopement with you, I might be attended by danger,
My company would titter and censor me too, my parents would frown and
     wonder.'
'Just then let them titter and censor away, consult with yourself, for it's
     drawing near day,
I don't care a fig what the whole of them say, if I once had you over the
     mountain.'

'Oh, then you're in earnest,' he said with a smile, 'kind providence be my director,
I've love in my bosom, I ne'er will deny,' though the sentence it seemed to
    affect her,
Between fiddling and dancing we spent the whole day, the fear of marriage it
    soon fades away,
And often times to my darling I say, 'You'll not rue going over the mountain.'

The moon was advancing and sunk in the west and the morning star shining
    so clearly,
And we did proceed our journey in haste and we joined at the alter of Hymen,
With peace and contentment we spent the long day, the anger of marriage
    will soon go away,
Oh, oft times I sat when I've little to say, of the trip we took over the mountain.

Paddy 'Stump' McCloskey, from Carnamenagh, Co. Antrim, made frequent trips to his
brother's home at Dunaghy and on these occasions he usually included a visit to the
neighbouring townland of Killyramer to visit the Holmes's. Sometimes he came alone and
sometimes he would be accompanied by his two nieces (see song No. 37). This song of
Paddy's was a particular favourite of Joe's mother and she got the words of the song from
him. *The Trip O'er the Mountain* was apparently written by a school teacher called Hugh
McWilliams, who taught locally in Loughgiel, Co. Antrim from *c.*1819 to 1831. I am grateful
to John Moulden for sharing his research on McWilliams.[3] McWilliams was born in
Glenavy, Co. Antrim in *c.*1783 and he published two books called *Poems and Songs on
Various Subjects* in 1816 and 1831. At least two of his songs entered the oral song tradition:
When A Man's in Love (see song No. 80) and *The Trip O'er the Mountain*. Versions of these
songs turn up all over Ireland, Britain and North America.
    Seamus Ennis (1919–82), uilleann piper, singer, storyteller and collector, played a
version of the air for *The Trip O'er the Mountain* and sang a few fragments of the words of
the song, which came from his grandfather.

75 The True-Born Sons of Levi

Come all you craftsmen that do wish,
To propagate the grand design,
Come enter into our high temple,
And learn the art that is divine.

Refrain:
For we are the true-born sons of Levi,
Non on earth with us compare,
We are the root and branch of David,
The bright and the glorious morning star.

Noah planted the first garden,
Moses planted Aaron's rod,
He smote the waters of the Egyptians,
And turned the Jordan into blood.

As Joshua and I crossed over Jordan,
We did twelve stones bear along,
'Twas the high priest and our grand master,
That moved the ark of God along.

Where, there seven trumpets of rams' horns,
Sounded along before the ark,
Gilgal was our resting quarter,
There we left our holy mark.

> Come all you brethren and join with me,
> And bear the ark as I have done,
> Come enter into our high temple,
> To this the new Jerusalem.

Eddie Butcher sang a verse and chorus of this masonic song for Joe Holmes and myself one night in his Magilligan home. Joe then and there followed this with another four verses. It was another song brought to life by two great men of song.

The *Songs of the People* published nine verses of the song under the title *The Knights of Malta* in 1926. Interestingly, Sam Henry credited a nineteenth-century broadside ballad by J. Nicholson of Belfast as his source for his text and an octogenarian from Magilligan for the air which he learned *c*.1855. The melody also serves the song *The Spanish Lady*. One of the nineteenth-century copies of the broadside ballad in the National Library of Scotland which has no printer's imprint, shows a title of *Sons of Levi – A New Masonic Song* (see appendix, p. 281).[4] Although Eddie Butcher was a Catholic and the Masonic Order in Ireland today draws its membership from the non-Catholic population, Eddie included another song involving the freemasons in his repertoire. This unusual song he sang for us was called *The Mason's Word*:

> He says, 'My dear, how would you like to undergo the toil,
> To mount upon a horned goat and ride for many a mile?'
> 'I am sure that it would be an action most absurd,
> For to ride astride all on a goat to learn the Mason's Word.'

The oldest material evidence of the freemasons existence in Ireland is a brass square bearing Masonic symbols and the date 1507, which was discovered in the foundations of Ball's Bridge in Limerick City. Unlike many of the other secret societies in Ireland, the freemasons are international and comparatively non-sectarian. Until the Vatican edict banning membership in the nineteenth century, many Irish Catholics practised freemasonry, including the illustrious Daniel O'Connell (see songs No. 16 and No. 19), who founded a Masonic Lodge in Tralee, Co. Kerry in the early nineteenth century. O'Connell defended freemasonry as a: 'philanthropy unconfined by sect, nation, colour or religion'. However, after much pressure and ecclesiastical censure from the Catholic hierarchy, he finally issued a public renunciation of freemasonry in the Catholic periodical *The Pilot* in April 1837. Interestingly, many prominent United Irishmen were freemasons including Henry Joy McCracken, Henry Munro, Samuel Neilson, Lord Edward Fitzgerald, Thomas Russell, John Napper Tandy, Theobald Wolfe Tone and many others. As part of the bi-centennial commemorations of the United Irish Rebellion, a plaque was unveiled at the Ulster Provincial Masonic Hall in Rosemary Street, Belfast to Freemason and United Irishman Henry Joy McCracken, who was executed at Cornmarket, Belfast on 7 June 1798.

76 True Lovers' Discussion

One pleasant evening, when pinks and daisies,
Closed in their bosom a drop of dew,
The feathered warblers of every species,
Together chanted their notes so true,
As I did stray, rapt in meditation,
It charmed my heart for to hear them sing,
Night's silent embers were just arising,
And the air in concert did sweetly ring.

With joy transported, each sight I courted,
While gazing round me with expecting eye,
Two youthful lovers, in conversation,
Closely engaged, I chanced to spy,
The couple spoke with such force of reason,
And their sentiments they expressed so clear,
That for to listen to their conversation,
My inclination was to draw near.

He pressed her hand and he said, 'My darling,
Tell me the reason you changed your mind,
Or have I loved you to be degraded,
While youth and innocence are in their prime?
For I am slighted and ill requited,
For all the favours I did bestow,

You will surely tell me before I leave you,
Why you're inclined to treat me so.'

With great acuteness she then made answer,
'If on your favours I would rely,
You might contrive to blast my glory,
And our marriage day you might hover by,
Young men in general are fickle-minded,
And oh, to trust you I am afraid,
If for your favours I am indebted,
Both stock and interest you shall be paid.'

'To blast your glory, love, I ne'er intended,
Nor fickle-minded will I ever be,
And as for my debts, you can never repay them,
Except by true love and loyally,
Remember, darling, our first engagement,
When childish pastime was all we knew,
Be true and constant and I'm thine forever,
I'll brave all dangers and go with you.'

'Your proffer's good, and I thank you for it,
But yet your offer I can't receive,
By soft persuasion and kind endearment,
The wily serpent beguiled Eve.
There's other reasons might be assigned,
The highest tide might ebb and fall,
Another fair maid might fit you better,
Therefore I can't obey your call.'

'Yes, I'll admit the tide in motion,
Is always moving from shore to shore,
But still its substance is never changing,
And never will, till time's no more.
I will sound the fame of all loyal lovers,
To fix their minds on whose love is pure,
Where no existence can ever change them,
Nor a physician prescribe a cure.'

She says, 'Young man, to tell you plainly,
For to refrain you I am inclined,
Another young man of birth and honour,
Has gained my favour and changed my mind,
My future welfare I have consulted,
On fickle footing I'll never stand,
Besides my parents would be affronted,
To see you walking at my right hand.'

'What had you, darling, when you were born?
What nature gave you, love, so had I,
Your haughty parents, I do defy them,
And ill-got riches I do deny,
An honest heart, love, is far superior,
Your gold and riches will fade away,
Sure, naked we came into this world,
And much the same shall we go away.'

'You falsify when you say you love me,
And slight my parents, whom I love dear,
I think it justice to degrade you,
When that's the course that you mean to steer,
By wealth or feature, or art, or nature,
You're not my equal in any line,
Since I conjure you, insist no further,
As to your wishes I'll not incline.'

'Oh, curb your passion, sir,' she then exclaimed,
'It was not to quarrel that I brought you here,
But to discourse with you in moderation,
With a real intention to make appear,
I speak with candour, I will surrender,
To what is proper in every way,
If you submit to a fair discussion,
And reason's dictates you will obey.'

'It is now too late to ask that question,
When you despised me before my friends,

Lebanon's plains, if you could command them,
Would not suffice to make amends,
There's not a tree in the Persian forest,
Retains its colour, excepting one,
And that's the laurel that I will cherish,
And always carry in my right hand.'

'The blooming laurel, sir you may admire,
Because its virtue seems always new,
But there's another, you can't deny it,
It's just as bright to the gardener's view.
It wisely rests throughout the winter,
And blooms again when spring draws near,
The pen of Homer has wrote its praises,
In June and July it doth appear.'

'You speak exceedingly, but not correctly,
By words supporting your cause in vain,
Had you the tongue of a Siren goddess,
Your exhortations I would distain.
It was your love that I required,
But since you placed it in a golden store,
I'll strike the string and my harp will murmur,
Farewell, my darling, for evermore.'

She seemed distracted, her eyes affected,
With exclamations she thus gave way,
'Sir, my denial was but a trial – ye Gods,
Be witness to what I say,
But if, my darling, you don't forgive me,
And quite forget my incredulity,
A single virgin for your sake I'll wander,
While a green leaf grows on yon laurel tree.'

So all young maidens, I pray take warning,
Let love and virtue be still your aim,
No worldly treasure should yield you pleasure,
With those whose features you do disdain.

All loyal lovers will then respect you,
And to your memory will heave a sigh,
The blooming rose and evergreen laurel,
Will mark the spot where your bodies lie.

From Ballynahinch, about two miles distant,
Where blackbirds whistle and thrushes sing,
With hills surrounding and valleys bounding,
A charming prospect all in the spring,
Where female beauty is never wanting,
The lonely stranger a refuge finds,
In Magheratimpany, if you inquire,
You will find the author of these simple lines.

Another of Joe's mother's songs, or marathon you could say, which was sung by both Eddie Butcher and Joe Holmes. Sometimes, they would sing verse about, like a conversation or 'discussion' to great effect. The melody and text with the eighteen verses they sang were similar and when I compare their texts with nineteenth-century broadside ballads and song books printed in Ireland and North America there are remarkable similarities. This also applies to the text published in the *Songs of the People* in 1927 and, according to a note by Sam Henry, the author of the song, of an unknown date, was a schoolteacher called McKittrick from Magheratimpany, Co. Down. Eddie Butcher's theory regarding this song and other big long songs, of which he had many, was that they pre-date the advent of the electric light and their purpose was to shorten the night and the winter! As if eighteen verses were not sufficient a Canadian version collected by Helen Creighton in the 1950s had an additional two verses. The singer was Angelo Dornan (see song No. 62), who had north Antrim connections:

'Misunderstandings if not adjusted,
Will cool the ardour of the staunchest friends,
The same is true of a lovers' quarrel,
On calm reflection does their fate depend.
If you won't come back love and quite forgive me,
And quite excuse my credulity,
A single virgin for your sake I'll mourn,
Till the silent tomb shall encompass me.'

Amazed, astounded, he stood dumbfounded,
His tender passion was ill concealed,
With doubt suspended and tension ended,

His true emotion was soon revealed,
Her declaration was so convincing,
His cold aloofness could not endure,
Those youthful lovers were reunited,
Their doubts dispelled and their trust assured.[5]

The poet, William Allingham (1824–89), from Ballyshannon, Co. Donegal worked as a customs officer in various north of Ireland locations from 1846 and one of his postings was in Coleraine, Co. Derry. In 1852, Allingham published an article in the London periodical *Household Words* entitled *Irish Ballad Singers and Irish Street Ballad*, which gives a vivid account of a fair day with all its trappings of cattle, horses, dealing-men, Cheap Johns and most importantly the ballad singers, peddling their ballad sheets. From the short references he makes in his article, we are able to identify many songs and ballads which are still current to this day. Here is his account of some of the ballad singers performing songs, including the *True Lovers' Discussion* at a fair day somewhere in Ulster in the mid nineteenth century:

At our elbow, a ballad-singer, a young woman in old plaid cloak and very old straw bonnet, strikes up, with a sweet Connacht lisp, and slightly nasal twang, *The Sorrowful Lamentation of Patrick Donohoe* – with the words, 'Come all you tender Christians!' – and soon summons around her a ring of listeners. She will sing da capo as long as the ballad appears to draw attention and custom, and then she will

Packie Manus Byrne, John Campbell, Hamish Henderson and Len Graham,
at the National Folk Music Festival, Sutton Bonington, Leicestershire, *c.*1990.
(photograph by John Heydon).

change it or move off to another part of the fair. The hour of melody seems to have struck; for, not far away we discover a second circle united by Orphean attraction. And here our curiosity is raised by the comment of a man who seems to be tearing himself away from the influence. The best ballad singer this, he declares, that he has heard these twenty years! To which another, assenting, says, 'In troth, it's worth a ha'penny to hear him go over it, let alone the paper.' The minstrel is found to be a tall, sad, stooping man, about thirty-five; his song, to the favourite tune of *Youghall Harbour*, is about two faithful lovers; his vocal excellence consists in that he twirls every word several times round his tongue, wrapt in the notes of a soft, husky, tremulous voice. In this style of gracing – which is considered highly artistic, and for which, I believe, 'humouring' is the country phrase – the words are delivered somewhat as follows:

> This pay-air disco-ooeyoor-cerced with sich foo-oocy-oorce o'ray-ayizin,
> Ther may-aynin they ay-apee-ayx-esprayss'd so-hoo-o-o clearrrr,
> That fau-hor to lae-ssen too-oo ther caw-aw-he-on-vairsay-ay-ashin,
> My ehe-ee-in-clinay-aheeay-ashin was for too-oo-hoo-draw-aw-haw-ee-aw-a-neerrrr.
> That is to say:
> This pair discoursed with such force of reasoning,
> Their meaning they expressed so clear,
> That for to listen to their conversation,
> My inclination was to draw near.

Urging our way slowly through the crowd, we come within ear-shot of a shriller strain, which proceeds from two female vocalists, standing face to face, and yelling down one another's throats. Agrarian politics, this time, and not of the most wholesome sort! That country lout – who tenders his copper with swaggering bashfulness, and, for careful preservation of the ballad, rolls it up into a wisp between his hands, and so thrusts it into his pocket – lout as he is, has not improbably, enough of musical ear and voice to enable him to revive the symphony and song of these strange damsels, by his winter fireside, and at subsequent wakes and gatherings; sprinkling into wild hearts the ignorance and foolishness – if it be no worse – of some poor conceited creature who perhaps bribed the printer with a few pence to exalt his trash into type.'[6]

My old friend the storyteller John Campbell from Mullaghbawn related a story regarding a Fair Day in Crossmaglen, Co. Armagh in the early 1950s, when a neighbour – man from Mullaghbawn – sold a cow, and was in Short's public house standing his customer a 'luck-penny' drink. Well, one drink led to another and after a while he was totally footless. He came out of the pub into the Fair and a ballad-singer with a sheath of ballads in his hand was singing with great gusto *The Wild Colonial Boy*. Our good man joined in with the song and bought a ballad off him, giving the ballad-singer a generous shilling for a penny ballad. This he folded and stuffed the ballad into his waistcoat pocket.

Ballad singers with ballad sheets from *Irish Street Ballads*
by John Hand of Castleblayney, Co. Monaghan, published in Liverpool
in 1875 in the *Denair's Penny Irish Library* series.

A good neighbour from Mullaghbawn saw our man staggering up the street and went over and linked unto him. 'Are you for Mullaghbawn?' 'I am,' says our man. 'Well you're in luck I'm heading that direction now and I have the tractor and link-box with me.' So the good neighbour oxtered our man into the link-box, along with the two pigs he was after buying at the Fair. When they arrived at the man's house, the neighbour let him out and pointed him in the direction of his front door. When the door opened the good neighbour put the boot down and took off before the wife would blame him for her husband's state. Well, the footless husband, when the wife opened the front door, he fell, mouth and nose onto the kitchen floor – out for the count. 'Ah!' says she. 'Now me chance to search his pockets.' And she started going through his trousers and then coat pockets, but she could only find loose change – coppers and brass and the odd shilling. Then she spotted something in his waistcoat pocket and she pulled it out, thinking it was one of those big white five pound notes that were in vogue at that time. She opened it out and when she saw what it was she burst out crying. At that the husband woke up and got up off the floor. 'Give me the damn thing,' says he. 'You haven't got the right air for the bloody ballad.' And he commenced to sing *The Wild Colonial Boy* – badly!

77 True Lover John

It happened for to be on a cold winter's evening,
A fair maid sat waiting all alone.
She was thinking of her father, likewise her aged mother,
Aye, and also her true lover John.

Young Johnny he was sweet and he promised for to meet,
But he tarried an hour too long.
He met with great delay which caused him for to stay,
Aye, and I weary waiting all alone.

Young Johnny came at last and he found the door was fast,
He slowly, slowly tinkled at the pane.
This fair maid she arose and hurried on her clothes,
In order to let young Johnny in.

He took her in his arms, aye, and off to bed they went,
And there they lay talking of their plans.
I wish, this maid says she, this night would prove to be,
As long since the world first began.

Fly up, fly up my pretty little cock,
And don't crow until it breaks day,
And your cage it shall become of the very shining gold,
And your wings of a silvery grey.

But this pretty little cock so cruel as he was,
He crowed out an hour too soon,
And he sent my love away before the break of day,
It being only the light of the moon.

This fair maid she arose and she quickly followed after,
Saying, when will you come to see me?
When the fishes they do fly and the seas they all run dry,
And seven moons shine brightly o'er yon lea.

There was once I thought my love was as constant unto me,
As the stones that lie under yon ground,
But now, since I do find he has altered his mind,
I would rather stay single as be bound.

As I have already mentioned in my introduction to the book this was the first song Joe sang for me – *True Lover John* – and he wrote the words out and presented them to me on my second visit to Killyramer (see facsimile below).[7] 'Fair exchange, no robbery,' says Joe. This was in 'payment' for the song *The Murlough Shore* I had given him on my first visit. I knew when I first heard *True Lover John*, as Joe's mother called it, that it was old and I eventually found a shorter text published by Professor F.J. Child. Child in his *The English and Scottish Popular Ballads* (No. 248) included it under the title *The Grey Cock*, which he had taken from David Herd's *Ancient and Modern Scottish Songs*, published in 1769. Herd published seven stanzas, while here in Killyramer nearly two hundred years later a fuller version was still in the oral tradition.

A six-verse version was collected in 1951 by Anne and Frank Warner from Hattie Hicks Presnell from Spice Creek, Tennessee, in which there is a chicken crowing!

My pretty little chicken, my pretty crowin' chicken,
Say, don't you crow before day.
I'll make your wings of a yeller beading gold,
And your comb of the silver so gay, gay, gay,
And your comb of the silver so gay.[8]

Another version was collected by Maud Karpeles in Newfoundland in 1929 which has a particularly poignant verse:

The sand is my soft bed of down, my love,
The sea is my white holland sheet,
And long hungry worms will feed off of me,
While I'm taking my long silent sleep.[9]

Song - True Lover John

I

It happened for to be on a cold Winters
evening. a fair maid sat waiting alone
She was thinking of her father like wise
her aged mother, and also her true lover John

II

Young Johnnie he was sweet and he Promosed
for to meet but he tarried an hour to long
he met with some delay, which caused
him for to stay and I weary waiting
all alone

III

Then Johnnie came at last and he found
the door was fast, and he slowley
slowley tinkled at the Pane
this fair maid she arose and hurried on
her clows, in order to let young Johnnie in

IIII

He took her in his arms, and off to bed
they went, and here they lay talking
off their Plan

P. T. O.

Facsimile of Joe Holmes's hand-written version of *The Grey Cock* ballad, c.1963.

78 Tumbling Through the Hay

It being in the month of July in the rosy time of the year,
Down by yon flowery meadows where the water does run clear,
Where the lambs and little fishes they do merrily sport and play,
And the lads and the lasses they go tumbling through the hay.

Refrain:
La de dee die de tol da lee, la de dee die la de die, la de dee die de tol da lee

Then up comes lovely Johnny with a pitchfork and a rake,
And up comes lovely Molly the hay then for to make,
They timed their notes so merrily as the nightingale did sing,
From morning until evening they were at their haymaking.

Then up comes the mowers the hay for to cut down,
With their scythes upon their shoulders and their hair a lovely brown.
Then up comes the labourers the hay for to shake out,
And when they had it all cut down they tossed it all about.

It was coming up to Saturday and all would get their pay,
Aye, and all these jolly hay-makers were feeling blithe and gay.
The number of these hay-makers as near as I can say,
Were five and twenty boys and girls a-tumbling through the hay.

When nine short months were over and all was passed and gone,
There were five and twenty boys and girls a-making their sad moan.
Hush-la-baa-baby these fair maids they did say,
And many a time they wished they ne'er had tossed among the hay.

Here we have a similar rustic theme to *The Jolly Ploughboy* (see song No. 38), only this time the Irish version sung by Joe's mother retains the frolicking in the hay and includes the pregnancy element. More often than not, when Sam Henry published a song in his *Songs of the People* series, he would provide his source with the names and addresses of his informants. In the case of this song which appeared on the 3 April 1937, he gives no source. It would appear that some censorship was in play, though mild as this song now appears to our modern eyes and ears, in the 1920s and 30s when this series ran in the Coleraine weekly *The Northern Constitution*, no songs of a bawdy, erotic or party political nature featured in the newspaper's columns. In the case of *Tumbling Through the Hay* the last verse

Haymaking at Montgomery's Farm, Lisnalinchy, Co. Antrim, 1904
(photograph courtesy of MAGNI).

would seem to have been 'modified' to lessen the promiscuity element. In the *Songs of the People* version the gestation period has been extended from 'nine months' to 'two years' and the last line of the final verse changed from Joe's 'And many a time they wished they ne'er had tossed among the hay', to Henry's published text 'And they wished that they were free again to tumble through the hay'.

The well-known Sussex family The Coppers sing a wonderful harmony version called *Pleasant Month of May* with not a baby in sight. The English folk in this instance are much better behaved than the Irish lads and lasses!

The Revd Baring-Gould and Cecil Sharp published an even more sanitised version of this song called *The Merry Haymakers* in 1906, which was taught in British schools in the early twentieth century. In their introduction to the *English Folk Songs for Schools*, the British Board of Education, in their 'Suggestions for the consideration of Teachers,' had this to say:

> Folk songs are the expression in the idiom of the people of their joys and sorrows, their zest for sport, and the simple pleasures of a country life. Such music is the early and spontaneous uprising of artistic power in a nation, and the ground on which all national music is built upon; folk songs are the true classics of the people and their survival, so often by tradition alone, proves that their appeal is direct and lasting.[10]

Noble words and 'lasting' indeed according to the Revd Baring-Gould, a version of this song appeared on an early broadside ballad in 1695, printed by C. Bates of West Smithfield, London.[11]

79 The Wedding of Lauchie McGrath

Oh listen a while and I'll tell you a prattle,
The night I fell in with some curious tattle,
To tell you the truth it was liker a battle,
The night of the wedding of Lauchie McGrath.

Refrain:
Oh, but that was a terrible tear,
Me and meself and me mother was there,
And should I get mixed up with the wheels of a train,
I'll never go back to a wedding again.

We had plenty to eat, we had frost-bitten liver,
As sure as I'm here, as sure as I'm never,
The look of the beef nearly gave us the flavour,
The night of the wedding of Lauchie McGrath.

The first thing we had was a cart-load of peelings,
A big Irish stew that was made in the Hielands,
And oh, but the look of it hurt-ed our feelings,
The night of the wedding of Lauchie McGrath.

Oh, the first one to sing was aul' Mrs O'Russell,
And she couldn'e sing, but she started to whistle,
And somebody gave her a kick on the bustle,
The night of the wedding of Lauchie McGrath.

Oh, the next one to sing was big Hughie O'Hara,
He started to give us a verse of tra-rarah,
But Hughie's remains was wheeled home on a barrow,
The night of the wedding of Lauchie McGrath.

The next one to sing was big Donal O'Glinty,
With several Peelers he kicked up a shinty,
He lifted the poker and killed about twenty,
The night of the wedding of Lauchie McGrath.

Eddie Butcher in full 'flight' – some of those present include Gracie Butcher, Paddy
Tunney, Hugh Shields, Micho Russell, Ted Hickey, Seán Corcoran, Cathal Goan, Frank
Harte … Photographed at Feile na Bóinne, Drogheda, Co. Louth, 1976
(photograph by Joe Dowdall, courtesy of ITMA).

Joe Holmes and Len Graham – some of those present include Finbar Boyle, Sinéad Cahir, John Slattery, Jackie Devenney, Eithne Ní Uallacháin, Hugh Shields, Tom Clarke, Tom and Meg Crehan, Mary Bergin (photograph by Joe Dowdall, courtesy of ITMA).

The street balladeers of earlier times sang songs on many and varied themes. One of the themes dealt with was people at play including sporting events, fair and market days, balls, wakes, weddings etc. Weddings seem to have been a particularly popular subject matter: *The Wedding of Ballyporeen, The Wedding of Biddy McCrane* – both appear on nineteenth-century broadside ballads. Eddie Butcher sang *The Wedding of Sandy McNabb*, Mary Anne Carolan from Co. Louth sang *The Wedding at Sweet Baltray*, John McGrath from Moneygran, Co. Derry sang another one, *The Wedding at Ballinderry*, and Micil 'Ned' Quinn from Mullaghbawn, Co. Armagh sings two wedding songs, which came down from Co. Dublin in the early years of the twentieth century. The harvest in Skerries, Co. Dublin was about six weeks earlier than south Armagh and Micil's father, John 'Ned' Quinn and other small farmers from south Armagh would walk the fifty-odd miles to Skerries and worked at the harvest on the large fertile Co. Dublin farms. The harvest-workers came from all arts and parts of Ireland and they were accommodated in the barns and out-houses of the farms. Micil's father came home with two wedding songs from these outings – *The Wedding of Larry Magee* and *The Wedding Above in Glencree*. When the Skerries harvest was saved, John 'Ned' and his neighbours would then walk the fifty-odd miles home, with money in their pockets, in time to harvest their own crops.

An interesting wedding song appears in the Hume MS of 1845 in the National Library, Dublin called *The Muntagh Wedding*. This song is laced with 'Montiaghisms', that is, dialect terms and Irish language words. The Montiaghs is a district of north-east Armagh on the shores of Lough Neagh. Not to be left out, Joe also sang a wedding song from his steam-roller days, *The Wedding of Lauchie McGrath*. This song was recorded in the early twentieth century by the popular Scottish music-hall entertainer, Harry Lauder (1870–1950).

John Kennedy, Cullybackey, Co. Antrim (photograph by Gary Parrott).

226

80 When a Man's in Love

When a man's in love he feels no cold, like me not long ago,
Like a hero bold to see his girl, he'll plough through frost and snow,
The moon she gently sheds her light along my dreary way,
Until I came to that sweet spot, where all my treasure lay.

I tapped at my love's window, 'My love are you within?'
And slowly she undid the latch and slyly I slipped in,
Her hand was soft, her breath was sweet, her tongue did gently glide,
I stole a kiss, it was no miss and I asked her to be my bride.

'Oh, take me to your chamber love, oh, take me to your bed,
Oh, take me to your chamber love, to rest my weary head,'
'To take you to my chamber love, my parents won't agree,
But sit you down by the fire-side and I'll sit close by thee.'

'Manys a night I courted you against your father's will,
You never once said you'd be my bride, but now my lass sit still,
The laws of nature bid us love and beauty whispered low,
May the Powers above look down on me, for I'm tormented so.'

'Manys a cold and stormy night I came to visit you,
When tossed about by the cold winter winds or wet by the morning dew,
But now I'm going to cross the sea, to far Columbia's shore,
And you will never, never see your youthful lover more.'

'Are you going to leave me, oh, pray what can I do?
I'll break through every bond of love, to go along with you,
Perhaps my parents won't forget, but surely they'll forgive,
For from this hour I am resolved along with you to live.'

This is another of Master Hugh McWilliam's songs, which like *The Trip O'er the Mountain* (see song No. 74) gained widespread popularity. Joe had this song from his neighbour Johnny Toland and it resembles the original one published by the author, McWilliams, in 1831 in his *Poems and Songs on Various Subjects.* Interestingly though, McWilliams wrote: 'and her tongue did gently chide', which is not quite the same as what Joe sang: 'her tongue did gently glide!'

Joe and I sang this in the Cosy Bar, Derrygonnelly, Co. Fermanagh one night back in the early 1970s. Mick Hoy, the local fiddler, singer, storyteller and great character, immediately played a different melody on the fiddle and sang a verse of *When a Man's in Love.* Joe and I often remarked on the wonderful full head of lovely, shiny black hair that Mick had, although he told us he was coming up on seventy. On another particularly hot summer's night in the Cosy Bar with a full house of musicians and singers, as the night progressed and the reels got faster and faster, we observed Mick was sweating and trickles of black beads of sweat were rolling down his forehead. 'Damn it all,' says Mick, wiping his brow with his handkerchief, 'but that bloody old *Cherry Blossom* boot polish isn't as good as it used to be!'

Part Two

FIDDLE PLAYING AND DANCING

Fiddle Playing and Dancing

A T THE AGE OF TWELVE IN 1918, Joe Holmes was presented with his first fiddle by his brother Harry. Harry had brought the fiddle back from France after the First World War and he soon taught his younger brother the rudiments of fiddle-playing. Very soon Joe was playing at house dances and harvest barn-dances, as well as learning tunes and tips from older neighbouring fiddlers. Most of his dance tunes were learned in his own locality and his repertoire and style is very much representative of the North Antrim fiddle tradition of the early twentieth century. The dances Joe played for included, music for reels, jigs, polkas, schottisches, strathspeys, hornpipes, mazurkas, quadrilles, four and eight-hand reels, lancers, as well as the more modern waltzes. According to Breandán Breathnach in his publication *Folk Music and Dances of Ireland*, the reel, schottische, and strathspey came from Scotland, hornpipes from England; that most of Europe had some form of the jig; polkas and mazurkas have an East European origin etc. All these dances were imported at one time or other, but of course the Irish love to dance and they put their own unique stamp on the imports and of course they composed many of their own dance tunes.

Joe Holmes at Antrim and Derry Fiddlers' Night in Smyth's Hall, Carnlough, Co. Antrim, *c.*1972 (photograph courtesy of Billy McKee).

231

Niel Gow (1727–1807) portrait by Henry Raeburn
(courtesy of the Scottish National Portrait Gallery).

Where a name for a dance tune was not known, it was common practice to name the tune after the person the tune was learned from. Hence some of Joe's tunes are named after his brother Harry; others were learned from Jimmy Kerr, Willie Clarke etc. The composers of the dance tunes were often unknown, with two exceptions in Joe's case – *Niel Gow's Farewell to Whisky* and *The Home Ruler*. Niel Gow (1727–1807), the Perthshire fiddler and composer, impressed Robert Burns (1759–96) when they met on Burns's Highland Tour in 1787. Interestingly, when I introduced Joe to the Sliabh Luachra, Co. Kerry fiddler Denis Murphy in the early 1970s, it was surprising how many tunes they had in common, albeit sometime known under different names. Denis called this tune after his fiddle teacher and mentor and it became *Pádraig O'Keefe's Farewell to Whiskey*. However, the tune is well documented and can most certainly be attributed to Niel Gow. *The Home Ruler* was composed by Frank McCollam (1910–73) of Ballycastle, Co. Antrim and this tune has wide currency with musicians and groups from all over the world playing this favourite hornpipe without knowing its composer. Back in the 1960s I asked Frank did he compose this tune in honour of the Revd J.B. Armour (1841–1928), the Ballymoney radical Presbyterian clergyman, who was a

Joe Holmes at Cross Keys public house, Toome Bridge, Co. Antrim, *c.*1975
(pencil sketch by Maurice Keenan).

THE FIDDLER

The fiddler with ancient art,
Fingering and bowing, heard and unheard melody,
The sensitive lug, the inherent part,
No man can drum into you.

Rhythm and time; notes with 'ghost'
Pass-over inept ears.
But to those who know – no mighty host,
A few unsung peers.

Triple – bowing, short and long,
Little finger to your aid,
Variations, notes prolong,
All tricks of the trade.[4]

233

Inaugural meeting of Comhaltas Ceoltóirí Éireann, Portglenone Branch, Co. Antrim, 1973.
L-R: Anne O'Brien, Joe Holmes, Len Graham, Willis Patton, Jeannie and
Paddy McGrath (photograph courtesy of Jeannie McGrath).

staunch supporter of Gladstone's Home Rule Bill. 'Not at all,' says Frank, 'I composed that wee hornpipe for my wife Sally – the home ruler!'

With the demise of the house and barn-dances after the Second World War, Joe became a member of the Antrim and Derry Fiddlers' Association in the 1950s and later in the mid 1960s, along with myself, Frank McCollam, Mickey McIlhatton and others, a branch of Comhaltas Ceoltóirí Éireann was formed in Ballycastle, Co. Antrim. Frank McCollam was the first chairman of the Ballycastle Comhaltas, as well as serving as the liaison officer with the already well-established Antrim and Derry Fiddlers' Association. Frank was also Master of the local Ballycastle Orange Lodge. It was marvelous to see the array of lapel badges at these gatherings – square and compass (Freemason), pioneer (alcohol abstinence), two-and-a-half (Orangeman), fáinne (Irish speaker) etc., and of course there were many who wore no lapel pin. As Alex Kerr, one of the founders of the Antrim and Derry Fiddlers' Association used to say – 'Traditional music knows no border, nor no creed'.

An old friend of my father's, Co. Antrim uilleann piper Willie Hope, along with members of the Dublin Pipers' Club – Jim Seery, Leo Rowsome and others – in June 1951 formed a committee in Mullingar, Co. Westmeath. This meeting led to the establishment of a steering organisation; in 1952 the name Comhaltas Ceoltóirí

234

Antrim and Derry Fiddlers' Association, *c.*1974 at Rathkenny Hall, Co. Antrim.
Front Row, L-R: Matt McAteer, Pat O'Hare, Bob Stevenson, Chris McCormick,
Willie Thompson, Willis Patton. *Middle Row, L-R:* Eileen Higgins, R.J. Hamilton,
Billy McKee. *Back Row, L-R:* Jim Johnston, Sam Stevenson and Mickey McIlhatton
(photograph courtesy of Antoin MacGabhann).

Éireann was adopted. In the same year the first Fleadh Cheoil was held in
Monaghan. Willie Hope once told my father that he was a direct descendant of
Jemmy Hope of 1798 fame. In 1953, Willie Hope, along with Alex Kerr, Mickey
McIlhatton and others, established the Antrim and Derry Fiddlers' Association.
Olivia Agnew, a Co. Antrim rustic bard, captured some of the atmosphere of these
gatherings in her poem of 1958, *The Antrim and Derry Fiddlers*:

> There's a group of fine musicians, who fill my heart with pride,
> The Antrim and Derry Fiddlers, may blessings on them bide;
> They keep alive within our hearts our Irish music rare,
> Those haunting old traditional tunes, that banish all our care.
>
> At concerts run for charities, you are sure to find them there,
> Each bow is plied with right good will, all led by Alex Kerr.
> The spice of life's variety and once again they cope,
> The uilleann pipes so ably played by our good friend William Hope.[1]

Uilleann pipers Leo Rowsome and Willie Hope, founder members of CCE in 1951 (photograph courtesy of Na Píobairí Uilleann).

The Co. Antrim Ordnance Survey Memoirs of the 1830s records a great love for dancing and this passion survived right up to the Second World War in the county and country in general.[2] Here are some observations in the Survey from various parishes of mixed religious denominations including the parish of Kilwaughter: 'Dancing is the only amusement. There are occasional dances in the farmhouses of the parish and at present a dancing school has just commenced. It consists of about six pupils, each pay 5s. per quarter'; from the parish of Derrykeighan: ' … principal amusements are dancing and a little cock-fighting'; the parish of Armoy: 'The inhabitants' principal amusement is dancing'; the parish of Ramoan: 'Dancing forms the principal amusement of the lower class and this they indulge frequently, particularly at the fairs and large markets in Ballycastle, at which time there is generally a room in each public house set apart for the purpose'; from the parish of Skerry – 'Their amusements are dancing and going to fairs and markets. At christenings and weddings they indulge in drinking and carousing and celebrate these events with great festivity'.

However, the Ordnance Survey Memoirs records a very different story regarding dancing in some parishes in the Glens of Antrim where the population was predominantly Catholic; for example, the parish of Ardclinis: 'There are no particular amusements though they are fond of cards, dancing and cock-fighting.

Dancing Couple. Sketch by William Conor (1881–1968) (courtesy of MAGNI).

Dancing has, however, lately been discontinued by orders of the priest'; and from the parish of Layd:

> The people in this parish cannot be said to have any particular amusement, though they are fond of it. Dancing, until very lately, was their favourite amusement and they frequently indulged in it both in their own houses and at the fairs at Cushendall, to which many came for no other purpose. But their priest, within the last year, put a total stop to it and since it has ceased, there has been much more drunken rioting at the fairs in this parish[3]

Over the years I recorded some of Joe's dance-tune repertoire. The following list represents some of the tune titles and dance types Joe played, but of course considering Joe's long fiddling career of some sixty years, this is in no way his entire repertory. It is followed by a selection of music for some of these dance tunes.

> Harry Holmes's Waltz
> The Peacock's Feather – Schottische
> Niel Gow's Farewell to Whisky – Polka
> The Blackberry Blossom – Reel
> The Pigeon on the Gate – Reel
> Harry Holmes's Jig

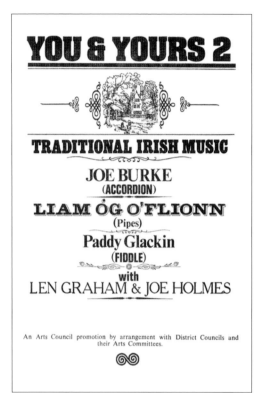

Arts Council of Northern Ireland – *You and Yours 2* Tour 1976.
Comhaltas Ceoltóirí Éireann Concert, Ballycastle, Co. Antrim, 1968.

The Green Fields of America – Reel
The Humours of Ballyconnell – Reel
Jeannie Put the Kettle On – Schottische
The Heather Breeze – Reel
Monymusk – Schottische
My Love Nell – Polka
Willie Clarke's Schottische
Green Grow the Rushes O – Schottische
Touch Me If You Dare – Reel
Wellington's Medal – Single Jig/Reel
The Girl That Broke My Heart – Reel
Maggie Picken – Schottische
The Leitrim – Hornpipe
The Quaker's Wife – Jig

238

Patsy McCann's Jig
Stirling Castle – Strathspey
Parnell's March
Miss Lyall – Strathspey
Harry Holmes's Schottische
My New Shoes – Mazurka
Royal Charlie – Single Jig
Rodney's Glory – Square Dance
Harry Holmes's Mazurkas No. 1, 2 & 3
The Fermoy Lasses – Reel
The Rakes of Kildare – Jig
The Rambling Pitchfork – Jig
Roaring Mary – Reel
If You Soon Don't Stop It – Polka
The Maid in the Corn – Jig
The Barren Rocks of Aden – Polka
Petronella – Polka and Last Figure of the Lancers
The Boys of Ballycastle – Schottische
The Old Antrim – Jig
Jimmy Kerr's Jig
The Little House Round the Corner – Jig
The Blackbird – Set Dance/Hornpipe
Down the Broom – Reel
The Flowers of Spring – Hornpipe
The White Cockade – March
St Anne's Reel
Slap the Churn – Single Jig
The Soldier's Joy – Reel
The Trumpet Hornpipe
The Flowers of Edinburgh – Reel
Chief O'Neill's Hornpipe
Centenary March
Harvest Home Hornpipe
Humours of Glendart – Jig
Lark in the Morning – Jig
The Tenpenny Bit – Jig
The Ewe With the Crooked Horn – Reel
The Muckin' O' Geordie's Byre – Schottische
Larry O'Gaff's Jig

Rights of Man – Hornpipe
Old Torn Petticoat – Reel
Boys of the Town – Jig
McMahon's Hornpipe
The Gold Ring – Jig
The Wind That Shakes the Barley – Reel
The Five Mile Chase – Reel
Miss McLeod's Reel
The Swallow's Tail – Reel
The Hunter's Purse – Reel
Cock of the North – Schottische
Drowsy Maggie – Reel
The Deal Among the Tailors – Reel
Saddle the Pony – Jig
The Laird of Drumblair – Strathspey
Cherish the Ladies Jig
Money in Both Pockets – Reel
The Home Ruler – Hornpipe
The Wandering Minstrel – Jig
Peter Street – Reel
Knights of St Patrick – Jig
Lucy Campbell – Reel
Tell Her I Am – Jig
George White's Fancy – Reel
The Maid on the Green – Jig
The Mountain Road – Reel
Tatter Jack Walsh – Jig
Jackson's Morning Brush – Jig
My Darling's Asleep – Jig
Roll Her in the Rye Grass – Reel
The Black Rogue Jig
The Frost Is All Over – Jig
The Sally Gardens – Reel
Drops of Brandy – Slip Jig
The Morning Star – Reel
The Flogging Reel
The Boyne Hunt – Reel
The Sligo Maid – Reel
Miss Monaghan – Reel

The Salamanca Reel
The Cuckoo's Nest – Hornpipe
The Sailor's Return – Reel
The Flax in Bloom – Reel
The Collier's Reel
O'er the Moor to Maggie – Reel
The Cup O' Tay – Reel
The Teetotaler – Reel
The Liverpool Hornpipe
The Belfast Hornpipe
Kitty's Wedding – Hornpipe
The Stack of Barley – Hornpipe
The Stack of Wheat – Hornpipe
Off to California – Hornpipe
The Scholar – Reel
The Honeysuckle Hornpipe
The Boys of Bluehill – Hornpipe
Madam Bonaparte – Set Dance
Rogue, Dare You Meddle Me – Reel
The Lass of Killiecrankie – Schottische
Dunphy's Hornpipe
Shandon Bells – Jig
Liverpool Hornpipe
The Peeler's Jacket – Reel

DANCE TUNES

1. The Barren Rocks of Aden

2. The Blackberry Blossom

3. The Blackbird

4. The Boys of Ballycastle

5. Down the Broom

6. The Fermoy Lasses

7. The Flowers of Spring

8. The Girl That Broke My Heart

9. The Green Fields of America

10. Green Grow the Rushes O

11. Harry Holmes's Jig

12. Harry Holmes's Mazurka No. 1

13. Harry Holmes's Mazurka No. 2

14. Harry Holmes's Mazurka No. 3

15. Harry Holmes's Waltz

16. Harry Holmes's Schottische

17. The Heather Breeze

18. The Home Ruler

19. The Humours of Ballyconnell

20. If You Soon Don't Stop It

21. Jeannie Put the Kettle On

22. Jimmy Kerr's Jig

23. The Lass of Killiecrankie

24. The Leitrim

25. The Little House Round the Corner

26. Maggie Picken

27. The Maid in the Corn

28. McMahon's Hornpipe

29. Miss Lyall

30. Monymusk

31. My Love Nell

32. My New Shoes

33. Niel Gow's Farewell to Whisky

34. O'er the Moor to Maggie

35. The Old Antrim

36. Parnell's March

37. Patsy McCann's Jig

38. The Peacock's Feather

39. Petronella

40. The Pigeon on the Gate

41. The Quaker's Wife

42. The Rakes of Kildare

43. The Rambling Pitchfork

44. Roaring Mary

45. Rodney's Glory

46. Royal Charlie

47. Stirling Castle

48. The Swallow's Tail

49. The Tenpenny Bit

50. Touch Me If You Dare

51. Wellington's Medal

52. Wellington's Medal Reel

53. Willie Clarke's Schottische

Part Three

OTHER TRADITIONS

The Killyramer Christmas Rhymers and Mummers

IN PARTS OF NORTH CO. ANTRIM before the Second World War the Christmas rhyming or mumming tradition flourished:

> As children, my sisters and I lived in terror of the Christmas Mummers, as they were called, and for some nights before Christmas our ears were strained as we sat by the fire to hear the shuffling of their feet which heralded their approach. A thundering knock would be given on our door and on opening it these big giants would enter shouting in a loud voice – 'Room, room for the Christmas Mummers' and we would scuttle into the farthest corner of the kitchen. They wore high straw helmets, their faces being blackened and peeping out through the straw which partly hid their faces. Coats of straw encased their bodies like coats of mail, and made us think of Goliath who fought with David. Straw encased their legs too and partly covered their leggings or strong boots. They carried big heavy cudgels and some of them used old bath lids as shields. The leader then began his rhyme.[1]

Title-page of a nineteenth-century Belfast Chapbook of the Christmas Rhymes.

Joe Holmes and some of his young male neighbours took an active part in these rustic seasonal traditions for many years in the weeks preceding Christmas. He told me that in his time, unlike other parts of Ulster, no straw was used in the costumes worn by the Killyramer Rhymers. Joe usually played the part of the Doctor and a bowler hat and a Gladstone bag or similar for the 'medicines' was borrowed. Any old hand-me-down coat would do, and the rest of the team would be togged-out in the best that could be procured to suit the character being played. Elaborate and colourful masks were hand-made, painted and sometimes flax, horse-hair or sheeps' wool was stuck to them for beards and hair styles. Joe referred to the masks as 'faceogs'. Some of the cast would blacken their faces. The Killyramer Rhymers usually had a melodeon, fife or mouth-organ player along for the march from house to house and the wee dance at the end of each visit. The money collected went towards a party for the cast and friends. Joe said he never took his fiddle on the Christmas Rhyming rounds, in case it would get damaged in the horse-play and sham-fighting, which was very much a part of the ritual. Joe recalled:

> We went round a lot of houses, as many as we could do in the one night, from the one place to the other. There weren't so many housing estates in those days and it took you going on to get to as many houses before the people had started to go to bed. Coming to a house we would ask permission at the door if there was any admittance for the Christmas Rhymers. Well sometimes we were admitted and sometimes we were not, but there was some good fun with it too. The leader always led the way in and started his rhyme.

Then without falter, he recited the entire play as it was performed in his youth:

LEADER: 'Room, room, brave, gallant boys, come give us room to rhyme. We're come to show activity upon this Christmas time. Active young or active age, the like was never acted on a stage, but if you don't believe what I say, enter in St George and clear the way.'

[Joe: 'That was the first rhyme – St George he would enter then.']

ST GEORGE: 'Here comes I, St George from England have I sprung one of those mighty deeds of valour to begin. Seven long years in a closed cave kept and from that to a prison kept and from that to a block of stone where I have manys a sad and grievous moan. Many a giant I did subdue I ran his fiery dragon through and through. I have fought them all courageously and still shall fight for liberty and still shall gain the victory. Show me the man that dare me challenge and I'll cut him down with my courageous hand.'

The Christmas Rhymers at Ballyboley, Co. Antrim, 1965
(photograph courtesy of MAGNI).

[Joe: 'The next to come in was the Turkish Champion – he comes in and he starts his rhyme.']

TURKISH CHAMPION: 'I am the man that dare you challenge with my sword I have made Dukes and Earls to quake.'

[Joe: 'Then St George he replies.']

ST GEORGE: 'Who are you, but a silly lad.'

TURKISH CHAMPION: 'Silly lad! I'm a Turkish Champion from Turkey land I came to fight you great George by name. I will cut you and slash you and make mince pies, baking and oven and when I am done I will fight all the champions in Christendom.'

ST GEORGE: 'You lie Sir, you lie Sir.'

TURKISH CHAMPION: 'Pull out your sword and try Sir.'

[Joe: 'So then there was a great fight with these two and the result of the fight, the Turkish Champion, St George put him down with a great blow of his sword, but he rose again and then he says.']

Woodcut of St George and St Patrick from nineteenth-century
Belfast Chapbook of the Christmas Rhymes.

TURKISH CHAMPION: 'St George, St George you missed your mark, you aimed
that blow for my tender heart, but since my sword is not yet broke I'll rise
and fight another stroke.'

[Joe: 'So then he went down for good this next time and St George he calls for the
doctor. The doctor comes in .']

DOCTOR: 'I am your doctor, pure and good and with my medicine I'll staunch
his blood, but if you want this young man's life to save – full fifty guineas I
must receive.'

ST GEORGE: 'What can you cure doctor ?'

DOCTOR: 'I can cure anything, within the plague without, the palsy or the gout.
Rather more if you bring to me an old woman of three score and ten with
the knuckle-bone of her big toe broken, I can fix it up again.'

ST GEORGE: 'What is your cure doctor?'

DOCTOR: 'My cure is hens' pens, peasy-weasy, turkey-treacle, midges-oil, the sap of the poker, the juice of the tongs, three turkey eggs nine yards long, all mixed up in a hen's bladder and stirred up with a Tom cat's feather. I carry a wee bottle in my hip coat, waistcoat pocket which contains; hokey-mokers, elegant pain, smell that dead man and fight again.'

[Joe: 'So as the man rises to fight again, here comes the next man in – Big Head and Little Wit, so he appears through the door.']

BIG HEAD AND LITTLE WIT: 'Here comes I that never came yet – Big Head and Little Wit, although I have but little wit I'll do all I can to please you yet. Rise up old woman and ruffle your feathers and don't imagine that we are all blethers, for we came here to show you some fun and to get a bit of your Christmas bun. Or a slice of your bacon, a cut of your cheese, or nine or ten shillings whichever you please. And if you don't believe what I say, enter in St Patrick and he'll soon clear the way.'

[Joe: 'And then St Patrick he steps over the door.']

ST PATRICK: 'Here comes I St Patrick in my shinning armour bright, I'm a famous champion and a worthy Knight. Who was St George but St Patrick's boy, who fed his horse on oats and hay and afterwards he ran away. If you don't believe what I say enter in Belzebub and he'll soon clear the way.'

BELZEBUB: 'Here comes I Belzebub and over my shoulder I carry my club and in my palm an old tin-can, I think myself a jolly old man. And if you don't believe what I say, enter in Oliver Cromwell and he'll soon clear the way.'

OLIVER CROMWELL: 'Here comes I Oliver Cromwell as you may all suppose, I have conquered many nations with my long copper nose. I have made my enemies tremble, I have made my foes to quake, I have beat back my oppressors and made their hearts to quake. And if you don't believe what I do say, enter in Devil Doubt and he'll soon clear the way.'

DEVIL DOUBT: 'Oh, here comes I wee Devil Doubt, the biggest wee devil that ever went out. Money I want and money I crave and if you don't give me money I'll sweep you all to your grave and if you don't believe what I say enter in Johnny Funny and he'll let you know the way.'

JOHNNY FUNNY: 'Here comes I wee Johnny Funny, I'm the man collects the money. Now ladies and gents this sport is now ended and this old box must now be recommended. This box could speak if it had a tongue, nine or ten shillings would do it no wrong. Or a slice of your bacon, a cut of your cheese or nine or ten shillings whichever you please.'

[Joe: 'Then altogether sing –]

ALL: With your pockets full of money
     And your barrel full of beer
     We wish you a Merry Christmas
     And a Happy New Year.

[Joe: 'Then members of the cast would take the oldest and youngest female out on the kitchen floor for a dance, while Johnny Funny went around the room collecting money.']²

Some attempts were made to suppress the mumming tradition in Ulster as this following nineteenth-century account from Donegal would indicate:

> The Cloghaneely mummers became embroiled in the Land War in 1897, with disastrous results. There had been evictions in the district and the parish-priest was in jail, but the mummers went down to the landlord's house at Ballyconnell as usual, and were kindly received and given money. The curate wrote to the famous Father McFadden in Gweedore to tell him what had happened, and to prevent them collecting in his parish. Neillí Uí Dubhtaigh, who tells the story, was in Bunbeg when the priest came round and ordered them out of the public house, and saw him knocking their big hats off with his stick, as they trooped out one by one.³

Many Irish poets and writers have dealt with the subject of the Christmas Rhymers or Mummers in their work – sometimes with fondness and sometimes with disdain – including Seamus Heaney, James Joyce, Patrick Kavanagh, John Montague and Michael J. Murphy. In a particularly caustic mood, writing in 1893 George Bernard Shaw comments on his gross dislike for Christmas, but was drawn to the mumming tradition associated with it:

> Like all intelligent people, I greatly dislike Christmas. It revolts me to see a whole nation refrain from music for weeks together in order that every man may rifle his neighbour's pockets under cover of a ghastly general pretence of festivity. ... I shall fly from it all tomorrow or next day to some remote spot miles from a shop, where nothing worse can befall me than a serenade from a few peasants, or some equally harmless survival of medieval mummery, shyly proffered, not advertised, moderate in its expectations, and soon over.⁴

The Ulster poet John Hewitt recalls his experience of contact with the mummers and some of the characters described by Joe Holmes, in a poem written in Ballynure in 1941: *The Christmas Rhymers* – an old woman remembers:

The Christmas Rhymers came again last year,
Wee boys with blackened faces at the door,
Not like those strapping lads that would appear,
Dressed for the mummers' parts in times before,
To act the old play on the kitchen floor;
At war-work now or fighting overseas,
My neighbours' sons; there's hardly one of these
That will be coming back here any more.

I gave them coppers, bid them turn and go;
And as I watched that rueful regiment
Head for the road, I felt that with them went
Those songs we sang, the rhymes we used to know,
Heart-some imagining the years without
The Doctor, Darkie and Wee Devil Doubt.[5]

I recall one occasion when Joe and I and other singers encountered the Wexford Mummers. We were attending the first Féile na Bóinne of 1976 in Drogheda (see song No. 39). As we arrived at the Ó Raghallaigh Gaelic Club in Drogheda we were welcomed by the committee. Eddie and Gracie Butcher, Joe Holmes, Jackie Devenney, our singing friend and driver to many of these occasions, and myself were taken to the bar for a drink with the compliments of the festival where we met up with some other old friends including the flute player Paddy Tyrell from Dundalk. Just then a bus arrived with Leo Carthy and his Wexford Mummers. They were dressed in ecclesiastical garb, complete with bishops' mitres and came in dancing. 'Holy God,' says Paddy Tyrell, 'I thought this was a Folk Festival and not a bloody Eucharistic Congress!'

The mumming and Christmas rhyming tradition still continues in parts of Ulster and is undergoing a revival in some districts, mainly in Armagh and Fermanagh.

Shinny Playing and Hurling

JOE AS A BOY and youth played the game of narrow-stick hurling or shinny,[6] as it was known in his area. Shinny would seem to be an early form of hurling, or shinty as it is known in the Highlands of Scotland. There is much evidence historically and in the oral tradition of shinny being organised informally into inter-parish/townland contests. Joe said his own townland of Killyramer would often play matches with the neighbouring townlands of Ballyboylands, Dunaghy and the Topp, usually around the New Year and Easter. The stick or cammon (Irish: *camán* – crooked) as Joe called it was a hooked stick, cut out of the hedge, trimmed and roughly smoothed and the ball was fashioned from a piece of wood. Examples of north Antrim narrow-stick *camáns* are in the National Museum in Dublin.[7] The game was usually played on roads around Joe's home-place, but he said that he had heard accounts of it being played on the beach at Portballintrae in north Antrim. Joe also said that the game was played by all denominations and both Catholics and Protestants played on the Killyramer team.

This was borne out when we had a conversation with Séamus Clarke in his Ballycastle pub one night in the 1960s. Séamus, it turned out, was a nephew of John 'Benmore' Clarke of Glenarm, who along with Belfast historian Francis Joseph Bigger and others formed the first North Antrim GAA hurling team, the Shane O'Neill's in Glenarm in 1903. The first big event was a match as part of the *Feis na nGleann* held in Glenarriff in 1904. This match was contested by Glenarm's Shane O'Neill's and Cary's Faughs. Interestingly, Roger Casement was one of the umpires. Cary's Faughs were the victors. My mother remembered

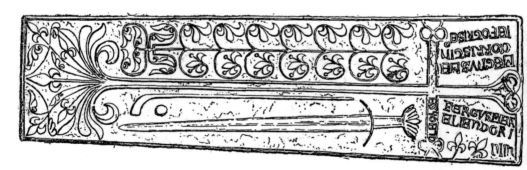

Carved fifteenth-century grave slab of a narrow-stick camán in Cloncha Churchyard, Inishowen, Co. Donegal (illustration from *UJA*, 1 (1895)).

Johnny 'Benmore' Clarke who was the proprietor of the Antrim Arms Hotel in Toberwine Street in Glenarm and she was able to tell me that her uncle Alec Robinson played for Glenarm's Shane O'Neill's in the original 1904 match.

The Co. Antrim Ordnance Survey Memoirs of the 1830s, records some instances of shinny/hurling, for example, the parish of Ballymoney: 'Ball-playing, hurling and suchlike is what they commonly resort to.' Parish of Finvoy: 'Cammon playing (a sort of hurling) at Christmas and certain seasons, particularly Easter.'[8]

In 1956 the *Ulster Folklife* published an article by Gerard B. Newe titled *From a Glens of Antrim Notebook*, which describes the 'shinny playing' at Christmas and an account of the efforts, and some resistance, to the introduction of hurling in the Glens of Antrim in the early years of the twentieth century:

> Down in the Glens we have several hurling teams, and glen is divided against glen on the hurling field. Yet my notes show that hurling is a comparatively modern game and was introduced by the late Mr Daniel De Largy some fifty years ago, when he taught in the little school at Tamlaght, in Glenariff. Until then 'shinny' was the popular game – as it was in my young days. Mr De Largy spent his summer holidays cycling through Ireland, 'discovered' hurling, and came home to Glenariff with sample hurley sticks and a ball. The youngsters and their elders were critical of the new game and it took time to catch on.
>
> A great Christmas Day event in the Glens was the gathering of men, young and not so young, to play 'shinny.' It was a game unencumbered with rules, or so I have recorded. As many as a hundred players could form a team – a hundred on each side and as many fields as they required as a playing pitch: one, two, even four acres, it didn't matter. If the 'ball' took a notion of wandering so did the players. Sides were chosen to represent Ballyeamon and Cushendall. The Ballyeamon captain chose a man; the Cushendall captain chose another, and so on, until ranged behind each of them stood every man on the field. The goal 'posts' were made up of heaps of stones and the 'ball' a hard wooden object, had to roll along the ground between the two heaps for a goal. If it went an inch above the ground it was 'no goal.' The game went on from early morning until nightfall, a test of stamina we wouldn't care to experience today.[9]

Today the game of hurling remains very popular in the Glens of Antrim and several flourishing GAA clubs continue to promote the game at senior, junior and minor levels. However, the game of shinny with its wild and informal 'rule-book' as recalled by Gerard B. Newe and Joe Holmes is just a memory and unfortunately is no longer played.

John Dickey of Donegore, Co. Antrim in his 1818 book *Poems on Various Subjects* includes a poem which mentions shinny: *Address to Parkgate*:

> Of Shinny Players, ended many a hail,
> Or buttons pitched, and then tossed head or tail.
> Blest days! When I the noisy mansion sought,
> Where Hefferen long thy clam'rous school has taught.[10]

More recently, William Clarke Robinson of Glenarm, Co. Antrim in 1907 published his *Antrim Idylls and Other Poems*, where refers to shinny in his poem *Glenarm: Antrim Coast*:

> By Cloney's wood we'll 'shinny' play,
> Where lovers all repair;
> We'll greet Deerpark, Carnalbanagh,
> Glencloy, and high Bellair.[11]

The townland of Ardicoan in Glendun in the Glens of Antrim is the scene of a song in Irish *Ard a'Chuain*, which is attributed to Glendun man Eoin Mac Ambróis (John McCambridge, *c.*1793–1873).[12] This song accords with Joe's account of shinny or hurling being played on the beaches of north Antrim and in the case of this song Cushendun's 'white strand'.

> Is ioma' Nollaig a bhí agam péin,
> I mBun Abhann Doinne is mé gan chéill,
> Ag iomáin ar an tráigh bhán,
> Mo chamán bán in mo dhorn liom.
>
> Many's a Christmas I would be,
> In Cushendun when [young and] foolish,
> Hurling on the white strand,
> My white hurl in my hand.
>
> (translation by Aodán Mac Póilín)[13]

Epilogue

WHEN JOE HOLMES DIED, musicians, singers, friends and relations from all over Ireland came to St Patrick's Parish Church in Ballymoney to pay their respects on Sunday, 8 January 1978. Two All-Ireland champion fiddlers, Anne O'Brien and Jim McKillop, played laments in the church and later at the graveside in Bushvale Presbyterian Churchyard, where Joe lies buried with his beloved mother and father. Joe's grandnephew, Robin Harper, published the following poem on 5 January 1980 in the *Belfast Telegraph* on the second anniversary of Joe's death:

Poster for Joe Holmes Memorial Concert, Ulster Museum, Belfast 22 September 1978.

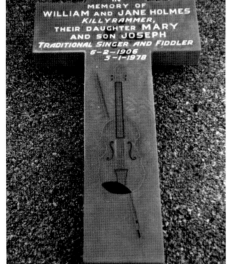

The memorial to Joe Holmes and his parents in Bushvale Presbyterian Churchyard, Co. Antrim, (photograph by Len Graham).

271

THE PEOPLE DANCED

(In memory of Joe Holmes, traditional singer and fiddle player)

His mother sang,
Poets and soldiers
Wandered in her songs.
Her singing bathed him
When he was a child,
His musicality belonged
To those times when
His mother sang.

The local fiddlers played
Through turf smoke in the evenings,
He loved and listened
To their easy hearts,
Their fingers light as bees' wings.
Out on a field of stars
He danced across the woven tunes
The local fiddlers played.

The children laughed,
Smothering giggles at Christmas
When rhymers called
To spit and whine a local drama,
Afterwards soda bread and melting butter.
Between the dresser and the wall
Crushed in a warmth of darkness
The children laughed.

The people danced
Around the silken tunes he minted
Deep in the sparking forge
Of summer nights,
And as he light-tapped out the steps
His music-making eyes were tinted
With a smile because
The people danced.

272

And when he died
Musicians gathered at the corner,
Slip-jigging reel-fast feet
Halting to an ache of shuffles.
A fiddle playing softly
On the wind alone was sweet
And all the birds were quiet
When he died.

Joe Holmes's niece and sister, Jean and Nancy Currie at Joe Holmes Memorial Concert in the Skerry Inn, Newtown Crommelin, Co. Antrim, 1979 (photograph by Len Graham).

SONGS OF THE PEOPLE.

CLOUGHWATER Or 'The Shamrock Shore'
Key D.

My friends and comrades, pray pay attention,
  Till I sing to you so far away;
I left my friends and my aged parents,
  In '56 in the month of May.

To try my fortune I took a notion,
  To cross the ocean where billows roar;
Our topsails set sweetly, she glided neatly
  And took me safe to Columbia's shore.

And when I landed my friends received me,
  Like Irish men that's kind and true;
I'm now quite happy and contented,
  All over the billows and life's journey through.

But while I ponder, my mind does wander,
  Though far away the Atlantic o'er,
To the fairest flower in Nature's garden,
  That happy place called the Shamrock shore.

I oftimes think, while in Philadelphia,
  Of the happy singings and scenes of fun,
And on the banks of the sweet Clough water,
  Where I oftimes wandered with my dog and gun.

But while the ocean keeps in its motion,
  And the surges dark on its rocky shore,
I will still revere thee with fond emotion,
  The land of my childhood, old Erin's shore.

So farewell, father, and farewell, mother,
  And farewell, brother, and sisters, too;
And to my comrades, both lads and lasses,
  I kindly send my respects to you.

Should fickle fortune to me prove kindly,
  I might once more in old Erin dwell,
When I hope to meet with a kindly welcome:
  I drop my pen with the word "Farewell."

As published by *The Northern Constitution* (SH610), Coleraine, Co. Derry, 10 August 1935.

THE EXILE OF ERIN.

In Irish and English.

There came to the beach a poor Exile of Erin,
   The dew on his thin robe was heavy and chill—
For his country he sigh'd, when at twilight repairing,
   To wander alone by the wind beaten hill ;
But the day star attracted his eyes and devotion,
   For it shone on his own native Isle of the ocean,
Where once in the fire of his youthful emotion,
   He sung the bold anthem of Erin go Bragh.

Du hanig chun na leedih, Deebiruh O Erin,
   A ylee fluich can speir agus Eaduch on ar ;
Is sgeesfur du cheenuch a her is ea aneanir,
   Sun Eehih fa vlean chunic na speirih gan agah,
Du vee huil agus intin gu creeng er an kealtan,
   Hugach fios an lee yo an eenshi na feile,
Mar a genach se le deegris a chree sheal an dreacht so,
   Buah agus treine leat Erin go Bragh.

Oh, hard is my sate, said the heart broken stranger,
   The wild deer and wolf to a covert can flee,
But I have no refuge from famine and danger—
   A home and a country remain not for me ;
A ! never again in the green shady bower,
   Where my forefathers lived shall I spend a gay hour
Or cover my harp with the wild woven flower,
   And strike to the numbers of Erin go Bragh.

Is trua ea mu chuis, er an sgnirling vocht ccasda,
   Gan sughis, gan feahiv o fean na o ya,
Neel a triv ma chudig a dtruceiv is beal lum,
   Fia puck is faolchuin kig feadir lco ail ,
Oh, nee ickid cheelii an cheel chluhir creavuch,
   Mar a mbeech mu heenshir, sheer cleaghla scar clas,
Nee chirfid blah nu meensgoher ma cheen crith da yreso,
   Is nee vuil fridsa leada orisa Erin go bragh.

Erin my country though sad and forsaken,
   In dreams I revisit thy sea beaten shore—
But alas ! in a far foreign land I awaken,
   And sigh for the friends that can meet me no more,
Ah ! cruel fate will thou ever replace me,
   In a mansion of peace where no peril can chase me.
Ah ! never again shall my brothers embrace,
   They died to defend me, or live to deplore.

Erin ma yuig cia dvoch is cia treakih,
   Is sooch nuise arn nealtiv a feachint du hra,
Is er voosgilt su doolih so is ur hillim deara,
   Gan suil le dul delia mu yealla gu Bragh ;
Och nu yachir cruag a viad cuard veg nag egin,
   Don theer shjn an luarchis gan beal dam,
O mu loma luain nee loaia kid mu yeagu,
   Mu chairde thaid treaghta nu paile da hauld.

Where is my cabin door fast by the wild wood,
   Sisters and sire have wept for its fall,
Where is the mother that watched on my childhood,
   Or where is the bosom friend dearer than all ;
Ah, my sad soul long abandoned by pleasure,
   Why should I doat on a fast fading treasure
Tears like the rain-drops shall fall without measure,
   But rapture and beauty they cannot recall.

Caoil doras mauria vee lauv lesh an Geel plish,
   'A chairdesu veentir an dceh liv ea er laur,
An vahir hug pairt agus gra dam am Neelucht,
   Is Brainhi mu chree stig is deelish nacaugh,
Tha an thanem soh mu yro lun le Bronyurt a trachlin,
   Ca vil ahis an sport sun bu yoil ling a yaul sheal,
Shillim deela deoragach lo mar a ml aistig,
   Gan suchis na dechus le sochus gu Bragh.

But yet all its sad recollections suppressing,
   One dying wish my fond bosom shall draw—
Erin on exile bequeaths thee his blessing,
   Land of my forefathers, Erin go bragh ;
Buried and cold when my heart still its motion,
   Green by thy fields sweetest Isle of the ocean—
And thy harp striking bards sing aloud with devotion,
   Erin ma vournean slan leat gu Bragh.

1g Erin O thaumshi or fann vahi deebirt,
   Faugirn is yeesho is me er centih an vaus—
Ig aind lah gach rail ylie a Glarlurk na meelig,
   Ig mahir mo heenshir is ig creeh chirt an aig,
Gur Blas iar du ceenuch a Reegan na Bochna,
   Gur Nartfur iad du heehr gur leenvur du blotih,
Gur fada veg du cheen crut gu shee vilis ceolour,
   Erin a vourneen slan leat go Bragh.

Sold by Alex. Mayne, 7½ High-street, Belfast.

RSAI/MSS/DON/012 Ballad Sheets (88 Archive Box 34). Printer Alex Mayne,
High Street, Belfast *c*.1850.

Sold Wholesale by Alex. Mayne, High-street, Belfast.

A NEW SONG CALLED

The Flowering Trade.

I hear that the flowering has become a good trade,
The girls of this country their fortune is made,
The dress they have got it makes me to say
That I think that the flowerers will carry the away.

When they rise in the morning their spirits are low,
The very first race to the tea-pot they'll go.
And then to the ashes their toes they'll present,
Saying mother my head is like for to rent

This cordial it drives the disorder away,
There is nothing for them like a wee drop of tea
It cheers up their spirits and makes them to sing,
Their head is so light that I think they'll take wing

Says Sally to Jane I must have a gold ring,
Says Jane I would rather have some other thing
If you listen a while I will soon tell you that,
She says its a necklace I want to be at,

Then down to the jewellers with smiles they do go,
They give 18 pence for the necklace you know,
Besides a white collar their neck to adorn
And a pair of side combs to be in full uniform.

These girls they have got so ill off for a man,
To entice the young boys they take many a plan,
They'll make up the feathers the roughs of the geese
And swear that it cost them a five shilling-piece,

Blame upon them for many's the trade they begin,
For the used to wear bandages tied round their chin,
Twelve yards of tape I do really believe,
And a full pound of feathers to every sleeve,

Their outside appearance it looks very gay,
With Dunstable bonnets and muslin delaine
To hide their bad stockings cloth boots they have got,
And on their shift tails there is many a knot.

Black bags they have got for to hang by their side,
And likewise white cuffs that do keep up their pride ;
Their hair so adorned with ribbons and toys
They think they will surely beguile the young boys.

Now their trades I have mentioned their names I'll not
    tell,
I give you a token you'll know them right well,
You could read the alphabet on their shin bone,
They are everywhere present, they'll not stay at home.

Now here I will give the young boys an advice
To keep out of their company if they be wise.
For if that they dont they're for ever undone.
They're the downfal of man since the world began.

RSAI/MSS/DON/012 Ballad Sheets (106 Archive Box 34). Printer Alex Mayne, High Street, Belfast c.1850.

LARK

IN

The Morning.

J. O. Bebbington. Printer, 26, Goulden-street, Oldham
Road, Manchester, and sold by John Beaumont. 176,
York-street, Leeds.'

As I was walking one morning in May,
I heard a pretty damsel those words for to say,
Of all the callings. whatever they may be,
No life like a plough boy all in the month of May.

The lark in the morning rises from her nest,
And mounts in the air with the dew around her breast,
Like the pretty plough-boy she'll whistle and sing,
And at night she'll return to her nest back again.

When his day's work is done that he's for to do,
Perhaps to some country wake he will go :
There with his sweetheart he'll dance and he'll sing,
And then he'll return with his lass back again,

And as they return from the wake in the town,
The meadows being mown and the grass cut down,
We chanc'd to tumble all on the new mown hay—
It's kiss me now or never, the maiden did say.

When twenty weeks were over and past
Her mamma ask'd her the reason why she so thickened
in the waist.
It was the pretty plough boy, the damsel did say,
That caused me to tumble on the new mown hay.

Come all you pretty maidens wherever you be.
You may trust a plough-boy to any degree :
They're used so much to plowing, their seed for to sow,
That all who employ them are sure to find it grow.

So good luck to the plough boys, wherever they be,
That will take a pretty lass to sit on their knee,
And with a jug of beer they will whistle and sing,
And a plough-boy is as happy as a prince or a king.

Broadside ballad from the Bodleian Library, Oxford University (Harding B11/2060).

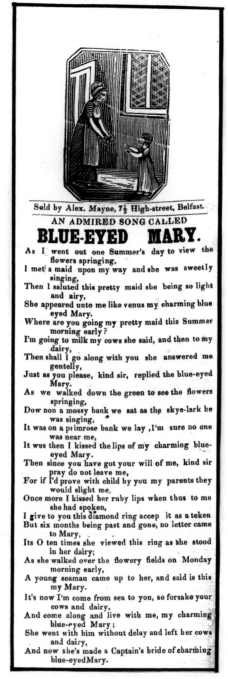

Sold by Alex. Mayne, 7½ High-street, Belfast.

AN ADMIRED SONG CALLED

BLUE-EYED MARY.

As I went out one Summer's day to view the
    flowers springing,
I met a maid upon my way and she was sweetly
    singing,
Then I saluted this pretty maid she being so light
    and airy,
She appeared unto me like venus my charming blue
    eyed Mary.
Where are you going my pretty maid this Summer
    morning early?
I'm going to milk my cows she said, and then to my
    dairy,
Then shall I go along with you she answered me
    gentelly,
Just as you please, kind sir, replied the blue-eyed
    Mary.
As we walked down the green to see the flowers
    springing,
Dow non a mossy bank we sat as the skye-lark he
    was singing,
It was on a primrose bank we lay ,I'm sure no one
    was near me,
It was then I kissed the lips of my charming blue-
    eyed Mary.
Then since you have got your will of me, kind sir
    pray do not leave me,
For if I'd prove with child by you my parents they
    would slight me,
Once more I kissed her ruby lips when thus to me
    she had spoken,
I give to you this diamond ring accep it as a teken
But six months being past and gone, no letter came
    to Mary,
Its O ten times she viewed this ring as she stood
    in her dairy;
As she walked over the flowery fields on Monday
    morning early,
A young seaman came up to her, and said is this
    my Mary.
It's now I'm come from sea to you, so forsake your
    cows and dairy,
And come along and live with me, my charming
    blue-eyed Mary;
She went with him without delay and left her cows
    and dairy,
And now she's made a Captain's bride of charming
    blue-eyedMary.

RSAI/MSS/DON/012 Ballad Sheets (100 Archive Box 34). Printer Alex Mayne,
High Street, Belfast c.1850.

THE RAMBLING
Boys of Pleasure.

Printed, and Sold Wholesale and Retail, by G.
Jacques, Oldham Road Library, Manchester.

You rambling boys of pleasure,
Give ear unto these lines I write,
It's true I am a rover,
And in roving I take great delight;
I placed my mind on a handsome girl
Who oftentimes did me slight,
But my mind was never easy,
But when my love was in my sight.

The first time that I saw my love,
I really thought her heart was mine,
Her graceful and her handsome face,
I thought that she was quite divine:
Curst gold is the root of evil
Altho' it shines with a glittering hue,
It causes many a lad and lass to part,
Let their hearts and minds be e'er so true.

Down by yon valley gardens,
One evening as I chanced to stray,
It's their I saw my darling,
I took her to be the queen of May,
She told me to take love easy,
not as the leaves grow on the trees,
J But I being young and foolish,
er then I did not agree.

There is one thing more that grieves me,
That to be called a runaway,
To leave where I was bred and born,
O, Cupid won't you set me free,
To leave my love behind me
Alack and alas what shall I do'
Must I become a rover into
The land I never knew.

When I am sitting o'er my quart,
And no one around me but strangers all,
I will think upon my own true love,
When I am booming far away,
Where I could have sweethearts plenty,
And flowing bowls on every side,
Let fortune never daunt you love,
For we are young and the world is wide.

I wish it was in Dublin,
And my own true love along with me,
And money to support us,
And keep us in good company;
Where I could have sweethearts plenty,
And flowing bowls on every side,
Let fortune never daunt you love,
For we are young and the world is wide.

(No. 59.)

Broadside ballad from the Bodleian Library, Oxford University (Harding B11/3222).

The Streams of Lovely Nancy.

Printed for W. Armstrong, Banastre-street.

O the streams of lovely Nancy divided in three parts,
Where young men and maidens do meet their sweethearts
For drinking good liquor makes my heart to sing,
And the noise in the valleys makes the rocks for to ring.

Upon yonder high mountain a castle does stand,
It is built up with ivory nigh to yon back strand,
It is built up with ivory and diamonds so bright,
It's a pilot for sailors on a dark winter's night.

Upon younder high mountain where wild fowls do fly,
There is one amongst them that flies very high,
If I had her on my galligan or all night on the strand,
O how soon I would tame her by the slight of my hand.

We got the rout on Sunday, on Monday march'd away,
Where drums loud did sound, boys, and fifes swoet did
    play.
Some hearts may be sorry for mine is full sad,
When I think on the pleasures my love and I had.

We march'd from Chester to Liverpool
    town,
Where there we spied girls, some fair and
    some brown;
But of all the fine lasses that I e'er I did see,
At the sign of the angel lives the girl for me.

I'll go up to the captain, on my knee beg
    at large,
That fifty bright guineas might buy your
    discharge;
And if that won't do, love, I have twice as
    much more,
Dare you let me go with you, O no my
    love, no.

I'll go down to you nunnery, and there end
    my life,
I never will be married, nor be made a wife,
So constant and true hearted for ever I'll
    remain,
And I'll never be married till my love
    comes again.

Broadside ballad from the Bodleian Library, Oxford University (Harding B28/29).

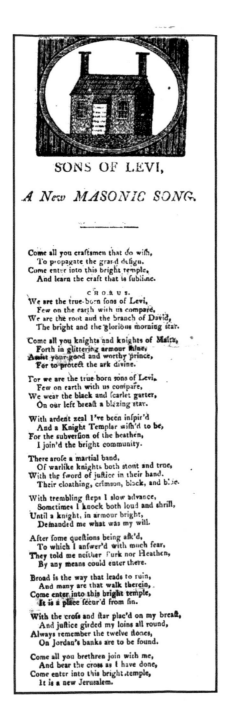

Broadside ballad from the National Library of Scotland, Edinburgh (RBm143/156).

Notes

INTRODUCTION

1 Antrim and Derry Fiddlers' Association was founded in 1953 with the aim of 'preserving the art of country fiddling'. It is largely responsible for promoting the rich tradition of north Ulster fiddle music. Founder-members included Alex Kerr and Mickey McIlhatton, both Co. Antrim fiddlers.

2 See Song No. 50, p. 144.

3 See Song No. 77, p. 217.

4 *Chaste Muses, Bards and Sages*, Free Reed, UK, #FR007 (1975). *After Dawning*, Topic Records, London, #12TS401 (1978).

5 *Early Ballads in Ireland, 1968–1985*, edited by Tom Munnelly and Hugh Shields (1985); Len Graham, *'It's of my Rambles …'* (1993).

6 John Hewitt, *The Rhyming Weavers* (1974), p. vi.

7 Sam Henry's *Songs of the People*. A song was published weekly in *The Northern Constitution* in Coleraine between 1923 and 1939. The full Henry collection published by G. Huntington and L. Herrmann, *Songs of the People* (1990).

8 The BBC carried out a survey in the early 1950s of the musical traditions of Britain and Ireland. Many of the recorded contributions were broadcast on the BBC radio series *As I Roved Out*.

9 Peter Kennedy, *Folksongs of Britain and Ireland* (1975).

10 See further information on dancing in Co. Antrim in 'The Dance Tunes', p. 241.

11 See further notes on scutching and the flax and linen traditions in Co. Antrim in Song No. 42, 'Long Cookstown', p. 127.

12 '… as a proof of the liberality entertained by the various sects towards each other, it may be remarked that the several places of public worship recently built in the town of Ballymoney, viz. for Unitarians, Covenanters, Roman Catholics and Presbyterians, were contributed to by persons of every persuasion, and in some instances the amount subscribed by the sect for whom the house was building was not as large as the sum received from their neighbours of different denominations …' *Ordnance Survey – Memoirs of Ireland – Parishes of County* Antrim (1830–1838), Vol. 16 (1992), 19.

13 Séamus Heaney, *The Sense of the Past* (1993), p. 33.

PART I: THE SONGS

1 Bedlam: St Mary of Bethlehem, an asylum in London.

2 R. Morton, *Folksongs Sung in Ulster* (1969), p. 29.

3 Broadside ballad collection in the Bodleian Library, University of Oxford (Harding B11/3432).

4 S. Baring-Gould, *Songs of the West* (1890), p. 84.

5 Library of Congress. Rare Books & Special Collections Division (#as101710).

6 D. Behan, *Ireland Sings* (1965), p. 12.

7 S. Henry, *Songs of the People* (1990), p. 201.

8 S. Henry, *Songs of the People* (1990), p. 490.

9 As published in *The Northern Constitution* (SH610), Coleraine, Co. Derry, 10 August 1935.

10 Thomas Paine (1737–1809), English political theorist and author of major influential works: *Common Sense* (1776) *Rights of Man* (1792) and *Age of Reason* (1794).

11 Theobald Wolfe Tone (1763–98), *Argument on Behalf of the Catholics of Ireland* (1791).

12 F.J. Child, *The English & Scottish Popular Ballads* (1965), p. 213.

13 See extensive information on placenames around Lough Neagh in P. McKay and K. Muhr, *Lough Neagh Places – Their Names and Origins* (2007).

14 *Ayr*: a river in Ayrshire in Scotland; *whinny knowes*: Gorse/furze clad round hillocks; *burnie*: a small stream; *awa*: away.

15 R. Ford, *Vagabond Songs & Ballads of Scotland* (1901), p. 244.

16 Broadside ballad collection in the Bodleian Library, University of Oxford (Harding B11/3947).

17 Michael J. Murphy, *Now You're Talking …* (1975), p. 54.

18 Library of Congress, *Rare Book and Special Collections* (sb20152a).

19 Broadside ballad collection in the Bodleian Library, University of Oxford (Harding B40/1).

20 S. Baring-Gould, *Songs of the West* (1890), p. 16.

21 M. Leach, *Folk Ballads & Songs of the Lower Labrador Coast* (1965), p. 64.

22 Broadside ballad collection in the Bodleian Library, University of Oxford (Harding B19/11).

23 E. & C.O. Moore, *Ballads & Folk Songs of the Southwest* (1964), p. 194. V. Randolph, *Ozark Folk Songs* (1946), p. 324, & J.H. Cox, *Folk-Songs of the South* (1963), p. 444.

24 Broadside ballad collection in the Bodleian Library, University of Oxford (28066/10/86).

25 H.T. Blethen & C.W. Wood, *Ulster and North America* (1997), 122.

26 PRONI. D/1828/18.

27 P. Fitzgerald & S. Ickringill, *Atlantic Crossroads* (2001), p. 42.

28 P.A. Walsh, *Exile of Erin – Who Wrote It?* (1921), p. 85.

29 The melody of the song *The Wounded Hussar* was popularised by the traditional musicians Seamus Ennis (1919–82) and Tony McMahon.

30 R. Bauerle, *The James Joyce Songbook* (1982), p. 431

31 RSAI/MSS/DON/012 Ballad Sheets (88 Archive Box 34). Printer Alex Mayne, High Street, Belfast, *c*.1850.

32 F. Purslow, *The Constant Lovers* (1972), p. 29.

33 Now UCD Delargy Centre for Irish Folklore and the National Folklore Collection.

34 RSAI/MSS/DON/012 Ballad Sheets (106 Archive Box 34). Printer Alex Mayne, High Street, Belfast, *c*.1850.

35 H. Marks, *An Old-Timer Talking* (1961), p. 52.

36 Piercers were a sharp instrument for making small holes in the handkerchiefs etc., around which fine stitching was done.

37 B. McKinney, 'Song of Eoghan – The Tradition of Singing in Inishowen', (MPhil, UCC, 2004), p. 43.

38 J.N. Healy, *Old Irish Street Ballads* (1967), p. 282.

39 The Black Rock is a rock in the bay between the villages of Glenarm and Carnlough.

40 Bobby Sands composed a song in praise of Mickey McIlhatton which was popularised by Christy Moore.

41 Derisory name for Ulster Catholics, derived from the Gaelic name *Tadhg*.

42 *Greig-Duncan Collection* (2004), vol. 8, 1516.

43 *Grá mo chroí*: Gaelic term of endearment 'love of my heart'.

44 P. Kennedy, *Folksongs of Britain & Ireland* (1975), p. 432.

45 S. Henry, *Songs of the People* (1990), p. 541.

46 M. Karpeles, *Folksongs from Newfoundland* (1971), 163; K. Peacock, *Songs of the Newfoundland Outposts* (1965), 698.

47 F. Purslow, *The Constant Lovers* (1972), p. 114.

48 Broadside ballad from the Bodleian Library, Oxford University (Harding B11/2060).

49 H. Shields, *Shamrock, Rose & Thistle* (1981), p. 124.

50 Eddie refers to the following: Jackie Devenney, Joe Holmes, Len Graham, Gracie Butcher from counties Derry and Antrim, Tom Munnelly from Co. Clare, Hugh and Lisa Shields, Frank Harte from Dublin and Sean Corcoran from Co. Louth. Words and music in Len Graham Collection. See also H. Shields, *Narrative Singing in Ireland* (1993), p. 240.

51 H. Creighton Nova Scotia Archive (AR5563/AC2318/2170 & AR5750/AC2347/ 2765).

52 Revd J. Dubourdieu, *Statistical Survey of the County Antrim* (1803), p. 444.

53 *Ordnance Survey Memoirs of Ireland – Parishes of Co. Antrim* (1830–8), vol. 16, (1992).

54 A.W. Tomlyn, *Gem Selection of Scottish Songs* (1890), p. xi.

55 J. Hunter, *The Fiddle Music of Scotland* (1979), p. 87. F. Collinson, *The Traditional and National Music of Scotland*.

56 Broadside ballad collection in the Bodleian Library, University of Oxford (Harding B11/2280).

57 H. Marks, *An Old-Timer Talking* (1961), p. 23.

58 Broadside ballad collection at the National Library of Scotland (LC. Fol. 178AZ).

59 H. Shields, *Ulster Folklife,* 18 (1972), p. 36.

60 H. Marks, *An Old-Timer Talking* (1961), p. 22.

61 RSAI/MSS/DON/012 Ballad Sheets (100 Archive Box 34). Printer Alex Mayne, High Street, Belfast *c.*1850.

62 Broadside ballad collection in the library of Cambridge University (Madden 20/87/452).

63 E.E. Gardner & G.J. Chickering, *Ballads & Songs of South Michigan* (1967), p. 131.

64 K. Peacock, *Songs of the Newfoundland Outposts* (1965), p. 1018.

65 L. Graham, *It's of My Rambles …* (1993), p. 62.

66 Broadside collection in the Bodleian Library, University of Oxford (2806C15/137).

67 G. Petrie, *The Complete Collection of Irish Music* (1902) 124.

68 *Max Hunter Folk Song Collection* (1960) 0563 (MFH194).

69 See collection of Joe's dance music, here No. 38, p. 253.

70 A. McMorland, *Herd Laddie O the Glen* (2006), p. 72.

71 K. Peacock, *Songs of the Newfoundland Outposts* (1965), p. 1007.

72 *The Greig-Duncan Folk Song Collection,* vol. 8 (2002), p. 1734.

73 B. Wannan, *The Wearing of the Green* (1965), p. 237.

74 J. Duffy, *The Dublin Comic Songster,* vol. 1 (1845), p. 270.

75 A. Noble, *The Canongate Burns* (2001), p. 803.

76 W.B. Yeats, *Selected Poetry* (1962), p. 209. R. Bauerle, *The James Joyce Songbook* (1982), p. 54.

77 H. Creighton, *Folksongs from South New Brunswick* (1971), p. 117.

78 S. O'Boyle, *The Irish Song Tradition* (1976), p. 84.

79 Broadside Ballad from the Bodleian Library, Oxford University (Harding B11/3222).

80 H. Henderson, *Tocher,* 11 (1973), p. 89.

81 *The Max Hunter Folk Song Collection* (1961) 0594 (MFH455).

82 E.E. Evans, *Ireland and the Atlantic Heritage* (1996), p. 99.

83 MS – Len Graham Collection.

84 C. Sandburg, *The American Songbag* (1927), p. 306

85 J.H. Combs, *Folk Songs of the Southern United States* (1967), p. 121.

86 Len Graham Collection: letter from Hamish Henderson, School of Scottish Studies, University of Edinburgh (19 Oct. 1992).

87 Broadside ballad in the Len Graham Collection.

88 K. Peacock, *Songs of the Newfoundland Outposts* (1965), p. 575.

89 P. Kennedy, *Folksongs of Britain and Ireland* (1975), p. 224.

90 P. Kennedy, *Folksongs of Britain and Ireland* (1975), p. 297.

91 F.J. Child, *The English & Scottish Popular Ballads* (1898), p. 299.

92 C. Sandburg, *The American Songbag* (1927), p. 44.

93 R. Ward, *The Penguin Book of Australian Ballads* (1964), p. 118.

94 Broadside ballad from the Bodleian Library, Oxford University (Harding B28/29).

95 Ibid.

96 R.V. Williams & A.L. Lloyd, *The Penguin Book of English Folk Songs* (1959), p. 98.

97 Broadside ballad from the National Library of Scotland (L.C.Fol.178.A.2.019).

98 R.V. Williams & A.L. Lloyd, *The Penguin Book of English Folk Songs* (1959), p. 52.

99 S. Henry, *Songs of the People* (1990), p. 343.

1 H. Shields, *Shamrock, Rose & Thistle* (1981), p. 59.

2 A. & F. Warner, *Traditional American Folk Songs* (1984), p. 427.

3 J. Moulden, *Songs of Hugh McWilliams* (1993), p. 109.

4 Broadside Ballad from the National Library of Scotland, Edinburgh (RBm143/156).

5 H. Creighton, *Folksongs from South New Brunswick* (1971) 117.

6 H. Shields, *Ceol, 3* (1967), p. 4.

7 Facsimile of Joe Holmes's hand-written version of *The Grey Cock*, ballad c.1963. (Child 248)

8 A. & F. Warner, *Traditional American Folk Songs* (1984), p. 225.

9 M. Karpeles, *Folksongs from Newfoundland* (1971), p. 100.

10 C. Sharp & S. Baring-Gould, *English Folk – Songs for Schools* (1906), p. iii.

11 S. Baring-Gould, *Songs of the West* (1890), p. 222.

PART 2: DANCING AND FIDDLE PLAYING

1 MS Poem – Len Graham Collection.

2 *Ordnance Survey Memoirs of Ireland – Parishes of County Antrim* (1830–8), vol. 16 (1992).

3 *Ordnance Survey Memoirs of Ireland – Parishes of County Antrim* (1830–8), vol. 13 (1992).

4 Len Graham for Joe Holmes on the occasion of his seventieth birthday, 6 February 1976.

PART 3: OTHER TRADITIONS

1 Mrs F. Stevenson of Portrush in *Ulster Folklife*, 6 (1960), p. 25.

2 The storyteller John Campbell had memories of the Christmas rhymers in south Armagh in the 1940s and 1950s and with his good memory he could recite most of the parts for the local version of the play. There were some similarities to Joe's text, but he had a character Joe didn't have called Big-bellied Ned: 'Here comes Big-bellied Ned, when I was a *gasúr* I wasn't very well fed, I can ate griddle and I can ate pan. If you don't get me something quick, I'm going to ate a man!' (*gasúr*: Gaelic for boy).

3 E.R.R. Green, *Ulster Journal of Archaeology*, 9 (1946), p. 3.

4 John Killen, *The Irish Christmas Book* (1985), p. 25.

5 F. Ormsby, *The Collected Poems of John Hewitt* (1991), p. 354. John Hewitt wrote this poem on the Christmas Rhymers during the Second World War – hence his note of pessimism – 'My neighbours' sons; there's hardly one of these that will be coming back here any more.'

6 See illustration published here of fifteenth century grave-slab of a narrow-stick *camán* which is in Cloncha Churchyard, Inishowen, Co. Donegal; *Ulster Journal of Archaeology*, 1 (1895), p. 170.

7 G. Law, *The Cultural Traditions Dictionary* (1998), p. 128.

8 *Ordnance Survey Memoirs of Ireland – Parishes of County Antrim* (1831–8), vol. 23 (1993).

9 G.B. Newe, *Ulster Folklife*, 2 (1956), p. 56.

10 J. Hewitt, *Rhyming Weavers* (1974), p. 114.

11 W.C. Robinson, *Antrim Idylls & Other Poems* (1907), p. 64. William Clarke Robinson (1851–1932) was educated in a small country school in Carncastle, Co. Antrim where he was taught by Master Patrick Magill; he went on to the Belfast Royal Academical Institute. Here he showed a special aptitude for languages and literature. Studying German at Bonn University one of his fellow students was Prince Wilhelm, who later became Emperor of Germany and the much-hated 'Kaiser Bill' of World War One. Having studied Italian in Florence and Rome, he secured posts as lecturer in modern languages at Durham University and later, lecturer of English literature at Kenyon College, Ohio, USA. He published many

books on English, German and French literature.

12 I am informed by Aodán Mac Poilin (in a letter dated 18 Feb. 2004) that John McCambridge was a Protestant who had been considering emigrating to the Mull of Kintyre, which is so close to the Antrim coast (*c*.12 miles) that you can see individual houses on a clear day. McCambridge apparently stood on the top of Ardichoan, imagining himself over in Kintyre looking back on his native soil and wrote this song of exile. The song made him so homesick that he decided not to go, and spent the rest of his days in Ireland. Ciarán Ó Duibhín gave Aodán some additional information that John McCambridge was born in Mullarts, near Glendun, and is buried in Layd Churchyard near Cushendall. His headstone is partly in Irish and begins: 'Tógthar a chlach so chun cuimhne a chongbháil ar a mhuintir atá marbh' which translates as: 'This stone is raised to preserve the memory of the people who are dead', and ends: 'Ná bain damh' 'disturb me not'. The remainder of the inscription is in English, and traces the family from Malcolm McCambridge who: 'came from Cantire (Kintyre) 1635 (1625?), located in Carnasheran, and died there,' through to John McCambridge himself. Glenarm man Eoin Mac Neill (1867–1945) was the first to publish a four versed version of *Ard a'Chuain* in the *Gaelic Journal* in 1895. Incidentally, Mac Neill and my maternal grandmother Ellen Robinson (née McClure) together attended the same primary school in Castle Street, Glenarm in the nineteenth century.

13 M. Maclean & T. Dorgan, *An Leabhar Mór – The Great Book of Gaelic* (2002), p. 126.

Abbreviations

CBE	Comhairle Bhéaloideas Éireann
CCE	Comhaltas Ceoltóirí Éireann
CLAJ	*County Louth Archaeological Journal*
EFDSS	English Folk Dance & Song Society
FMJ	*Folk Music Journal*
G-D	Greig-Duncan Folk Song Collection
ITMA	Irish Traditional Music Archive
JFSS	*Journal of the Folk-Song Society*
JIFSS	*Journal of Irish Folk Song Society*
KR	Killyramer
LoC	Library of Congress, Book and Special Collections
MAGNI	National Museums & Galleries of Northern Ireland
MG	Magilligan
NITB	Northern Ireland Tourist Board
RSAI	Royal Society of Antiquaries of Ireland
SCR	Sony Cassette Recorder
SoP SH	Songs of the People – Sam Henry
SRR	Sharp Reel to Reel Recorder
UF	*Ulster Folklife*
UJA	*Ulster Journal of Archaeology*

Further Song References

1 Annie Moore
SoP SH191 9.7.1927 (1990), p. 142
Roud 2881
Cooper (2009), p. 43
Morton (1970), p. 68
Leyden (1989), p. 161
O'Byrne (1982), p. 77 (story only)
19th-century broadside ballads
Len Graham Collection:
Joe Holmes rec. KR 27.1.1971 SRR

2 The Banks of Boyne
Laws P22
Roud 2891
Morton (1970), p. 28
Dean (1973), p. 104
Fowke (1965), p. 13
MacKenzie (1963), p. 384
19th-century broadside balladsheets
Len Graham Collection:
Joe Holmes rec. KR 26.11.1968 SRR
Jane Holmes MS
Bridget Morgan, Oran, Co. Roscommon.
Hugh Lee, Aughakillymaud, Co. Fermanagh.

3 The Banks of Claudy
SoP SH5 15.12.1923 and SH693 6.3.1937 (1990),
    313
Laws N40
Roud 266
Bunting (1840), p. 33
Cooper (2009), p. 43
Moloney (2000), p. 239
Petrie (1905), p. 107
Shields (1993), p. 236
Shields, *UF*, 21 (1975), p. 27
Shields, *UF*, 33 (1987)
Ó Lochlainn (1939), p. 116
O'Neill (1913), p. 114
Meek (1997), p. 12
Morton (1970), p. 3
Morton (1973), p. 134
Fleischmann (1998), p. 1078

Mac Con Iomaire (2007), p. 479
McMahon (1991), p. 108
Come-All-Ye (1916), p. 27
Walton, vol. 4 (1966), p. 34
Belden (1940), p. 154
Combs (1967), p. 214
Cox (1963), p. 321
Fowke (1965), p. 58
Mackenzie (1963), p. 70
O'Connor (1901), p. 39
Randolph (1982), p. 47
Wehman (1898), p. 118
Creighton (1971), p. 48
Creighton (1962), p. 65
Gardner & Chickering (1967), p. 191
Kennedy (1884), p. 70
Kidson (1891), p. 88
Copper (1972), p. 248
Sharp (2003), p. 81
Ord (1930), p. 130
Ford (1901), p. 211
G-D 1036, vol. 5 (2002)
Eddy (1964), p. 157
Meredith & Anderson (1967), p. 166
Library of Congress #as100610
19th-century broadside ballads
Len Graham Collection:
Joe Holmes rec. KR 10.9.1968 SRR
Pat Neeson, Mill Quarter, Co. Antrim
Colm Lynn, Moneystaghan, Co. Derry
Davy McKee, Taylorstown, Co. Antrim
John Johnson, Ballymoney, Co. Antrim
Lizzie McKeever, Cross Keys, Co. Antrim
Jeannie McKeown, Ballybeg, Co. Antrim
Eddie Butcher, Magilligan, Co. Derry
Willie Johnson, Magherafelt, Co. Derry
John 'Jock' Maguire, Rosslea, Co. Fermanagh

4 The Banks of the River Ness
SoP SH205. 15.10.1927 (1990), p. 319
Roud 3813
Fowke (1965), p. 100
McKinney MS (2004), p. 98

G-D 1047, vol. 5 (2002)
19th-century broadside ballads
Len Graham Collection:
Joe Holmes rec. KR 24.9.1968 SRR

5 The Beggarman
Child 279 (Appendix)
SoP SH810 3.6.1939 (1990), p. 269
Laws P19
Roud 118/119
Bronson (1972), p. 481
Bunting (1840), p. 63
Moloney (2000), p. 235
Petrie (1905), p. 170
JIFSS, 14 (1914), p. 32
Shields (1993), p. 236
Smith & Clarke (2009), p. 45
Fleischmann (1998), p. 61
Cooper (2002), p. 277
Cooper (2009), p. 43
Baring-Gould (1895), p. 24
Cameron (1856), vol. 2, p. 124
Collinson (1966), p. 134, 153
Kennedy (1975), p. 419
Henderson (1992), pp 141/319
Herd vol. 2 (1869), p. 49
Johnson (1787), p. 234
Kinsley (1969), p. 626
G-D 275, vol. 2; 1311 vol. 7 (2002)
Lyle (1994), p. 62
Ord (1930), p. 375
Percy, vol. 3 (1766), p. 46
Ramsay, vol. 1 (1871), p. 80
MacColl (1965), p. 34
MacColl & Seeger (1977), p. 102
MacColl & Seeger (1986), p. 12
Palmer (1980), p. 225
Tocher, 15 (1974), p. 278
Ritson (1869), p. 241
Moore (1964), p. 128
Brunnings (1981), p. 103
Milner (1983), p. 45
19th-century broadside ballads
Len Graham Collection:
Joe Holmes rec. KR 5.1.1969 SRR
Maggie Murphy, Tempo, Co. Fermanagh
John Campbell, Mullaghbawn, Co. Armagh

6 Bonny Brown Jane
SoP SH613 31.8.1935 (1990), p. 396

Laws P5
Roud 7000
Kennedy (1975), p. 365
19th-century broadside ballads
Len Graham Collection:
Joe Holmes rec. KR 18.6.1968 SRR
Mickey Doherty, Stranolar, Co. Donegal
    (melody)
Willie Johnson, Magherafelt, Co. Derry

7 The Bonny Bunch of Roses
Laws J5
Roud 664
Petrie (1905), p. 170
JIFSS, 15 (1915), p. 31 & 27 (1930), p. 43
Hughes, vol. 2 (1915), p. 92
Hayward (1925), p. 17
Hayward (n.d.), p. 18
JIFSS, 27 (1930), p. 43
Ó Lochlainn (1939), p. 32
Behan (1965), p. 8
Shields, *UF*, 21 (1975), p. 45
Fleischmann (1998), p. 893
Mac Con Iomaire (2007), p. 299
Moylan (2000), p. 141
Treoir, 4 (1972), p. 14
Walton (1968), p. 118
Zimmermann (1967), p. 190
Baring-Gould (1890), p. 54
Buchan & Hall (1973), p. 148
Dallas (1972), p. 132
G-D 155, vol. 1 (2002)
Ord (1930), p. 301
MacColl & Seeger (1977), p. 270
Purslow (1965), p. 7
Sharp (2003), p. 85
Reeves (1960), p. 63
Brunnings (1981), p. 35
Creighton (1966), p. 140
Greenleaf & Mansfield (1933), p. 170
Huntington (1970), p. 207
MacKenzie (1963), p. 188
Milner (1983), p. 162
Peacock (1965), p. 988
Warner (1984), p. 50
Wehman (1898), p. 78
O'Connor (1901), p. 127
19th-century broadside ballads
Len Graham Collection:
Joe Holmes rec. KR 24.9.1968 SRR

Willie Nicholl, Cullybackey, Co. Antrim
John Maguire, Newtownbutler, Co. Fermanagh
Paddy Gamble, Loughgiel, Co. Antrim
John Johnson, Ballymoney, Co. Antrim
Eddie Butcher, Magilligan. Co. Derry
Peter Cassidy, Galbally, Co. Tyrone

8 The Bonny Wee Lass o' the Glen
SoP SH14a 16.2.1924 (1990), p. 356
Roud 6879
JIFSS, 2 (1905), p. 23
Cooper (2009), p. 43
Shields, *UF*, 21 (1975), p. 51
Len Graham Collection:
Joe Holmes rec. KR 16.7.1969 SRR
Jim McAuley, Ballycastle, Co. Antrim
Tommy McQueston, Ballymoney, Co. Antrim
Johnny McClelland, Magherafelt, Co. Derry

9 Brian O'Lynn
SoP SH480a 11.2.1933 (1990), p. 52
Roud 294
Duffy (1845), p. 17
Hand (2004), p. 9
Shields, *UF*, 21 (1975), p. 58
Ó Lochlainn (1939), p. 30
O'Neill (1913), p. 429
Behan (1965), p. 12
McMahon (1991), p. 52
Baring-Gould (1890), p. 84
Bauerle (1982), p. 568
Kennedy (1975), p. 644
Kane (1983), p. 32
Joyce, James, Hodgart & Worthington (1959)
Dick & Fitzgerald (1863), p. 13
Reeves (1960), p. 65
Sharp (1932), p. 202
O'Connor (1901), p. 64
Wehman (1898), p. 91
Flanders (1966), p. 178
Hunter (1967), p. 1441
Kennedy (1884), p. 393
Pankake (1989), p. 35
Randolph (1982), p. 471
LoC #as101710
19th-century broadside ballads
Len Graham Collection:
Joe Holmes rec. KR 5.10.1970 SRR
Willie McKeever, Cross Keys, Co. Antrim
Joe Toner, Toomebridge, Co. Antrim

10 The Brown-Haired Girl
SoP SH116 30.1.1926 (1990), p. 201
McKinney MS (2004), p. 149
Len Graham Collection:
Joe Holmes rec. KR 10.7.1969 SRR

11 Captain Wedderburn's Courtship
Child 46
Roud 36
Bronson (1972), p. 120
SoP SH681 12.12.1936 (1990), p. 490
Breathnach (1971), p. 30
Mac Con Iomaire (2007), p. 299
MacLochlainn, *DalgCais*, 11 (1993), p. 53
Munnelly (1994), p. 126
Munnelly, *DalgCais*, 1 (1977), p. 105
Murphy (1940), p. 49
Shields (1993), p. 248
Shields, *UF*, 10 (1972), p. 87
Shields, *UF*, 21 (1975), p. 377
Shields & Munnelly (1985), p. 5
Smith & Clarke (2009), p. 65
uí Ogáin (2009), p. 53
Baring-Gould (1890), p. 96
G-D 842, vol. 4 (2002)
Ord (1930), p. 416
Boswell (1997), p. 30
Creighton (1966), p. 6
Creighton (1962), p. 6
Fowke (1954), p. 136
Gardner & Chickering (1967), p. 139
Karpeles (1971), p. 39
Sharp (1932), p. 190
Sharp & Karpeles (1968), p. 80
Eddy (1964), p. 25
Milner (1983), p. 24
Ives (1953), p. 38
Hunter 0041 (1958)
19th-century broadside ballads
Len Graham Collection:
Joe Holmes rec. KR 16.7.1969 SRR
Bob McConaghie, Ballymoney, Co. Antrim
Lizzie Clarke, Bennefreaghan, Co. Tyrone

12 Clough Water
SoP SH610 10.8.1935 (1975), p. 208
Moloney (2002), p. 6 (from SoP)
Wright (1975), p. 120 (from SoP)
Len Graham Collection:
Joe Holmes rec. KR 14.8.1973 SRR

13 Come Tender-Hearted Christians
Roud 5279/9756
Petrie (1905), p. 185
Ó Lochlainn (1965), p. 42
Shields (1993), p. 247
Cooper (2002), p. 249
Cooper (2009), p. 43
Moylan (2000), p. 91
Fay (1989) (history)
McLaughlin (2003), p. 100
Zimmermann (1967), p. 158
Jolliffe (1970), p. 11
Len Graham Collection:
Joe Holmes rec. KR 10.11.1970 SRR
Barney Henry, Cloghogue, Toomebridge,
     Co. Antrim
Sarah Anne Campbell, Ahoghill, Co. Antrim

14 The Corncrake Among the Whinny Knowes
SoP SH18b 15.3.1924 (1990), p. 272
Roud 2736
Tunney (1991), p. 18
Vallely (John Kennedy) (2001), p. 29
Ford (1901), p. 244
G-D 945, vol. 5 (2002)
19th-century broadside ballads
Len Graham Collection:
Joe Holmes rec. KR 11.12.1971 SRR
Mary Magill, Ballynacaird, Co. Antrim
Barney McManus, Torbradan, Co. Fermanagh
Micil 'Ned' Quinn, Mullaghbawn, Co. Armagh
John Kennedy, Cullybackey, Co. Antrim

15 The County Tyrone
SoP SH153a 16.10.1926 (1975), p. 480
Roud 1991
Bunting (1840), p. 97
Moloney (2000), p. 229
Petrie (1905), p. 132
Moulden (1979), p. 19
Shields, *UF*, 17 (1971), p. 18
Shields, *UF*, 18 (1972), p. 48
Fleischmann (1998), p. 1100
Healy (1967), p. 316
Causeway (n.d.), p. 66
Huntington (1970), p. 218
19th-century broadside ballads
Len Graham Collection:
Joe Holmes rec. KR 5.10.1970 SRR
Jane Holmes MS

16 Daniel O'Connell and His Steam Engine
uí Ogáin (1995), p. 193
Roud 2313
Library of Congress Recording 3745B1
Meek (1997), p. 60
Fowke (1965), p. 50
Murphy (1975), p. 54 (story)
O'Connell (1990), p. 93 (history)
Ó Faoláin (1938) (history)
MacDonagh (1989) (history)
Len Graham Collection:
Joe Holmes rec. MG 31.3.1974 SRR
Eddie Butcher, Magilligan, Co. Derry

17 The Dark-Eyed Gypsy
Child 200
SoP SH124 27.3.1926 (1990), p. 509
Roud 1
Bronson (1972), p. 349
Johnson (1787), p. 189
JIFSS, 1 (1904), p. 42
Harding (1900), p. 296
Joyce (1909), p. 154
Shields (1981), p. 66
Shields (1993), p. 212
Shields, *UF*, 10 (1972), p. 77
Shields, *UF*, 21 (1975), p. 108
Shields & Munnelly (1985), p. 3
Kennedy (1975), p. 571
MacLochlainn, *DalgCais*, 11 (1993), p. 53
Munnelly, *Ceol,* 4 (1972), p. 6
Munnelly, *DalgCais,* 6 (1982), p. 82
Hammond (1978), p. 57
O'Boyle (1986), p. 62
Smith & Clarke (2009), p.76
Treoir, 11 (1979), p. 17
Tunney (1979), p. 110
Herd (1869), p. 54
Baring-Gould (1890), p. 102
Beattie (1952), p. 239
Causeway (n.d.), p. 52
Cooper (2009), pp 41 & 43
Collinson (1966), p. 134
Kinsley (1969), p. 249
G-D 278, vol. 2 (2002)
Butterworth (1977), p. 14
Henderson (1992), p. 115
Lyle (1994), p. 68
Ord (1930), p. 411
Ramsey (1871), p. 241

MacColl (1965), p. 39
MacColl & Seeger (1986), p. 7
Palmer (1980), p. 117
Reeves (1960), p. 141
Sharp & Baring-Gould (1906), p. 2
Sharp & Campbell (1917), p. 112
Sharp (1932), p. 233
Sharp (1959), p. 13
Boswell (1997), p. 28
Belden (1940), p. 73
Brunnings (1981), p. 68
Cox (1963), pp 130, 524
Creighton (1971), p. 12
Eddy (1964), p. 67
Flanders (1963), p. 193
Fowke (1965), p. 18
Fowke (1973), p. 176
Greenleaf & Mansfield (1933), p. 38
Hunter 0118 (1958)
Karpeles (1971), p. 81
Linacott (1990), p. 207
Moore (1964), p. 97
Randolph (1982), p. 27
Sandburg (1927), p. 311
Sharp & Karpeles (1968), p. 46
Warner (1984), p. 133
LoC #sb20152a
19th-century broadside ballads
Len Graham Collection:
Joe Holmes rec. KR 9.8.1972 SRR
Lizzie Clarke, Bennefreaghan, Co. Tyrone
Tilly Quigley, Magilligan, Co. Derry

18 Dick the Dasher
Roud 5280
Cooper (2009), p. 43
Smith & Clarke (2009), p. 63
Leach (1965), p. 64
Len Graham Collection:
Joe Holmes rec. KR 14.5.1976 SCR
Bob McConaghie, Ballymoney, Co. Antrim
Michael Kealey, Killerfaith, Co. Derry
Rose McManus, Corradiller, Co. Fermanagh

19 Erin's Green Shore
Laws Q27
Roud 280
Munnelly, *DalgCais* 6 (1982), p. 91
Munnelly (1994), p. 81
Harding (1900), p. 762

Cooper (2009), p. 43
Ó Cróinín (2000), p. 111
O'Neill (1915), p. 45
Shields, *UF*, 21 (1975), p. 132
Zimmermann (1967), p. 178
Ó Lochlainn (1965), p. 262
Moloney (2002), p. 6
Smith & Clarke (2009), p. 41
Wright (1975), p. 355
uí Ógáin (1995), p. 215
Belden (1940), p. 282
Brunnings (1981), p. 86
Cox (1963), p. 442
Creighton (1966), p. 171
Creighton (1962), p. 164
Fowke (1965), p. 88
Gardner & Chickering (1967), p. 479
Greenleaf & Mansfield (1933), p. 142
Hubbard (1961), p. 134
Hunter 0038 (1958)
Hyland (2009), p. 72
Moore (1964), p. 194
Peacock (1965), p. 362
Randolph (1982), p. 324
Wehman (1898), p. 107
O'Connor (1901), p. 38
Milner (1983), p. 129
LoC #as200830
19th-century broadside ballads
Len Graham Collection:
Joe Holmes rec. MG 27.2.1971 SRR
Rose McManus, Corradiller, Co. Fermanagh
Eddie Butcher, Magilligan, Co. Derry
Meena and Evelyn McManus, Torbradan,
    Co. Fermanagh

20 Erin's Lovely Home (A)
SoP SH46 27.9.1924 (1990), p. 438
Laws M6
Roud 1427
JIFSS 1 (1904), p. 11
Harding (1900), p. 756
McBride (1988), p. 58
O Lochlainn (1939), p. 202
O'Neill (1915), p. 49
Shields, *UF*, 33 (1987), p. 132
Shields, *Ceol*, 3 (1967), p. 8
G-D 1098, vol. 6 (2002)
Ord (1930), p. 106
Purslow (1974), p. 27

Sharp (1975), p. 124
MacColl & Seeger (1977), p. 250
Yates (2006), p. 61
Creighton (1962), p. 64
Fowke (1965), p. 12
Huntington (1970), p. 198
Hyland (2009), p. 73
Kenedy (1884), p. 12
Leach (1965), p. 48
MacKenzie (1963), p. 117
O'Connor (1901), p. 38
Randolph (1982), p. 356
Wehman (1898), p. 92
Wright (1975), p. 358
19th-century broadside ballads
Len Graham Collection:
Joe Holmes rec. KR 5.10.1970 SRR
Jim McAuley, Ballycastle, Co. Antrim
Mary O'Donnell, Dungloe, Co. Donegal
Archie McKeegan, Glenann, Co. Antrim

21 Erin's Lovely Home (B)
Roud 5175
Shields SRT (1981), p. 76
Shields, *UF*, 21 (1975), p. 133
McBride & McFarland (1985), p. 13
Moulden (1994), p. 30
Wright (1975), p. 104
Blethen & Wood (1997), p. 122 (history)
Green (1969), p. 97 (history)
19th-century broadside ballads
Len Graham Collection:
Joe Holmes rec. KR 3.8.1972 SRR
Martha Mullan, Portrush, Co. Antrim
Eddie Butcher, Magilligan, Co. Derry
Mary Ellen Butcher, Drumavally, Co. Derry
Geordie Hanna, Derrytresk, Co. Tyrone

22 The Exile of Erin
Roud 4355
Bunting (1809), p. 65
Moloney (2000), p. 339
Shields, *UF*, 17 (1971), p. 19
Shields, *UF*, 33 (1987), p. 88
Shields (1993), p. 240
Harding (1900), p. 421
Moylan (2000), p. 94
Walsh (1921), p. 85
Hodgart & Worthington (1959)
Walton (1968), p. 104

Bauerle (1982), p. 431
Brunnings (1981), p. 88
Dean (1922), p. 53
Dick & Fitzgerald (1863), p. 80
Fowke (1965), p. 58
Gardner & Chickering (1967), p. 479
Kennedy (1884), p. 62
O'Connor (1901), p. 41
Wehman (1898), p. 9
Wright (1975), p. 242
Levy #038–045
LoC #as103590
19th-century broadside ballads
Len Graham Collection:
Joe Holmes rec. KR 27.1.1971 SRR

23 The Factory Girl
SoP SH127 17.4.1926 (1990), p. 368
Roud 1659
Hayward (n.d.), p. 7
Morton (1970), p. 31
Morton (1973), p. 129
Shields, *Ceol*, 1 (1963), p. 8
Shields, *UF*, 21 (1975), p. 137
Shields (1993), p. 240
Ó Cróinín (2000), p. 240
Carroll & Mackenzie (2003), p. 22
Mac Mathúna (1977), p. 39
Kennedy (1975), p. 501
Dallas (1974), p. 32
Purslow (1972), p. 29
Brunnings (1981), p. 88
19th-century broadside ballads
Len Graham Collection:
Joe Holmes rec. KR 7.11.1969 SRR
Lizzie McKeever, Cross Keys, Co. Antrim
David McKee, Taylorstown, Co. Antrim
Bill John Gordon, Ballymoney, Co. Antrim
Bob McConaghie, Ballymoney, Co. Antrim
Sarah Anne O'Neill, Derrytresk, Co. Tyrone
Eddie Butcher, Magilligan, Co. Derry

24 Farewell Ballymoney
SoP SH615 14.9.1935 & SH625 23.11.1935 (1975),
    p. 342
Roud 454
JIFSS, 8 (1910), p. 12; 13 (1913), p. 28
Shields, *Ceol*, 1 (1965), p. 8
Shields, *UF*, 21 (1975), p. 167
Kennedy (1975), p. 355

McBride (1988), p. 90
Irvine (1988), p. 35 (via Holmes)
McKinney MS (2004), p. 176
Slow Air, 1:1 (1976), p. 5
Treoir, 8 (1976), p. 24; (1981), p. 18
G-D 1192, vol. 6 (2002)
Sharp (1927), p. 16
Brunnings (1981), p. 91
Creighton (1962), p. 71
Peacock (1965), p. 465
Randolph (1982), p. 749
Wright (1975), p. 382
Meredith & Anderson (1967), p. 172
Len Graham Collection:
Joe Holmes rec. KR 10.8.1969 SRR
Jane Holmes MS
Peter McArdle, Dundalk, Co. Louth
Bill John Gordon, Ballymoney, Co. Antrim

25 Faughanvale
SoP SH167 22.1.1927 (1990), p. 369
Cooper (2009), p. 43
Len Graham Collection:
Joe Holmes rec. KR 3.8.1971 SRR
Jane Holmes MS

26 The Flowering Trade
Shields, *UF*, 33 (1987), p. 106
Marks (1961), p. 52 (not this song)
Jones (1989), p. 64 (history & lore)
McKinney MS (2004), p. 43 (history & lore)
19th-century broadside ballads
Len Graham Collection:
Joe Holmes rec. KR 11.1.1969 SRR

27 The Gallant Hussar
SoP SH243a 7.7.1928 (1990), p. 473
Roud 1146
Shields, *UF*, 31 (1987)
Cooper (2009), p. 43
Healy, vol. 1 (1967), p. 282
Joyce (1909), p. 137
G-D 982, vol. 5 (2002)
Ford (1901), p. 91
Kidson (1926), p. 42
Sharp (2003), p. 39
Dallas (1972), p. 89 (SoP)
Brunnings (1981), p. 103
Eddy (1964), p. 313
Fowke (1965), p. 100

Kennedy (1884), p. 38
LoC #sb10149b
19th-century broadside ballads
Len Graham Collection:
Joe Holmes rec. MG 18.4.1970 SRR

28 Glenarm Bay
SoP SH102 24.10.1925 (1990), p. 464
Roud 3575
Moulden (1979), p. 63
Shields (1975), p. 161
Graham (1993), p. 59
McKillop (1987), p. 103
Vallely (John Kennedy) (2001), p. 26
McKinney MS (204), p. 10
Len Graham Collection:
Joe Holmes rec. KR 12.9.1968 SRR
Jane Holmes MS
Eveline Robinson, Glenarm, Co. Antrim
Agnes McAuley, Carnlough, Co. Antrim
Bill John Gordon, Ballymoney,
    Co. Antrim
David McKee, Taylorstown, Co. Antrim
Lizzie McKeever, Cross Keys, Co. Antrim
Johnny McClelland, Magherafelt,
    Co. Derry
John Kennedy, Cullybackey, Co. Antrim

29 Good Friends and Companions
Roud 1801/1836
Shields (1981), p. 89
Shields, *UF*, 21 (1975), p. 183
Morton (1970), p. 91
Tunney (1979), p. 172
Boyce (2004), p. 252
G-D 1516, vol. 8 (2002)
Ord (1930), p. 350
Creighton (1966), p. 120
Creighton & Senior (1950), p. 222
Milner (1983), p. 118
Len Graham Collection:
Joe Holmes rec. MG 7.2.1970 SRR
Paddy McGinley, Ballyboyland, Co. Antrim
Cathal McConnell, Bellanaleck, Co.
    Fermanagh
Kathleen MeEntee, Threemilehouse,
    Co. Monaghan
John Johnson, Ballymoney, Co. Antrim
Willie McElroy, Brookeborough,
    Co. Fermanagh

30 Grá mo Chroí
SoP SH582 26.1.1935 (1990), p. 238
Roud 2329
O Lochlainn (1939), p. 26
Cooper (2009), p. 43
Joyce (1909), p. 103
Ord (1930), p. 127
G-D 1469, vol. 7 (2002)
Boyce (2004), p. 153
Fowke (1965), p. 70
Len Graham Collection:
Joe Holmes rec. KR 4.8.1972 SRR

31 The Green Brier Bush
Roud 1506
Johnson (1787), p. 508
Buchan & Hall (1973), p. 69
Cameron (1856), vol. 1, p. 94; vol. 2, p. 292
Noble & Hogg (2001), p. 923
Ford (1901), p. 157
Ford (1900), p. 205
Henderson (1992), p. 142
Kennedy (1975), p. 432
McCarthy (1972), p. 28
Palmer (1979), p. 155
Fleischmann (1998), p. 455
19th-century broadside ballads
Len Graham Collection:
Joe Holmes rec. KR 11.9.1971 SRR

32 Green Broom
SoP SH147 4.9.1926 (1990), p. 474
Roud 379
D'Urfey (1959), p. 100
Baring-Gould (1890), p. 20
Broadwood & Maitland (1893), p. 88
Cooper (2009), p. 43
Kennedy (1975), p. 503
Kidson & Moffa (1926), p. 86
Danaher (1964), p. 119
Reeves (1960), p. 131
Sharp (1959), p. 76
Sharp (1975), p. 110
G-D 950, vol. 5 (2002)
Karpeles (1971), p. 230
19th-century broadside ballads
Len Graham Collection:
Joe Holmes rec. KR 17.9.1968 SRR
John Morgan, Ballintoy, Co. Antrim
Packy Russell, Doolin, Co. Clare

33 Here I Am Amongst You
Roud 5278
Cooper (2009), p. 43
Len Graham Collection:
Joe Holmes rec. KR 8.6.1974 SRR
Paddy Joe Kelly, Rocktown, Co. Derry

34 India's Burning Sands
SoP SH120 27.2.1926 (1990), p. 332
Roud 550
Laws N2
Shields (1981), p. 96
Shields, *UF*, 21 (1975), p. 204
McBride (1988), p. 65
G-D 185, vol. 1 (2002)
Flanders (1939), p. 19
Creighton & Senior (1950), p. 192
Creighton (1962), p. 158
Doerflinger (1951), p. 308
Gardner & Chickering (1967), p. 222
MacKenzie (1963), p. 143
19th-century broadside ballads
Len Graham Collection:
Joe Holmes rec. KR 10.9.1971 SRR
Frank McCollum, Ballycastle, Co. Antrim
Bill Quigley, Magilligan, Co. Derry
Frank McKenna, Omagh, Co. Tyrone

35 Johnny Doyle
SoP SH137 26.6.1926 (1990), p. 431 and
     Appendix C 541
Laws M2
Roud 455
Petrie (1905), p. 112
JIFSS, 1 (1904), p. 66
Shields (1981), p. 106
Shields (1993), p. 242
Shields, *UF*, 17 (1971)
Shields, *UF*, 18 (1972)
Shields, *UF*, 21 (1975), p. 224
Shields, *UF*, 33 (1987), p. 87
Hughes (1936), p. 72
G-D 1020, vol. 5 (2002)
Eddy (1964), p. 187
Flanders (1939), p. 248
Flanders (1953), p. 279
Fowke (1965), p. 58
Fowke (1970), p. 107
Gardner & Chickering (1967), p. 69
Henry (1938), p. 162

Hubbard (1961), p. 56
Hunter 0062 (1958)
Karpeles (1971), p. 212
Leach (1965), p. 64
MacKenzie (1963), p. 106
Peacock (1965), p. 687
Randolph (1982), p. 350
Sharp & Campbell (1917), p. 251
Sharp (1932), p. 27
Warner (1984), p. 209
O'Connor (1901), p. 16
Wehman (1898), p. 27
Levy #192–018
LoC #as201890
19th-century broadside ballads
Len Graham Collection:
Joe Holmes rec. MG 11.1.1971 SRR
Willie Johnson, Magherafelt, Co. Derry
Eddie Butcher, Magilligan, Co. Derry

36 Johnny and Molly
SoP SH755 14.5.1938 (1990), p. 297
Laws K14
Roud 527
Joyce (1912), p. 95
Hughes (1936), p. 2
Shields, *UF*, 10 (1964), p. 37
Graham (1993), p. 27
Cooper (2009), p. 43
O Lochlainn (1965), p. 44
Tunney (1979), p. 98
Boys of the Lough (1977), p. 29
Sharp (1959), p. 62
Sharp (1975), p. 70
Creighton (1971), p. 101
Creighton (1962), p. 40
Huntington (1970), p. 266
Karpeles (1971), p. 176
19th-century broadside ballads
Len Graham Collection:
Joe Holmes rec. MG 5.12.1969 SRR
Pat Magee, Carnhugh, Co. Donegal
Sandy McConnell, Bellanaleck,
    Co. Fermanagh,
Eddie Butcher, Magilligan, Co. Derry

37 John Reilly the Sailor
SoP SH468 19.11.1932 (1990), p. 441
Laws M8
Roud 270

Petrie (1905), p. 89
Shields, *UF*, 21 (1975), p. 223
Ó Lochlainn (1965), p. 14
Munnelly, *Bealoideas* (1980), p. 43
O'Hara (1997), p. 196
Slow Air, 1:1 (1976), p. 6
Treoir, 8 (1976), p. 25
Vallely (John Kennedy) (2001), p. 31
G-D 22, vol. 1 (2002)
Purslow (Gardiner MSS), p. (1972), p. 114
Reeves (1960), p. 60
Sharp (1959), p. 32
Sharp (1961), p. 107
Cox (1963), p. 323
Creighton (1971), p. 133
Creighton (1962), p. 102
Eddy (1964), p. 116
Fowke (1965), p. 58
Fowke (1973), p. 156
Greenleaf & Mansfield (1933), p. 182
Hunter 1172 (1971)
Huntungton (1964), p. 105
Mackenzie (1928), p. 43
Karpeles (1971), p. 163
Peacock (1965), p. 698
Warner (1984), p. 338
O'Connor (1901), p. 49
Randolph (1982), p. 56
Wehman (1898), p. 121
Wright (1975), p. 268
19th-century broadside ballads
Len Graham Collection:
Joe Holmes rec. KR 10.3.1971 SRR
Jane Holmes MS
Barney McManus, Torbradan, Co. Fermanagh
Sarah Anne O'Neill, Derrytresk, Co. Tyrone
John Kennedy, Cullybackey, Co. Antrim

38 The Jolly Ploughboy
Roud 151
Moloney (2000), p. 250
Shields (1981), p. 134
Fleischmann (1998), p. 1067
Baring-Gould (1895), p. 27
Copper (1972), p. 264
Kennedy (1975), p. 317
McCarthy (1972), p. 61
Palmer (1979), p. 129
Purslow (1965), p. 51
Reeves (1960), p. 172

Sharp (1959), p. 107
Sharp (1961), p. 61
Sharp (1975), p. 141
Kidson (1891), p. 145
Lloyd (1967), p. 203
Randolph (1982), p. 374
19th-century broadside ballads
Len Graham Collection:
Joe Holmes rec. KR 5.10.1970 SRR
Eddie Butcher, Magilligan, Co. Derry

39 Laurel Hill
SoP SH8 5.1.1924 (1990), p. 311
Roud 2917
Moulden (1979), p. 88
Moulden (1992), p. 6
Shields (1981), p. 112
Shields (1993), p. 244
Moylan (2000), p. 147
Len Graham Collection:
Joe Holmes rec. MG 5.12.1969 SRR
John Johnson, Ballymoney, Co. Antrim
Eddie Butcher, Magilligan, Co. Derry

40 The Lily of the West
SoP SH578 29.12.1934 (1990), p. 416
Laws P29
Roud 957
Ó Lochlainn (1939), p. 184
Baring-Gould (1890), p. 118
Belden (1940), p. 132
Cooper (2009), p. 43
Creighton (1966), p. 84
Eddy (1964), p. 147
Hunter 0299 (1958)
Huntington (1970), p. 133
Milner (1983), p. 184
Moore (1964), p. 191
Peacock (1965), p. 473
Randolph (1982), p. 75
Sandburg (1927), p. 61
Sharp (1932), p. 199
LoC #as107790
19th-century broadside ballads
Len Graham Collection:
Joe Holmes rec. KR 10.3.1971 SRR
Jane Holmes MS
Bob McConaghie, Ballymoney, Co. Antrim
John Johnson, Ballymoney, Co. Antrim
Willie Devlin, Arboe, Co. Tyrone

41 The Load of Kail Plants
SoP SH25b 3.5.1924 (1990), p. 261
Roud 6919
Blair (2007), p. 44
Len Graham Collection:
Joe Holmes rec. KR 11.8.1969 SRR
Willie Stevenson, Ballybrakes, Co. Antrim
John Twaddle, Ballymoney, Co. Antrim
Sammy Wade, Ballymoney, Co. Antrim
Bill John Gordon, Ballymoney, Co. Antrim
John Johnson, Ballymoney, Co. Antrim

42 Long Cookstown
SoP SH745 5.3.1938 (1990), p. 47
Roud 883
Moulden (1979), p. 91
Shields (1993), p. 245
Shields, *UF*, 21 (1975), p. 296
Irvine (1988), p. 62
Kennedy (1975), p. 611
Ord (1930), p. 372
G-D 603, vol. 3 (2002)
McMorland (2006), p. 132
19th-century broadside ballads
Len Graham Collection:
Joe Holmes rec. KR 7.9.1973 SCR
Eddie Butcher, Magilligan, Co. Derry

43 Lovely Armoy
SoP 9 12.1.1924 (1990), p. 186
Roud 13541
JIFSS, 1 (1904), p. 12
Shields, *UF*, 21 (1975), p. 251
Len Graham Collection:
Joe Holmes rec. KR 18.6.1968 SRR
Alec McFarland, Armoy, Co. Antrim
Eddie Butcher, Magilligan, Co. Derry
Jeannie McGrath, Rasharkin, Co. Antrim

44 Maggie Picken
Roud 8945
Cooper (2009), p. 43
Meek (1985), p.92
Moloney (2000), p. 195
Shields, *UF*, 21 (1975), p. 270
Shields (1981), p. 120
Henderson (1992), p. 151
Herd (1869), p. 208
Johnson (1787), p. 258
Cameron (1856), p. 81

Collinson (1966), pp 205, 213
Tomlyn (1890), pp xi & 65
G-D 1414/1657 (2002)
Hunter (1979), p. xxix
Len Graham Collection:
Joe Holmes rec. KR 11.1.1971 SRR
John Campbell, Mullaghbawn, Co. Armagh
Eddie Butcher, Magilligan, Co. Derry
Elspeth Barnes, Ballyurnanellan, Co. Down
John Fyfe, Omagh, Co. Tyrone

45 A Maid in a Flowery Garden
SoP SH471 10.12.1932 & SH818 29.7.1939
    (1990), p. 317
Laws N42
Roud 264
Hughes (1936), p. 63
Shields (1981), p. 110
McBride (1988), p. 106
Munnelly *Bealoideas* (1980), p. 44
O'Boyle (1976), p. 34
Ó Lochlainn (1939), p. 4
Ó Cróinín (2000), p. 280
Carroll & Mackenzie (2003), p. 3
Cooper (2009), p. 43
Treoir, 11 (1979), p. 17
Reeves (1960), p. 64
Summers (2004), p. 15
G-D 1038, vol. 5 (2002)
Belden (1940), p. 148
Cox (1963), p. 316
Creighton (1966), p. 56
Creighton (1971), p. 57
Eddy (1964), p. 152
Fowke (1973), p. 152
Hunter 0445 (1960)
Moore (1964), p. 187
Peacock (1965), p. 584
Randolph (1982), p. 55
Sandburg (1927), p. 68
Sharp & Campbell (1917), p. 281
Sharp (1932), p. 70
19th-century broadside ballads
Len Graham Collection:
Joe Holmes rec. KR 16.7.1969 SRR
Colm Lynn, Moneystaghan, Co. Derry
Sarah & Rita Keane, Caherlistrane,
    Co. Galway
Jim McAuley, Ballycastle, Co. Antrim
Willie Devlin, Ardboe, Co. Tyrone

Sarah Anne O'Neill, Derrytresk, Co. Tyrone
Maggie Murphy, Tempo, Co. Fermanagh

46 The Maid of Erin's Isle
SoP SH57b 13.12.1924 (1990), p. 228
Roud 7978
Cooper (2009), p. 43
19th-century broadside ballads
Len Graham Collection:
Joe Holmes rec. KR 9.8.1972 SRR
Joe Holmes MS
John Johnson, Ballymoney, Co. Antrim
John Campbell, Mullaghbawn, Co. Armagh

47 The Maid of Mourne Shore
SoP SH564 22.9.1934 (1990), p. 344
Roud 5282
Petrie (1905), p. 75
JIFSS, 5 (1907), p. 13
Joyce (1909), p. 302
Cooper (2009), p. 43
Marks (1961), p. 23
Boyce (2004), p. 120 (via Holmes)
Len Graham Collection:
Joe Holmes rec. KR 5.10.1970 SRR
Bill John Gordon, Ballymoney, Co. Antrim
Paddy Gamble, Loughgiel, Co. Antrim
John Johnson, Ballymoney, Co. Antrim

48 Mary of the Wild Moor
Laws P21
Roud 155
Cooper (2009), p. 43
Glassie (2006), p. 539
O'Hara (1997), p. 198
Kennedy (1975), p. 376
G-D 1175, vol. 6 (2002)
Kidson (1891), p. 77
Purslow (1972), p. 57
Belden (1940), p. 207
Cox (1963), p. 437
Eddy (1964), p. 209
Fowke (1965), p. 101
Gardner & Chickering (1967), p. 481
Henry (1938), p. 372
Hunter 0070 (1958)
Leach (1965), p. 733
Moore (1964), p. 232
Pound (1972), p. 81
Randolph (1982), p. 72

Sandburg (1927), p. 466
Wehman (1898), p. 85
Levy #125–073
LoC #as108620
19th-century broadside ballads
Len Graham Collection:
Joe Holmes rec. KR 22.10.1969 SRR
Tommy Kelly, Newtown Crommelin,
    Co. Antrim

49 Molly Bán Lavery
SoPSH114 16.1.1926 (1990), p. 143
Laws O36
Roud 166
Cooper (2009), p. 43
Moloney (2000), p. 246
JIFSS, 3 (1905), p. 25
Joyce (1909), p. 220
Shields (1993), p. 245
Shields, *UF*, 18 (Hume MS) (1972), p. 36
Shields, *UF*, 21 (1975), p. 272
Ó Cróinín (2000), p. 151
O Lochlainn (1939), p. 58
Morton (1973), p. 99
Jones (1989), p. 163
McMahon (1991), p. 85
Summers (2004), p. 5
Walton (1968), p. 162
Dubliners (1968), p. 14
Kennedy (1975), p. 716
Palmer (1980), p. 55
Boswell (1997), p. 44
Cox (1963), p. 339
Creighton (1962), p. 111
Eddy (1964), p. 194
Fowke (1965), p. 100
Gardner & Chickering (1967), p. 66
Hunter 0108 (1958)
Karpeles (1971), p. 113
Kennedy (1884), pp 80 & 321
Leach (1965), p. 176
Linscott (1990), p. 274
Moore (1964), p. 169
Pound (1972), p. 78
Randolph (1982), p. 54
Sharp & Campbell (1917), p. 159
Sharp (1932), p. 328
Milner (1983), p. 51
Meredith & Anderson (1967), p. 196
19th-century broadside ballads

Len Graham Collection:
Joe Holmes rec. KR 29.8.1974 SRR
Jim Hamilton, Balinamore, Co. Antrim
Joe Scott, Ballygillan, Co. Derry
Packy Manus Byrne, Ardara, Co. Donegal
Maggie Murphy, Tempo, Co. Fermanagh

50 The Murlough Shore
SoPSH27a 5.7.1924 (1990), p. 371
Roud 2946
Moulden (1979), p. 102
Shields (via Graham), p. (1981), p. 124
Shields, *UF*, 21 (1975), p. 258
Marks (1961), p. 22
O'Boyle (1979), p. 54
Foley (191), p. 32
Boyce (2004), p. 166 (via Graham)
Len Graham Collection:
Joe Holmes rec. KR 31.7.1971 SRR
Ellen & Eveline Robinson, Glenarm,
    Co. Antrim
Bill John Gordan, Ballymoney, Co. Antrim
Jim McAuley, Ballycastle, Co. Antrim
Eddie Butcher, Magilligan, Co. Derry
John McKeown, Newtown Crommelin,
    Co. Antrim
Colm Lynn, Moneystaghan, Co. Derry
Sarah and Rita Keane, Caherlistrane,
    Co. Galway

51 My Charming Blue-Eyed Mary
SoP SH785 10.12.1938 (1990), p. 399
Roud 3230
Shields, *UF*, 33 (1987)
Cooper (2009), p. 43
McBride & McFarland (1985), p. 18
Carroll & Mackenzie (2003), p. 7
19th-century broadside ballads
Len Graham Collection:
Joe Holmes rec. KR 4.11.1969 SRR
Joe Holmes MS

52 My Father's Servant Boy
SoP SH198 27.8.1927 (1990), p. 481
Laws M11
Roud 1910
Shields, *UF*, 21 (1975), p. 284
Blair (2007), p. 186
MacColl & Seeger (1977), p. 252
Summers (2004), p. 10

MacKenzie (1963), p. 119
Wright (1975), p. 395
19th-century broadside ballads
Len Graham Collection:
Joe Holmes rec. KR 5.9.1971 SRR
Jane Holmes MS
Willie Johnson, Magherafelt, Co. Derry
Maggie Murphy, Tempo, Co. Fermanagh
Willie McElroy, Brookborough, Co. Fermanagh

53 My Love is on the Ocean
Roud 3720
Belden (1940), p. 491
Cooper (2009), p. 43
Gardner & Chickering (1967), p. 131
Hunter (1973), p. 1484
Randolph (1982), p. 236
SoP SH504 29.7.1933 (1990), p. 347
    (*Farewell He*)
Baring-Gould (1895), p. 43 (*Farewell He*)
Purslow (1972), p. 32 (*Farewell He*)
19th-century broadside ballads (*Farewell He*)
Len Graham Collection:
Joe Holmes rec. KR 10.3.1971 SRR
Jane Holmes MS

54 My Parents Reared Me Tenderly
SoP SH466 5.11.1932 (1990), p. 79
Roud 8003
McBride & McFarland (1985), p. 15
Slow Air, 1:1 (1976), p. 6
Treoir, 8 (1976), p. 25
Peacock (1965), p. 1018
Len Graham Collection:
Joe Holmes rec. KR 11.1.1969 SRR
Eddie Butcher, Magilligan, Co. Derry
Malachy Clerkson, Threemilehouse,
    Co. Monaghan

55 My Willie O
Child 77/248?
Roud 50/179?
Bronson (1972), p. 440
Cooper (2009), p. 43
Joyce (1909), p. 219
Shields (1993), p. 250
Shields, *UF*, 10 (1972), p. 80
Shields, *UF*, 21 (1975), p. 436
Morton (1973), p. 5
McBride (1988), p. 22

Gmelch (1975), p. 137
Slow Air, 1:1 (1976), p. 3
Graham (1993), p. 62
Carroll & Mackenzie (2003), p. 12
G-D 338 vol. 2 (2002)
Creighton (1962), p. 113
19th-century broadside ballads
Len Graham Collection:
Joe Holmes rec. KR 16.7.1969 SRR
John McLaughlin Skerry, Co. Antrim,
Jimmy McGinley Ros Ghoill, Co. Donegal
Dan 'Bartley' McGlynn, Largnalore,
    Co. Donegal
Robbie Haldane, Craryville, NY, USA

56 The Nobleman's Wedding
SoP SH60a 3.1.1925 (1990), p. 400
Laws P31
Roud 567
Petrie (1905), p. 124
Shields (1993), p. 246
Shields (1982), p. 41
Shields, *UF*, 21 (1975), p. 302
Allingham (1865), p. 162
Cooper (2009), p. 43
Fleischmann (1998), p. 1243
Cooper (2002), p. 203
FMJ (2009), p. 506
Graves (1894), p. 146
Munnelly, *JMI* 3:2 (2003), p. 15
Joyce (1909), p. 224
McBride (1988), p. 12
McKinney MS (2004), p. 171
Causeway (n.d.), p. 36
Kennedy (1975), p. 364
G-D 1199 vol. 6 (2002)
Ord (1930), p. 132
Purslow (1965), p. 61
MacColl & Seeger (1986), p. 40
Belden (1940), p. 165
Reeves (1960), p. 44
Sharp & Campbell (1917), p. 292
Sharp (1932), p. 83
Greenleaf & Mansfield (1933), p. 155
Karpeles (1971), p. 124
Kennedy (1884), p. 81
Peacock (1965), p. 691
19th-century broadside ballads
Len Graham Collection:
Joe Holmes rec. KR 8.10.1968 SRR

Eddie Butcher, Magilligan, Co. Derry
Bob McConaghie, Ballymoney, Co. Antrim
John Kennedy, Cullybackey, Co. Antrim
Joe McGrath, Boho, Co. Fermanagh
Margaret Reilly, Dowra, Co. Cavan
Bobby Kilkenny, Ballinasloe, Co. Galway

57 The Old Oak Tree
SoP SH207 29.10.1927 (1990), p. 417
Laws P37
Roud 569
Shields (1993), p. 246
Shields, *UF*, 33 (1987), p. 66
Morton (1970), p. 24
Morton (1973), p. 141
Munnelly, *DalgCais*, 6 (1982), p. 91
Munnelly (1994), p. 34
Doerflinger (1951), p. 283
Flanders (1939), p. 74
Gardner & Chickering (1965), p. 107
Leach (1965), p. 52
Peacock (1965), p. 628
19th-century broadside ballads
Len Graham Collection:
Joe Holmes rec. KR 4.11.1969 SRR
Jimmy Spallin, Castlerock, Co. Derry
Bill John Gordon, Ballymoney, Co. Antrim
Sarah and Rita Keane, Caherlistrane,
    Co. Galway
Pat Carolan, Drogheda, Co. Louth

58 Once I Loved
Roud 459
Harding (1900), p. 602
G-D 1145, vol. 6 (2002)
Ord (1930), p. 181
Belden (1940), p. 209
Hunter 0563 (1960)
Peacock (1965), p. 453
Randolph (1982), p. 249
Sandburg (1927), p. 323
McKinney MS (2004), p. 179
19th-century broadside ballads
Len Graham Collection:
Joe Holmes rec. KR 5.10.1970 SRR
Jane Holmes MS
Sarah and Rita Keane, Caherlistrane,
    Co. Galway
Eddie Butcher, Magilligan, Co. Derry
John Campbell, Mullaghbawn, Co. Armagh

Micil 'Ned' Quinn, Mullaghbawn,
    Co. Armagh

59 The Parting Glass
SoP SH769 20.8.1938 (1990), p. 65
Roud 3004
Ó Lochlainn (1939), p. 138
O'Neill (1915), p. 25
Cooper (2009), p. 43
Clancy (1964), p. 64
Boyce (2004), p. 256 (via Holmes)
MacLochlainn, *DalgCais* (1993), p. 53
Meek (1997), p. 95
G-D 1531, vol. 8 (2002)
Fowkes (1965), p. 59
Peacock (1965), p. 573
19th-century broadside ballads
Len Graham Collection:
Joe Holmes rec. KR 22.9.1971 SRR
Tommy McQueston, Ballymoney,
    Co. Antrim

60 The Plains of Waterloo
Laws N31
Roud 622
Dallas (Willie Scott) (1972), p. 87
McMorland (Willie Scott) (2006), p. 72
Tocher, 25 (Willie Scott) (1977), p. 46
Brunnings (1981), p. 31
Cooper (2009), p. 43
Fowkes (1965), p. 58
Gardner & Chickering (1967), p. 227
Greenleaf & Mansfield (1933), p. 178
Peacock (1965), p. 1007
19th-century broadside ballads
Len Graham Collection:
Joe Holmes rec. KR 16.7.1969 SRR

61 The Quaker's Wife
Roud 6479
Duffy (1845), p. 270
Cooper (2009), p. 43
G-D1734, vol. 8 (2002)
Noble (2001), p. 803
Opie (1951), p. 358
Wannan (1965), p. 237
Fleischmann (1998), p. 274 (melody)
Ní Uallacháin (2003), p. 440 (melody)
Len Graham Collection:
Joe Holmes rec. KR 7.12.1969 SRR

62 The Rambling Boys of Pleasure
Roud 386
Graham (1993), p. 10
Cooper (2009), p. 43
Shields (1993), p. 246
O'Boyle (1976), p. 84
Smith & Clarke (2009), p. 21
Traditional Music, 6 (1977), p. 4
Tunney (1991), p. 80
Irvine (1988), p. 35 (via Holmes)
O'Toole (2006), p. 264 (via Holmes)
Purslow (1974), p. 77
Bauerle (1982), p. 54
Creighton (1971), p. 117
Creighton (1966), p. 95
Fowke (1973), p. 138
Tocher 11 (1973), p. 89
Yeats (1962), p. 209
LoC #sb40467b
19th-century broadside ballads
Len Graham Collection:
Joe Holmes rec. KR 10.10.1972 SRR

63 The Rambling Irishman
Roud 3572
Graham (1993), p. 13
Boys of the Lough (1977), p. 37
Cooper (2009), p. 43
SoP 334 (1930)
Hunter 0594 (1961)
Blethen & Wood (1997), p. 118 (history)
Evans (1965), p. 86 (history)
Green (1969), p. 100 (history)
McClure (1889), p. 178 (history)
Montgomery (1965), p. 26 (history)
NIPRO, *18th-Century Emigration* (1972)
Len Graham Collection:
Joe Holmes rec. KR 16.7.1969 SRR
Mary McQueston, Lisboy, Co. Antrim
John Johnson, Ballymoney, Co. Antrim
Eddie Butcher, Magilligan, Co. Derry
Bertha Lauderdale, Fayetteville, Arkansas, USA

64 The Ride in the Creel
Child 281
SoP SH201 17.9.1927 (1990), p. 265
Roud 120
Bronson (1972), p. 486
Moulden (1979), p. 126
Tunney (1979), p. 92

Shields (1993), p. 239
Shields, *UF*, 10 (1972), p. 102
Shields, *UF*, 21 (1975), p. 93
Shields & Munnelly (1985), p. 17
Clune (2007), p. 109
O'Boyle (1979), p. 32
Boyce (2004), p. 116
Jones (1989), p. 218
Cowan (1980), p. 92
Henderson (1992), p. 151
Kinsley (1969), p. 631
G-D 317, vol. 2 (2002)
Ford (1901), p. 139
Lyle (1994), p. 195
McCarthy (1972), p. 54
MacColl (1965), p. 52
Palmer (1980), p. 223
Yates (2006), p. 52
Flanders (1965), p. 136
Len Graham Collection:
Joe Holmes rec. KR 24.9.1968 SRR
Jimmy Currie, Dunluce, Co. Antrim
Mary Keane, Caherlistrane, Co. Galway
Packy Manus Byrne, Ardara, Co. Donegal
John Kennedy, Cullybackey, Co. Antrim

65 The Roving Sea Captain
Laws Q12
Roud 947
Graham (1993), p. 39
G-D 1502, vol. 7 (2002)
Combs (1967), p. 121
19th-century broadside ballads
Len Graham Collection:
Joe Holmes rec. KR 11.1.1969 SRR
Hamish Henderson MS (19.10.1992)
Willie McKeever, Cross Keys, Co. Antrim

66 Sandy and Paddy
Cooper (2009), p. 43
Murphy (2002) (history)
19th-century broadside ballads
Len Graham Collection:
Joe Holmes rec. KR 22.10.1969 SRR
20th-century broadside ballad

67 The Sea-Apprentice
SoP SH739 22.1.1938 (1990), p. 291
Roud 1671
Cooper (2009), p. 43

G-D 54, vol. 1 (2002)
Creighton (1966), p. 304
Greenleaf & Mansfield (1933), p. 214
Peacock (1965), p. 575
19th-century broadside ballads
Len Graham Collection:
Joe Holmes rec. KR 5.10.1970 SRR
Paddy Gamble, Loughgiel, Co. Antrim

68 Seventeen Come Sunday
SoP SH152 9.10.1926 & SH793 4.2.1939 (1990),
    p. 266
Child 299?
Laws O17
Roud 277/162
Bronson (1972), p. 517
Shields, *UF*, 21 (1975), p. 357
Mac Con Iomaire (2007), p. 479
Henderson (1992), p. 150
Kennedy (1975), p. 224/297
Kidson (1926), p. 2
McCarthy (1972), p. 106
Purslow (1968), p. 104
Reeves (1960), p. 238
Sharp(1959), p. 104
Sharp (1975), p. 138
MacColl & Seeger (1977), p. 168
Palmer (1979), p. 138
Dallas (1972), p. 54
G-D 1470, vol. 7 (2002)
Cole (1961), p. 14
Cox (1963), p. 394
Creighton (1961), p. 32
Creighton (1971), p. 44
Lomax (1960), p. 212
Moore (1964), p. 213
Niles (1960), p. 341
Peacock (1965), p. 284
Sharp & Campbell (1917), p. 149
Sharp (1932), p. 156, 305
Warner (1984), p. 148
Milner (1983), p. 50
19th-century broadside ballads
Len Graham Collection:
Joe Holmes rec. KR 10.1.1972 SRR
Eddie Butcher, Magilligan, Co. Derry

69 The Shamrock Sod No More
SoP SH235 12.5.1928 (1990), p. 203
Roud 2747

Kennedy (1827), p. 182
Graham (1993), p. 66
Cooper (2009), p. 43
Ord (1930), p. 352
Wright (1975), p. 505
Len Graham Collection:
Joe Holmes rec. KR 5.10.1970 SRR
Jane & Joe Holmes MSS
Mary Magill, Ballynacaird, Co. Antrim
Bob McAllister, Dunaghy, Co. Antrim
Sarah Anne O'Neill, Derrytresk, Co. Tyrone
    (via Holmes)

70 Slieve Gallen Braes
Bunting (1840), p. 21
Moloney (2000), p. 245
Hardebeck (1910), p. 3
Ó Lochlainn (1965), p. 18
Meek(1978), p. 58
O'Neill (1987), p. 18
Walton (1966), p. 40
Fleischmann (1998), p. 1067
Wright (1975), p. 192
Len Graham Collection:
Joe Holmes rec. KR 27.1.1971 SRR
John McKeown, Newtown Crommelin,
    Co. Antrim

71 The Son of a Gamble-eer
SoP SH741 5.2.1938 (1990), p. 50
Roud 2964
Shields (1981), p. 135
Shields, *UF*, 21(1975), p. 327
Sandburg (1927), p. 44
Hodgart & Worthington (1959)
Ward (1964), p. 118
LoC#sb40466b
Len Graham Collection:
Joe Holmes rec. MG 11.1.1972 SRR
Tom Anderson, Clooney, Co. Derry
Eddie Butcher, Magilligan, Co. Derry

72 The Strands of Magilligan
SoP SH520 18.11.1933 (1990), p. 259
Roud 688
Shields (1981), p. 142
Shields (1993), p. 248
Shields, *UF*, 21 (1975), p. 379
Treoir, 11 (1979), p. 16
Baring-Gould (1890), p. 190

Reeves (1960), p. 251
Williams & Lloyd (1959), p. 98
Gardner & Chickering (1967), p. 95
Karpeles (1971), p. 205
19th-century broadside ballads
Len Graham Collection:
Joe Holmes rec.KR 24.9.1968 SRR
Eddie Butcher, Magilligan, Co. Derry
John Butcher, Drumavally, Co. Derry
David McKee, Taylorstown, Co. Antrim
Tom Anderson, Clooney, Co. Derry
Jimmy Spallin, Castlerock, Co. Derry
Mary Osborne, Dunboe, Co. Derry

73 The Sweet Bann Water
SoP SH722 25.9.1937 (1990), p. 343
Child 248?
Laws M4
Roud 179/402
Joyce (1909), p. 85
Shields (1981), p. 59
Shields (1993), p. 238
Shields, *Ceol*, 3 (1968), p. 44
Shields, *UF*, 21 (1975), p. 86
Cooper (2009), p. 43
Glassie (1982), p. 685
Henderson (1992), p. 147
Kennedy (1975), p. 359
McKinney MS (2004), p. 187
Treoir, 12 (1980), p. 15
G-D 783/792, vol. 4 (2002)
Ord (1930), p. 89
Palmer (1980), p. 49
Reeves (1960), p. 176
Sharp (1959), p. 72
Sharp (1961), p. 194
Williams & Lloyd (1959), p. 52
MacColl & Seeger (1986), p. 13
Belden (1940), p. 118
Brunnings (1981), p. 80
Cox (1963), p. 348
Creighton (1962), p. 63
Doerflinger (1951), p. 314
Eddy (1964), p. 92
Fowke (1965), p. 105
Gardner & Chickering (1967), p. 86
Greenleaf & Mansfield (1933), pp 55 & 76
Hunter 0003 (1958)
Moore (1964), p. 196
Peacock (1965), p. 733

Pound (1972), p. 51
Randolph (1982), p. 52
Sharp & Campbell (1917), p. 173
Sharp (1932), p. 358
Sharp & Karpeles (1968), p. 68
Warner (1984), p. 427
19th-century broadside ballads
Len Graham Collection:
Joe Holmes rec. KR 22.12.1972 SRR
Jane Holmes MS
Eddie Butcher, Magilligan, Co. Derry
John Butcher, Drumavally, Co. Derry
Peter 'P' Flanegan, Drumbargy,
    Co. Fermanagh

74 The Trip O'er the Mountain
SoP 61a 7 61b 10.1.1925 (1990), p. 459
Roud 9632
Bunting (1809), p. 25
Moloney (2000), p. 242
Mac Con Iomaire (2007), p. 478
McWilliams (1831), p. 109
Moulden (1993), p. 9
JIFSS, 8 (1910), p. 13; 11 (1912), p. 14; vol. 26
    (1929), p. 79
Tunney (1991), p. 27
Joyce (1909), p. 128
Healy (1967), p. 294
O'Hara (1997), p. 198
Walton (1966), p. 63
Ní Uallacháin (2003), p. 506 (melody)
Fowkes (1965), p. 13
19th-century broadside ballads
Len Graham Collection:
Joe Holmes rec. KR 11.8.1969 SRR
Eddie Butcher, Magilligan, Co. Derry
Teddy Hagan, Aneterbeg, Co. Tyrone

75 The True-Born Sons of Levi
SoP SH146 28.8.1926 (1990), p. 180
Roud 2430
G-D 470, vol. 3 (2002)
Ord (1930), p. 3
Williams (de Vere White on Freemasonry),
    (1973), p. 46
Mirala (Freemasonry) (2007), p. 274
19th-century broadside ballads
Len Graham Collection:
Joe Holmes rec. MG 7.3.1971 SRR
Eddie Butcher, Magilligan, Co. Derry

76 True Lovers' Discussion
SoP SH164 1.1.1927 (1990), p. 362
Laws O22
Roud 2948
JIFSS, 14 (1914), p. 32
Shields (1981), p. 153
Shields (1993), p. 249
Shields, *Ceol*, 3 (1967), p. 4 (Allingham article)
O Croinin (2000), p. 177
Munnelly, *DalgCais*, 8 (1986), p. 69
O'Boyle (1979), p. 26
Boyce (2004), p. 84
Causeway (nd), p. 74
Creighton (1971), p. 87
Fowkes (1965), p. 59
O'Connor (1901), p. 79
Wehman (1898), p. 5
19th-century broadside ballads
Len Graham Collection:
Joe Holmes rec. KR 10.9.1972 SRR
Joe Holmes MS
Eddie Butcher, Magilligan, Co. Derry
Paddy Lyons, Listowel, Co. Kerry
Frank McKenna, Omagh, Co. Tyrone
Sam Doherty, Ballymoney, Co. Antrim

77 True Lover John
SoP SH699 17.4.1937 (1990), p. 383
Child 248
Roud 179
Bronson (1972), p. 438
Cooper (2009), p. 43
Joyce (1909), p. 219
Hughes (1915), p. 64
Yeats & Higgins, *Broadsides* (1935)
Shields (1993), p. 241
Shields & Munnelly (1985), p. 4
Clune (2007), p. 101
Slow Air, 1:1 (1976), p. 5
Traditional Music, 6 (1977), p. 4
Treoir, 8 (1976), p. 24; 12 (1980), p. 15
Herd (1776), p. 324
Johnson (1787), p. 77
Reeves (1960), p. 136
Williams & Lloyd (1959), p. 52
Brunnings (1981), p. 116
Cameron (1856), vol. 2, p. 57
Karpeles (1971), p. 100
Moore (1964), p. 113
Sharp & Campbell (1917), p. 128

Sharp (1932), p. 259
Warner (1984), p. 225
Len Graham Collection:
Joe Holmes rec. KR 10.9.1968 SRR
Jane & Joe Holmes MSS
Sam Mulholland, Bushmills, Co. Antrim
John Johnson, Ballymoney, Co. Antrim
Sam Doherty, Ballymoney, Co. Antrim

78 Tumbling Through the Hay
SoP SH697 3.4.1937 (1990), p. 278
Roud 153
D'Urfey (1720), p. 22
Baring-Gould (1890), p. 222
Cooper (2009), p. 43
Kennedy (1975), p. 56
Sharp & Baring-Gould (1906), p. 54
Lloyd (1967), p. 220
Copper (1972), p. 228
Palmer (1979), p. 29
Purslow (1972), p. 58
17th–19th-century broadside ballads
Len Graham Collection:
Joe Holmes rec. KR 5.10.1970 SRR
John Johnson, Ballymoney,
    Co. Antrim

79 The Wedding of Lauchie McGrath
Shields, *UF*, 21 (1975), p. 422
Clune (2007), p. 57
uí Ogáin (2009), p. 494
Len Graham Collection:
Joe Holmes rec.KR 11.8.1971 SRR
Jim McQuillan, Dunloy, Co. Antrim

80 When a Man's in Love
SoP SH211 26.11.1927 (1990), p. 479
Laws O20
Roud 990
McWilliams (1831), p. 116
Moulden (1993), p. 2
Ó Cróinín (2002), p. 227
Shields (1981), p. 158
Shields, *UF*, 21 (1975), p. 427
Kennedy (1975), p. 320
Tunney (1979), p. 96
Brunnings (1981), p. 339
Creighton & Senior (1950), p. 214
Karpeles (1971), p. 194
Lomax (1960), p. 146

Len Graham Collection:
Joe Holmes rec. KR 11.8.1971 SRR
Eddie Butcher, Magilligan, Co. Derry
Mick Hoy, Derrygonnelly, Co. Fermanagh

The Killyramer Christmas Rhymers and Mummers
Murphy (1940), p. 81
Patterson, *CLAJ*, 11 (1945), p. 44
Green, *UJA*, 9 (1946), p. 3
Evans (1951)
Gailey (1969)
Buckley (2007)
UF, 6 (1960), p. 25
Gailey, *UF*, 13 (1967), p. 18
Gailey, *UF*, 21 (1975), p. 73
Gailey, *UF*, 24 (1978), p. 59
Corcoran, *Ceol*, 4 (1972)
Glassie (1976)
Slow Air, 1:1, (1976), p. 6; 1:2 (1976), p. 4
Treoir, 8 (1976), p. 25
Tunney (1979), p. 61
Fowke (1976), p. 153

McKillop (1987), p. 83
Ormsby, Frank (1991), p. 354
Len Graham Collection:
Joe Holmes rec. KR 10.3.1971 SRR
John Campbell, Mullaghbawn, Co. Armagh

Shinny Playing and Hurling
UJA, 1 (1895), p. 170
Robinson (1907), p. 64
Clarke, *The Glensman*, 9:1 (1932), p. 30
Newe, *UF*, 2 (1956), p. 56
Foster, *UF*, 9 (1963)
Ó Maolfabhail (1973)
Hewitt (1974), p. 114
Bell, *Slow Air*, 1:3 (1977)
McKillop (1987), p. 83
Colhoun (1995)
King (1996)
Tocher, 36 (1965), SA126
Phoenix, *Feis na nGleann* (2005), p. 158
Maclean & Dorgan (2002), p. 126
Len Graham Collection:
Aodán MacPoilin MS (18.2.04)

307

Bibliography

Allingham, William, *The Ballad Book: A Selection of the Choicest British Ballads* (Sever & Francis, Cambridge, 1865).

Baring-Gould, Sabine, *Songs of the West* (Methuen & Co., London (1890), 1928).

Baring-Gould, Sabine, *A Garland of Country Song* (1895, reprinted Llanerch Books, Wales, 1998).

Barnett, Correlli, *Bonaparte* (Book Club Associates, London, 1978).

Bauerle, Ruth, *The James Joyce Songbook* (Garland Reference Library, NY, 1982).

Bealoideas. The Journal of the Folklore of Ireland Society, Dublin (1927–).

Beattie, William, *The Penguin Border Ballads* (Penguin Books, London, 1952).

Behan, Dominic, *Ireland Sings* (Essex Music, London, 1965).

Belden, Henry M., *Ballads and Songs Collected by the Missouri Folklore Society* (University of Missouri, 1940).

Bell, Jonathan, 'Narrow Stick Hurling', *Slow Air*, 1:3 (Belfast, 1977).

Bell, Margaret, *The Ould Lammas Fair Ballycastle* (Ballycastle Urban District Council, 1966).

Blair, May, *Hiring Fairs and Market Places* (Appletree Press, Belfast, 2007).

Blethen, H. Tyler & Curtis W. Wood, *Ulster and North America – Transatlantic Perspectives on the Scotch-Irish* (University of Alabama Press, AL, 1997).

Boswell, George, *Folk Songs of Middle Tennessee* (University of Tennessee, TN, 1997).

Boyce, Jackie, *Songs of the County Down* (Ballyhay Books, Donaghadee, 2004).

Boyle, Finbar, *Well Situated in the North of Old Ireland* (Sinsear, UCD, Dublin 1988).

Boys of the Lough Music & Song Book (Gilderoy Music, Edinburgh, 1977).

Breathnach, Breandán, *Folk Music & Dances of Ireland* (Talbot Press, Dublin, 1971).

Breathnach, Breandán (ed.), *Ceol: A Journal of Irish Music* (Dublin, 1963–85).

Broadwood, Lucy & J.A. Fuller Maitland, *English County Songs* (Leadenhall Press, London, 1893).

Bronson, Bertrand, *The Traditional Tunes of the Child Ballads*, 4 vols (Princeton University Press, NJ, 1959–72).

Bronson, Bertrand, *The Singing Tradition of Child's Popular Ballads* (Princeton University Press, NJ, 1976).

Brunnings, Florence E., *Folk Song Index – A Comprehensive Guide* (Library of Congress, Washington, DC, 1981).

Buchan, Norman & Peter Hall, *The Scottish Folksinger* (Wm. Collins, London, 1973).

Buckley, Anthony D. etc., *Border-Crossing – Mumming in Cross-Border and Cross-Community Contexts* (Dundalgan Press, Dundalk, 2007).

Bunting, Edward, *A General Collection of the Ancient Music of Ireland* (Clementi & Co., London, 1809).

Bunting, Edward, *The Ancient Music of Ireland* (Hodges & Smith, Dublin, 1840).

Burns, Robert, *The Merry Muses of Caledonia* (Panther Books, London, 1965).

Burns, Robert, *Burns – Poems and Songs*, ed. James Kinsley (Oxford University Press, Oxford, 1969).

Butterworth, George, *The Ploughboy's Glory* (EFDSS, London, 1977).

Cameron, John, *The Lyric Gems of Scotland* (Glasgow, 1856).

Campbell, Olive Dame & Cecil Sharp, *English Folk Songs from the Southern Appalachians* (1917, reprinted Kessinger Publishing, MT, 2008).

Carroll, Jim and Pat Mackenzie, *From Puck to Appleby* (Music Traditions, Stroud, 2003).

Carson, Ciarán, *Irish Traditional Music* (Appletree Press, Belfast, 1986).

Carson, Ciarán, *Last Night's Fun* (Jonathan Cape, London, 1996).

Causeway Press, *The Ulster Song Book* (Causeway Press, Derry, n.d.).

Ceol. Journal of Irish Music, Dublin (1963–85).

Child, Francis James, *The English and Scottish Popular Ballads*, 5 vols (1882–98, reprinted Dover Publications, NY, 1965).

Clancy Bros., & Tommy Makem Song Book (Oak Publications, NY, 1964).

Clune, Anne (ed.), *Dear Far-Voiced Veteran – Essays in Honour of Tom Munnelly* (The Old Kilfarboy Society, Miltown Malbay, 2007).

Cole, William, *Folk Songs of England, Ireland, Scotland and Wales* (Doubleday & Co., NY, 1961).

Colhoun, Mabel R., *The Heritage of Inishowen* (NW Archaeological & Historical Society, Derry, 1995).

Collins, Peter, *The Making of Irish Linen* (Friar's Bush Press, Belfast, 1994).

Collinson, Francis, *The Traditional and National Music of Scotland* (Routledge and Kegan Paul, London, 1966).

Combs, Josiah H., *Folk Songs of the Southern United States* (1925, reprinted University of Texas Press, Austin, 1967).

Come-All-Ye – Popular Ballads of the North-West (*Derry Journal*, 1916).

Cooper, David (ed.), *The Petrie Collection of Ancient Music of Ireland* (Cork University Press, Cork, 2002).

Cooper, David, *The Musical Traditions of Northern Ireland and its Diaspora* (Ashgate Publishing, 2009).

Copper, Bob, *A Song for Every Season* (Country Book Club, UK, 1972).

Co. Louth Archaeological Journal [*CLAJ*] (Dundalk, 1904–).

Cowan, Edward J. (ed.), *The People's Past* (Polygon Books, Edinburgh, 1980).

Cox, J.H., *Folk-Songs of the South* (1925, reprinted Folklore Associates, US, 1963).

Creighton, Helen & Doreen Senior, *Traditional Songs from Nova Scotia* (Ryerson Press, Toronto, 1950).

Creighton, Helen, *Maritime Folk Songs* (Ryerson Press, Toronto, 1962).

Creighton, Helen, *Songs & Ballads from Nova Scotia* (Dover Publications, NY, 1966).

Creighton, Helen, *Folksongs from South New Brunswick* (National Museums of Canada, Ottawa, 1971).

Dal gCais. The Co. Clare Magazine (1977–).

Dallas, Karl, *The Cruel Wars* (Wolfe Publishing, London, 1972).

Dallas, Karl, *Songs of Toil* (Wolfe Publishing, London, 1974).

Danaher, Kevin, *In Ireland Long Ago* (Mercier Press, Cork, 1964).

Danaher, Kevin, *The Year in Ireland – A Calendar* (Mercier Press, Cork, 1972).

Dean, M.C., *The Flying Cloud* (1922, reprinted Norwood Editions, PA, 1973).

Dick & Fitzgerald, *The Emerald* (Dick & Fitzgerald, NY, 1863).

Doerflinger, William M., *Shantymen and Shantyboys: Songs of the Sailor and Lumberman* (Macmillan Co., NY, 1951).

Donnelly, Liam S., *Echoes from Fair Head* (Phoenix Printing, Belfast, 2008).

Dubliners Song Book (Scott Solomon, London, 1968).

Dubourdieu, Revd John, *Statistical Survey of the County Antrim* (1803, reprinted Graisberry & Campbell, Dublin, 1812).

Duffy, James, *The Dublin Comic Songster* (Duffy, Dublin, 1845).

D'Urfey, Thomas, *Pills to Purge Melancholy*, 6 vols (1719–20, reprinted Folklore Library Publishers, NY, 1959).

Eddy, Mary O., *Ballads & Songs from Ohio* (Folklore Associates, PA, 1964).

Evans, E. Estyn, *Mourne County: Landscape and Life in South Down* (Dundalgan Press, Dundalk, 1951).

Evans, E. Estyn, *Irish Folk Ways* (Routledge & Kegan Paul, London, 1957).

Evans, E. Estyn, *The Scotch-Irish – Their Cultural Adaptation and Heritage in the American Old West* ed. E.R.R. Green (Routledge & Kegan Paul, London, 1965).

Evans, E. Estyn, *Ireland and the Atlantic Heritage* (Lilliput Press, Dublin, 1996).

Fay, Anne, *Roddy McCorley: A Study of Evidence* (NEELB, Ballymena, 1989).

Fegan, Tommy, *The Sweets of May* (Ceol Camlocha, South Armagh, 2008).

Fitzgerald, Patrick & Steve Ickringill, *Atlantic Crossroads* (Newtownards, 2001).

Flanders, H.H. & G. Brown, *Vermont Folk Songs & Ballads* (1931, reprinted Folklore Associates Inc., 1968).

Flanders, H.H., *The New Green Mountain Songster – Traditional Folk Songs of Vermont* (1939, reprinted Folklore Associates, 1966).

Flanders, Helen Hartness & Margaret Olney, *Ballads Migrant in New England* (Farrar, Straus & Young, NY, 1953).

Flanders, Helen Hartness, *Ancient Ballads Traditionally Sung in New England* (University of Pennsylvania Press, PA, 1961–5).

Fleischmann, Aloys, *Sources of Irish Traditional Music* (Garland Publishing, London, 1998).

Foley, James, *Songs and Crack from West Tyrone* (Arts Council of NI, Belfast, 1991).

Folk Music Journal: English Folk Dance and Song Society [FMJ] (London, 1965–).

Ford, Ira W., *Traditional Music in America* (1940, reprinted Folklore Associates, PA, 1965).

Ford, Robert, *Song Histories* (Wm. Hodge, Edinburgh, 1900).

Ford, Robert, *Vagabond Songs & Ballads of Scotland* (Alex. Gardner, London, 1901).

Fowke, Edith, *Folk Songs of Canada* (Waterloo Music, Ontario, 1954).

Fowke, Edith, *Traditional Singers and Songs from Ontario* (Folklore Associates, PA, 1965).

Fowke, Edith, *Lumbering Songs from the Northern Woods* (University of Texas Press, TX, 1970).

Fowke, Edith, *The Penguin Book of Canadian Folk Songs* (Penguin Books, London, 1973).

Fowke, Edith, *Folklore of Canada* (McClelland & Stewart, Toronto, 1976).

Gailey, Alan, *Irish Folk Drama* (Mercier Press, Cork, 1969).

Gardner, E.E. & G.J. Chickering, *Ballads and Songs of Southern Michigan* (Folklore Associates, PA, 1967).

Glassie, Henry, *All Silver and No Brass – An Irish Christmas Mumming* (Dolman Press, Dublin, 1976).

Glassie, Henry, *Passing the Time* (O'Brien Press, Dublin, 1982).

Glassie, Henry, *The Stars of Ballymenone* (Indiana University Press, IN, 2006).

Gledhill, Christopher, *Folksongs of Prince Edward Island* (Williams & Crue, PEI, 1973).

Gmelch, Sharon, *Tinkers and Travellers* (O'Brien Press, Dublin, 1975).

Graham, Len, *It's of My Rambles ...*, *Treoir*, 8 (Dublin, 1976 & *Slow Air*, 1:1, Belfast, 1976).

Graham, Len, *Strands of Magilligan, Treoir*, 11 (Dublin, 1979).

Graham, Len, *It's of My Rambles ...* (Arts Council of NI, Belfast, 1993).

Graham, Len, *Meeting Child on the Road,* ed. Anne Clune (The Old Kilfarboy Society, Miltown Malbay, 2007).

Graves, A.P., *The Irish Song Book* (Fisher Unwin, London, 1894).

Green, E.R.R. (ed.), *Essays in Scotch-Irish History* (Routledge & Kegan Paul, London, 1969).

Greenleaf, Elisabeth Bristol & Grace Yarrow Mansfield, *Ballads and Sea Songs of Newfoundland* (Harvard University Press, MA, 1933).

Greig – Duncan Folk Song Collection [G-D: (1981–2002)], 8 vols (Aberdeen University Press, 1981–2002).

Guthrie, Woody, *Bound for Glory* (1943, reprinted Penguin Books, London, 2004).

Hamilton, James B., *Ballymoney & District* (J.C. Scarlett, Ballycastle, 1957).

Hammond, David, *Songs of Belfast* (Gilbert Dalton, Dublin, 1978).

Hand, John, *Irish Street Ballads* (1875, reprinted Carraig Books, Dublin, 1976).

Hand, John, *Irish Street Songs & Ballads* (19th century, reprinted Fredonia Books, Amsterdam, 2004).

Hardeback, Carl, *Gems of Melody: Seoda Ceoil* (Pigott, Dublin, 1910).

Harding, N., *Harding's Dublin Songster* (N. Harding, Dublin, c.1900).

Hastings, Gary, *With Fife & Drum* (Blackstaff Press, Belfast, 2003).

Hayward, Richard, *Ulster Songs and Ballads of the Town and the Country* (Duckworth, London, 1925).

Hayward, Richard, *Ireland Calling* (Mozart Allan, Glasgow, n.d.).

Healy, James N., *Old Irish Street Ballads*, 4 vols (Mercier Press, Cork, 1967–9).

Henderson, Hamish, *Alias MacAlias* (Polygon, Edinburgh, 1992).

Henry, Mellinger E., *Folksongs from the Southern Highlands* (J.J. Augustin, NY, 1938).

Henry, Sam, *Songs of the People*, ed. Gale Huntington and Lani Herrmann (University of Georgia Press, GA, 1990).

Herd, David, *Ancient and Modern Scottish Songs* (1776, reprinted Kerr and Richardson, Glasgow, 1869).

Hewitt, John, *Rhyming Weavers* (Blackstaff Press, Belfast, 1974).

Hodgart, M.J.C. & Mabel Worthington, *Song in the Works of James Joyce* (Columbia University Press, NY, 1959).

Hubbard, Lester A., *Ballads and Songs from Utah* (University of Utah Press, 1961).

Hughes, Herbert, *Irish Country Songs,* 4 vols (Boosey & Hawkes, London, 1909–36).

Hunter, James, *The Fiddle Music of Scotland* (Chambers, Edinburgh, 1979).

Hunter, Max, *The Max Hunter Folk Song Collection* (http://maxhunter.missouristate.edu).

Huntington, Gale, *Songs the Whalemen Sang* (1964, reprinted Dover Publications, NY, 1970).

Huntington, Gale & Lani Herrmann (eds), *Songs of the People* (University of Georgia Press, GA, 1990).

Hyland, J.S., *Hyland's Mammoth Hibernian Songster* (1901, reprinted Chelsea Books, Quebec, 2009).

Irvine, Andy, *Aiming for the Heart* (Heupferd Music, Germany, 1988).

Ives, Burl, *The Burl Ives Song Book* (Ballantine Books, NY, 1953).

Journal of the Folk-Song Society [JFSS] (London, 1889–1931).

Journal of the English Folk Dance and Song Society [JEFDSS] (London,1932–64).

Johnson, James, *The Scots Musical* Museum *(1787–1803)* (Folklore Associates, 1962).

Jolliffe, Maureen, *The Third Book of Irish Ballads* (Mercier Press, Cork, 1970).

Jones, Stephen, *Recollections of a Donegal Man – Packie Manus Byrne* (Millington, Lampeter, 1989).

Joyce, P.W., *Irish Peasant Songs* (M.H. Gill, Dublin, 1906).

Joyce, P.W., *Old Irish Folk Music and Songs* (University Press, Dublin, 1909).

Joyce, P.W., *Ancient Irish Music* (M.H. Gill, Dublin, 1912).

Judd, Denis, *The Crimean War* (Book Club Associates, London, 1976).

Kane, Alice, *Songs and Sayings of an Ulster Childhood* (Wolfhound Press, Dublin, 1983).

Karpeles, Maud, *Folk Songs from Newfoundland* (Faber & Faber, London, 1971).

Kennedy, Peter, *Folksongs of Britain and Ireland* (Oak Publications, London, 1975).

Kenedy, P.J., *New Universal Irish Song Book* (P.J. Kennedy, New York, 1884).

Kennedy, William, *Fitful Fancies* (Oliver & Boyd, Edinburgh, 1827).

Kidson, Frank, *Traditional Tunes* (Chas. Taphouse, Oxford, 1891).

Kidson, Frank & Alfred Moffat, *A Garland of English Folk Songs* (Ascherberg, Hopwood & Crew, London, 1926).

Killen, John, *The Irish Christmas Book* (Blackstaff Press, Belfast, 1985).

King, Seamus J., *A History of Hurling* (Gill & Macmillan, Dublin, 1996).

Kinsley, James, *The Oxford Book of Ballads* (Oxford University Press, Oxford, 1969).

Law, Gary, *The Cultural Traditions Directory* (Blackstaff Press, Belfast, 1998).

Laws, G. Malcolm, *American Balladry from British Broadsides* (American Folklore Society, PA, 1957).

Leach, MacEdward, *Folk Ballads and Songs of the Lower Labrador Coast* (National Museum of Canada, 1965).

Levy, The Lester S. Collection of Sheet Music, Special Collections at the Sheridan Libraries of the John Hopkins University (http://levysheetmusic.mse.jhu.edu/otcgi/llscgi60).

Leyden, Maurice, *Belfast City of Song* (Brandon Books, Dingle, 1989).

Library of Congress. Rare Book & Special Collections (http://memory.loc.gov/ammem/amsshtml/amsshome.htm/).

Linscott, Eloise Hubbard, *Folk Songs of Old New England* (Dover Publications, NY, 1990).

Lloyd, A.L., & R.V. Williams, *The Penguin Book of English Folk Songs* (Penguin Books, London, 1959).

Lloyd, A.L., *Folk Song in England* (Granada Publishing, 1967).

Lomax, John & Alan, *American Ballads & Folk Songs* (Macmillan Co., NY, 1934).

Lomax, Alan, *The Folk Songs of North America* (Doubleday Inc., NY, 1960).

Lyle, Emily, *Scottish Ballads* (Canongate Press, Edinburgh, 1994).

McBride, Jimmy & Jim McFarland, *My Parents Reared Me* (Wm. Doherty, Buncrana, Co. Donegal, 1985).

McBride, Jimmy, *The Flower of Dunaff Hill* (Wm. Doherty, Buncrana, Co. Donegal, 1988).

McCarthy, Tony, *Bawdy British Folk Songs* (Wolfe Publishing, London, 1972).

McClure, A.K., *Scotch-Irish Achievement* (R. Clarke, Cinicinnati, OH, 1889).

MacColl, Ewan, *Folk Songs and Ballads of Scotland* (Oak Publications, NY, 1965).

MacColl, Ewan & Peggy Seeger, *Travellers' Songs from England & Scotland* (Routledge & Kegan Paul, London, 1977).

MacColl, Ewan & Peggy Seeger, *Till Doomsday in the Afternoon* (Manchester University Press, Manchester, 1986).

McCollam, Frank, *Echoes from Fair Head* (Phoenix Printing, Belfast, 2008).

Mac Con Iomaire, Liam, *Seosamh Ó hÉanaí* (Cló Iar-Chonnachta, Conamara, 2007).

MacDonagh, Oliver, *The Emancipist – Daniel O'Connell* (Weidenfeld & Nicholson, London, 1989).

McGuffin, John, *In Praise of Poteen* (Appletree Press, Belfast, 1978).

McKay, Patrick, *A Dictionary of Ulster Place-Names* (Cló Ollscoil na Banríona, QUB, Belfast, 2007).

McKay, Patrick & Kay Muhr, *Lough Neagh Places – Their Names and Origins* (Cló Ollscoil na Banríona, QUB, Belfast, 2007).

MacKenzie, W.R., *Ballads and Sea Songs from Nova Scotia* (1928, reprinted Folklore Associates, PA, 1963).

McKillop, Felix, *Glenarm – A Local History* (Ulster Journals, Belfast, 1987).

McKinney, Breda, 'Song of Eoghan – The Tradition of Singing in Inishowen, Co. Donegal' (MPhil, NUI, Cork, 2004).

McLaughlin, John, *One Green Hill – Journeys through Irish Songs* (BTP Publications, Belfast, 2003).

Maclean, Malcolm & Theo Dorgan, *An Leabhar Mór – The Great Book of Gaelic* (Canongate Books, Edinburgh, 2002).

McMahon, Sean, *The Poolbeg Book of Irish Ballads* (Poolbeg Press, Dublin, 1991).

MacMathúna, Séamus, *Traditional Songs and Singers* (CCE, Dublin, 1977).

McMorland, Alison, *Herd Laddie O The Glen – Songs of a Border Shepherd* (Scottish Borders Council, 2006).

McSparran, Malachy, Cahal Dallat & Jimmy Irvine, *Oh Maybe It Was Yesterday* (Glens of Antrim Historical Society, Ballycastle, 1980).

McWilliams, Hugh, *Poems and Songs on Various Subjects* (Belfast, 1831, only copy in Linen Hall Library, Belfast).

Maguire, W.A., *Up In Arms – The 1798 Rebellion in Ireland* (Ulster Museum, Belfast, 1998).

Marks, Hugh, *An Old-Timer Talking* (Mourne Observer Press, Newcastle, 1961).

Meek, Bill, *Songs of the Irish in America* (Gilbert Dalton, Dublin, 1978).

Meek, Bill, *Irish Folk Songs* (Gill & Macmillan, Dublin, 1997).

Meek, Bill, *Moonpenny* ... a collection of rhymes, songs and play-verse for and by children gathered in Ireland (Ossian Publications, Cork, 1985).

Meredith, John & Hugh Anderson, *Folk Songs of Australia* (Ure Smith Ptg., Sydney, 1967).

Messenger, Betty, *Picking Up the Linen Threads* (Blackstaff Press, Belfast, 1988).

Milner, Dan & Paul Kaplan, *Songs of England, Ireland & Scotland – A Bonnie Bunch of Roses* (Oak Publications, NY, 1983).

Mirala, Petri, *Freemasonry in Ulster, 1733–1813* (Four Courts Press, Dublin, 2007).

Moloney, Colette, *The Irish Music Manuscripts of Edward Bunting (1773–1843)* (Irish Traditional Music Archive, Dublin, 2000).

Moloney, Mick, *Far From the Shamrock Shore* (Collins Press, Cork, 2002).

Montgomery, Eric, *The Scotch-Irish in America's History* (Ulster-Scot Historical Society, Belfast, 1965).

Moore, E. & C.O., *Ballads & Folk Songs of the Southwest* (University of Oklahoma Press, Norman, OK, 1964).

Morton, Robin, *Folksongs Sung in Ulster* (Mercier Press, Cork, 1970).

Morton, Robin, *Come Day, Go Day, God Send Sunday* (Routledge & Kegan Paul, London, 1973).

Morrison, H.S., *Modern Ulster* (H.R. Allenson, London, 1920).

Moulden, John, *Songs of the People – Part One* (Blackstaff Press, Belfast, 1979).

Moulden, John, *The Trim Little Borough* (Coleraine Borough Council, Coleraine, 1992).

Moulden, John, *Songs of Hugh McWilliams* (Ulstersongs, Portrush, 1993).

Moulden, John, *Thousands are Sailing* (Ulstersongs, Portrush, 1994).

Moylan, Terry, *The Age of Revolution in the Irish Song Tradition* (Lilliput Press, Dublin, 2000).

Mulcahy, Michael & Marie Fitzgibbon, *The Voice of the People* (O'Brien Press, Dublin, 1982).

Munnelly, Tom & Hugh Shields, *Early Ballads in Ireland* (Folk Music Society of Ireland, TCD, Dublin, 1985).

Munnelly, Tom, *The Mount Callan Garland – Songs from the Repertoire of Tom Lenihan* (Dundalgan Press, Dundalk, 1994).

Murphy, David, *Ireland and the Crimean War* (Four Courts Press, Dublin, 2002).

Murphy, Michael J., *At Slieve Gullions Foot* (Dundalgan Press, Dundalk, 1940).

Murphy, Michael J., *Now You're Talking …* (Blackstaff Press, Belfast, 1975).

Niles, Jack J., *The Ballad Book of Jack J. Niles* (Dover Publications, NY, 1960).

NIPRO – Northern Ireland Public Record Office, *18th Century Emigration* (HMSO, Belfast, 1972).

Ní Uallacháin, Pádraigín, *A Hidden Ulster –People, Songs and Traditions of Oriel* (Four Courts Press, Dublin, 2003).

Noble, Andrew & Patrick Scott Hogg, *The Canongate Burns* (Cannongate Books, Edinburgh, 2001).

O'Boyle, Carmel, *Cut the Loaf – The Irish Childrens' Songbook* (Mercier Press, Dublin, 1986).

O'Boyle, Cathal, *Songs of County Down* (Gilbert Dalton, Dublin, 1979).

O'Boyle, Sean, *The Irish Song Tradition* (Gilbert Dalton, Dublin, 1976).

O'Byrne, Cathal, *As I Roved Out* (Blackstaff Press, Belfast, 1982).

O'Connell, Maurice, *Daniel O'Connell – The Man and His Politics* (Irish Academic Press, Dublin, 1990).

O'Connor, Manus, *Irish Come-All-Yes and Ballads of Ireland* (Popular Publishers, NY, 1901).

Ó Cróinín, Dáibhí, *The Songs of Elizabeth Cronin* (Four Courts Press, Dublin, 2000).

O'Faoláin, Seán, *King of the Beggars – A Life of Daniel O'Connell the Irish Liberator* (Nelson, London, 1938).

O'Hara, Aidan, *I'll Live Till I Die – The Story of Delia Murphy* (Drumlin Publications, Manorhamilton, 1997).

Ó Lochlainn, Colm, *Irish Street Ballads* (Three Candles Press, Dublin, 1939).

Ó Lochlainn, Colm, *More Irish Street Ballads* (Three Candles Press, Dublin, 1965).

Ó Maolfabhail, Art, *Camán* (Dundalgan Press, Dundalk, 1973).

O'Neill, Francis, *Irish Minstrels & Musicians* (1913, reprinted Mercier Press, Cork, 1987).

O'Neill, Francis, *O'Neill's Irish Music* (1915, reprinted Mercier Press, Cork, 1987).

Opie, Rona & Peter, *The Oxford Dictionary of Nursery Rhymes* (Oxford University Press, Oxford, 1951).

Ord, John, *Bothy Songs and Ballads* (John Donald Publishers, Edinburgh, 1930).

Ordnance Survey – Memoirs of Ireland. Parishes of County Antrim, 1830–1838 (Institute of Irish Studies, QUB, Belfast, 1992).

Ormsby, Frank, *The Collected Poems of John Hewitt* (Blackstaff Press, Belfast, 1991).

O'Sullivan, Patrick (ed.), *The Creative Migrant* (Leicester University Press, London, 1994).

O'Toole, Leagues, *The Humours of Planxty* (Hodder Headline Ireland, 2006).

Palmer, Roy, *Everyman's Book of English Country Songs* (J.M. Dent & Sons, London, 1979).

Palmer, Roy, *Everyman's Book of British Ballads* (J.M. Dent & Sons, London, 1980).

Pankake, Marcia & Jon, *A Prairie Home Companion Folk Song Book* (Faber & Faber, London, 1989).

Peacock, Kenneth, *Songs of the Newfoundland Outposts*, 3 vols (Queen's Printer, Ottawa, ON, 1965).

Percy, Thomas (bishop of Dromore), *Reliques of Ancient English Poetry*, 3 vols (P. Wilson & E. Watt, Dublin, 1766).

Petrie, George, *Ancient Music of Ireland*, 2 vols (M.H. Gill, Dublin, 1855).

Petrie, George, *The Complete Collection of Irish Music*, 3 vols (Boosey & Co., London, 1902–5).

Phoenix, Éamon et al., *Feis na nGleann* (Stair Uladh, Belfast, 2005).

Pound, Louise, *American Ballads and Songs* (Charles Scribner, NY, 1972).

Purslow, Frank, *Marrow Bones* (Hammond & Gardiner MSS) (EFSDS, London, 1965).

Purslow, Frank, *The Wanton Seed* (Hammond & Gardiner MSS) (EFSDS, London, 1968).

Purslow, Frank, *The Constant Lovers* (Hammond & Gardiner MSS) (EFSDS, London, 1972).

Purslow, Frank, *The Foggy Dew* (Hammond & Gardiner MSS) (EFSDS, London, 1974).

Ramsay, Allan, *The Tea-Table Miscellany*, 2 vols (1724, reprinted John Crum, Glasgow, 1871).

Randolph, Vance, *Ozark Folk Songs* (1946, reprinted University of Illinois Press, Champaign, IL, 1982).

Ranson, Joseph, *Songs of the Wexford Coast* (Redmond Bros., Wexford, 1948).

Reeves, James, *The Everlasting Circle* (Hammond & Gardiner MSS) (Heinemann, London, 1960).

Ritson's Scottish Songs (1794, reprinted Hopkins, Glasgow, 1869).

Robinson, Wm. Clarke, *Antrim Idylls* (W. Mullan & Sons, Belfast, 1907).

Ross, Susan, *Castles of Scotland* (Chambers, Edinburgh, 1987).

Roud, Steve, *The Folk Song Index and The Broadside Index* (EFDSS, London and ITMA, Dublin) (database continually updated).

Sandburg, Carl, *The American Songbag* (Harcourt Brace & Co., NY, 1927).

Scott, Stanley & Dorothea E. Hast, *Music in Ireland* (Oxford University Press, Oxford, 2004).

Sharp, Cecil & S. Baring-Gould, *English Folk-Songs for Schools* (J. Curwen & Sons, London, 1906).

Sharp, Cecil, *English Country Folk Songs*, 5 vols (1908–12, Novello & Co., London, 1961), vol. 1.

Sharp, Cecil, *One Hundred English Folksongs* (1916, reprinted Dover Publications, NY, 1975).

Sharp, Cecil & Olive Dame Campbell, *English Folk Songs from the Southern Appalachians* (1917, reprinted Kessinger Publishing, Whitefish, MT, 2008).

Sharp, Cecil, *English Folk Songs*, 2 vols (1920, reprinted in 1 vol., Novello & Co., London, 1959).

Sharp, Cecil, *English Folk-Songs from the Southern Appalachians*, 2 vols (Oxford University Press, London, 1932).

Sharp, Cecil & Maud Karpeles, *Eighty English Folk Songs from the Southern Appalachians* (Faber & Faber, London, 1968).

Sharp, Cecil, *Still Growing* (EFDSS, London, 2003).

Shepard, Leslie, *The Broadside Ballad: A Study in Origins and Meaning* (Folklore Associates, Hatboro, PA, 1965).

Shields, Hugh, *Shamrock, Rose and Thistle* (Blackstaff Press, Belfast, 1981).

Shields, Hugh & Tom Munnelly, *Early Ballads in Ireland* (Folk Music Society of Ireland, TCD, Dublin, 1985).

Shields, Hugh, *Narrative Singing in Ireland* (Irish Academic Press, Dublin, 1993).

Sinsear: The Folklore Journal (UCD 1979–).

Slow Air (Arts Council of Northern Ireland, Belfast, 1976–7).

Smith, Peter & Francis Clarke, *Songs from the Sperrins* – Traditional Singing from Mid and North Tyrone (Beaghmore Publications, Pomeroy, 2009).

Summers, Keith, *The Hardy Sons of Dan* (Musical Traditions, UK, 2004).

Tocher (School of Scottish Studies, Edinburgh, 1971–).

Tomlyn, Alfred W., *Gem Seletion of Scottish Songs* (Valentine & Sons, Edinburgh, 1890).

Traditional Music (London, 1975–8).

Treoir (CCE, Dublin, c.1969–).

Tunney, Paddy, *The Stone Fiddle* (Gilbert Dalton, Dublin, 1979).

Tunney, Paddy, *Where Songs Do Thunder* (Appletree Press, Belfast, 1991).

Ulster Folklife [*UF*] (Belfast, 1955–).

uí Ógáin, Ríonach, *Immortal Dan – Daniel O'Connell in Irish Folk Tradition.* (Geography Publications, Dublin, 1995).

uí Ógáin, Ríonach, *Going to the Well for Water – The Séamus Ennis Field Diary 1942–46* (Cork University Press, Cork, 2009).

Ulster Journal of Archaeology [*UJA*] (Belfast, 1853–).

Vallely, Fintan, *Companion to Irish Traditional Music* (Cork University Press, Cork, 1999).

Vallely, Fintan, *Together in Time – John Kennedy* (Loughshore Traditions Group, Belfast, 2001).

Walker, Brian, M., *Sentry Hill – An Ulster Farm and Family* (Blackstaff Press, Belfast, 1981).

Walsh, P.A., *Exile of Erin – Who Wrote It?* (Fallon Bros., Dublin, 1921).

Walton's, *New Treasury of Irish Songs & Ballads,* Part One & Two (Walton's, Dublin, 1966 & 1968).

Walton's, *A Ballad Selection,* vol. 4 (Walton's, Dublin, 1966).

Wannan, Bill, *The Wearing of the Green – The Lore, Literature, Legend and Balladry of the Irish in Australia* (Lansdowne Press, 1965).

Ward, Russel, *The Penguin Book of Australian Ballads* (Penguin Books, London, 1964).

Warner, Anne & Frank, *Traditional American Folk Songs* (Syracuse University Press, Syracuse, NY, 1984).

Wehman Bros., *Six Hundred and Seventeen Irish Songs and Ballads* (Wehman Bros, NY, c.1898).

Whistle-Binkie – A Collection of Songs for Social Circle (David Robertson & Co., Glasgow, 1878).

Whitlock, Ralph, *A Calendar of Country Customs* (Batsford Publishers, London, 1978).

Williams, R.V. & A.L. Lloyd, *The Penguin Book of English Folk Songs* (Penguin Books, London, 1959).

Williams, T. Desmond, *Secret Societies in Ireland* (Gill & Macmillan, Dublin, 1973).

Wright, Robert L., *Irish Emigrant Ballads & Songs* (Bowling Green University Press, OH, 1975).

Yates, Janelle, *Woody Guthrie – American Balladeer* (Ward Hill Press, NY, 1995).

Yates, Mike, *Traveller's Joy – Songs of English & Scottish Travellers & Gypsies* (EFDSS, London, 2006).

Yeats, W.B, F.R. Higgins et al., *Broadsides – A Collection of Old and New Songs* (Cuala Press, Dublin, 1933).

Yeats, W.B., *Selected Poetry* (Macmillan, London, 1962).

Zimmermann, Georges-Denis, *Songs of Irish Rebellion* (Allen Figgis, Dublin, 1966).

Towns, Townlands and Place-Names in Counties Antrim and Derry

Place-name	Parish	Gaeilge	Interpretation
Aghadolgan (A)	Glenavy	*Achadh Dealgán*	'field of pegs/thorns'
Aghagallan (A)	Aghagallon	*Achadh Gallán*	'field of standing stones'
Ahoghill (A)	Ahoghill	*Achadh Eochaille*	'field of the yew wood'
Ardclinis (A)	Ardclinis	*Ard Claonais*	'height of the slope'
Ardicoan (A)	Grange of Inispollan	*Ard an Chuain*	'height of the bay'
Armoy (A)	Armoy	*Oirthear Ma í*	'the east of the plain'
Ballynacaird (A)	Racavan	*Baile an Chearda*	'townland of the artisan or tradesman'
Ballintoy (A)	Ballintoy	*Baile an Tuathaigh*	'townland of the ruler of the *tuath*'
Ballybeg (A)	Ahoghill	*An Baile Beag*	'the little townland'
Ballyboley (A)	Ballycor	*Baile na Buaile*	'townland of the *booley* or summer dairying place'
Ballyboyland (A) (Upper/Lower)	Ballymoney	*Baile Uí Bhaolláin*	'(O')Boylan's townland'
Ballybrakes (A)	Ballymoney	*An Baile Breac*	'the speckled townland'
Ballycastle (A)	Ramoan	*Baile an Chaistil*	'townland of the castle'
Ballyeamon (A)	Layd	*Baile Éamainn*	'Edmund's homestead'
(minor place-name in the townland of Tavnagharry)			
Ballygillan (D) (Beg/More)	Artrea	*Baile Mhic Giolláin*	'Gillan's townland'
Ballyinderry (D)	Ballinderry	*Baile an Doire*	'townland of the oak wood'
Ballymena (A)	Kirkinriola	*An Baile Meánach*	'the middle townland or settlement'
Ballymoney (A)	Ballymoney	*Baile Monaidh*	'townland of the moor'
Ballynure (A)	Ballynure	*Baile an Iúir*	'townland of the yew tree'
Ballyscullion (A)	Ballyscullion	*Baile Uí Scolláin*	'Scullion's townland'
Balnamore (A)	Ballymoney	*Béal an Átha Móir*	'mouth of the big ford'
Belfast (A)	Shankill	*Béal Feirste*	'mouth of the sandbank ford'
Bellaghy (D)	Bellaghy	*Baile Eachaidh*	'Eochy's town'
Bellair (A)	Tickmacrevan	*An Baile Láir*	'the middle townland'
Bovevagh (D)	Bovevagh	*Boith Mhéabha*	'Maeve's hut or monastic cell'
Breen (A)	Armoy	*Bruíon*	'fairy dwelling, fairy fort'
Buckna (A)	Racavan	*Bocshnámh*	'stag ford'
Carncastle (A)	Carncastle	*Carn an Chaistil*	'cairn of the castle'
Cary (A)	Culfeightrin	*Cothraí*	– a tribal name
Carnalbanagh (A	Tickmacrevan	*Carn Albanach*	'cairn of the Scotsmen'
Carnamenagh (A)	Loughguile	*An Carn Meánach*	'the middle cairn'
Carnlough (A)	Ardclinis	*Carnlach*	'place of cairns'

Place-name	Parish	Gaeilge	Interpretation
Cashel (A)	Racavan	*Caiseal*	'stone ring-fort'
Clooney (D)	Magilligan	*Cluanaigh*	'place of meadows'
Clough (A)	Dunaghy	*An Chloch*	'the stone (castle)'
Cloghogue (A)	Drummaul	*Clochóg*	'stony place'
Cloyfin (D)	Ballywillin	*An Chloich Fhionn*	'the white stone'
Coleraine (D)	Coleraine	*Cúil Raithin*	'corner/nook of ferns'
Croaghan (D)	Macosquin	*An Cruachán*	'the round hill'
Cullybackey (A)	Craigs	*Cúil na Baice*	'corner/angle of the river bend'
Culmore (D)	Templemore	*An Chúil Mhór*	'the large corner/peninsula'
Cushendall (A)	Layd	*Bun Abhann Dalla*	'bottom of the river Dall'
Cushendun (A)	Culfeightrin	*Bun Abhann Doinne*	'bottom of the river Dun'
Derry (D)	Templemore/ Clondermot	*Doire*	'oak wood'
Derrykeighan	Derrykeighan	*Doire Chaocháin*	'*Caochán*'s oak wood'
Donegore (A)	Donegore	*Dún Ó gCorra*	'oak wood of the Corrs'
Drummaul (A)	Drummaul	*Droim Málla*	'pleasant ridge'
Drumavally (D)	Magilligan	*Droim an Bhealaigh*	'ridge of the road or pass'
Dunaghy (A)	Dunaghy	*Dumha Achaidh*	'mound of the field'
Dunboe (D)	Dunboe	*Dún Bó*	'fort of the cows'
Duneane (A)	Duneane	*Dún Dá Éan*	'fort of the two birds'
Dungiven (D)	Dungiven	*Dún Geimhin*	'fort of the hide or skin'
Dunloy (A)	Finvoy	*Dún Lathaí*	'fort of the muddy place'
Dunluce (A)	Dunluce	*Dún Libhsí*	'fort of the …' (obscure)
Dunminning (A)	Rasharkin	*Droim Fhionnáin*	'*Fionnán*'s ridge'
Dunseverick (A)	Billy	*Dún Sobhairce*	'*Sobhairce*'s fort'
Faughanvale (D)	Faughanvale	*Nuachongbháil*	'new (church) habitation'
Finvoy (A)	Finvoy	*An Fhionnbhoith*	'the white hut/monastic cell'
Fish Loughan (A)	Kildollagh	*Inis Locháin*	'island of the little lake'
Glarryford (A)	Rasharkin		Scots *glarry* 'muddy' + English '*ford*'
Glenann (A)	Layd	*Gleann Athain*	'glen of the burial chamber' (may refer to 'Ossian's Grave')
Glenarm (A)	Tickmacrevan	*Gleann Arma*	'glen of the army'
Glenariff (A)	Ardclinis	*Gleann Airimh*	'glen of arable land'
Glenavy (A)	Glenavy	*Lann Abhaigh*	'church of the dwarf'
Glencloy (A)	Tickmacrevan	*Gleann Cloiche*	'glen of the stone'
Glendun (A)	Layd/Grange of Layd	*Gleann Doinne*	'glen of the river Dun'
Glenshesk (A)	Ramoan	*Gleann Seisc*	'barren glen'
Killerfaith (D)	Dungiven	*Coiléar Fraoich*	'quarry in the heather'
Killyramer (A)	Ballymoney	*Coillidh Ramhar*	'broad wood'
Killywool (D)	Faughanvale	*Coill an Bhuaile*	'wood of the *booley* or summer dairying place'
Kilwaughter (A)	Kilwaughter	*Cill Uachtair*	'upper church'
Layd (A)	Layd	*Leithead Lachtmhaí*	'territory of the milk plain'
Lisboy (A)	Kilraghts	*Lios Buí*	'yellow fort'
Lisburn (A)	Blaris	*Lios na gCearrbhach*	'fort of the gamesters/gamblers'
Liscolman (A)	Billy	*Lios Cholmáin*	'*Colmán*'s fort'

Place-name	Parish	Gaeilge	Interpretation
Lisnagunogue (A) (Upper/Lower)	Billy	*Lios na gCuinneog*	'fort of the churns'
Loughguile (A)	Loughguile	*Loch gCaol*	'lake of narrows'
Loughinsholin (D) (name of a barony in S. Derry)		*Loch Inse Uí Fhloinn*	'lake of O'Flynn's island' (a crannog outside Desertmartin)
Loughlynch (A)	Billy	*Loch Leithinse*	'lake of the peninsula'
Macfinn (A) (Upper/Lower)	Ballymoney	*Ard Mhaoilfhinn*	'*Maoilfhinn's* height'
Macosquin (D)	Macosquin	*Maigh Choscáin*	'*Coscán's* plain'
Magherafelt (D)	Magherafelt	*Machaire Fíolta*	'*Fíolta's* plain'
Magilligan (D)	Magilligan	*Aird Mhic Giollagáin*	'Magilligan's point'
Moneystaghan (D) (Ellis/Macpeake)	Tamlaght-O'Crilly	*Muine Steacháin*	'*Steachán's* thicket'
Murlough (A)	Culfeightrin	*An Murlag*	'the sea bay'
Portballintrae (A)	Dunluce	*Port Bhaile an Trá*	'the port of Ballintrae'
Portglenone (A)	Portglenone	*Port Chluain Eoghain*	'port of Owen's meadow'
Portrush (A)	Ballywillin	*Port Rois*	'port of the headland'
Ramoan (A)	Ramoan	*Ráth Muáin*	'*Muán's* fort'
Rasharkin (A)	Rasharkin	*Ros Earcáin*	'*Earcán's* wooded height'
Skerry (A)	Skerry	*Sciridh*	(meaning uncertain)
Slemish (A)	Racavan	*Sliabh Mis*	'*Mis's* mountain'
Stranocum (A)	Ballymoney	*Sraith Nócam*	'river-plain of…' (obscure)
Tamlaght (A)	Rasharkin	*Tamhlacht*	'(pagan) burial place'
Toomebridge (A)	Duneane	*Droichead Thuama*	'bridge of the tumulus or burial mound'

I am grateful to Dr Patrick McKay of the Northern Ireland Place-Name Project, Irish and Celtic Studies, School of Languages, Literature and Arts at Queen's University, Belfast for the information on all the place-names listed above, with the exception of Killerfaith, the information for which was provided by Colm Hasson of Dungiven, Co. Derry.

Index

Page entries in *italics* refer to illustrations.